How to Become a Winning Crew Chief

HOW TO BECOME
A WINNING CREW CHIEF

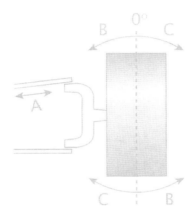

LARRY McREYNOLDS

WITH JEFF HUNEYCUTT

DESIGN BY TOM MORGAN

DAVID BULL PUBLISHING

Library of Congress Control Number: 2005921037

ISBN: 1 893618 47 1

David Bull Publishing, logo, and colophon are trademarks of David Bull Publishing, Inc.

Book and cover design: Blue Design (www.bluedes.com)

Printed in Hong Kong

10 9 8 7 6 5 4 3 2 1

David Bull Publishing
4250 East Camelback Road
Suite K150
Phoenix, AZ 85018

602-852-9500
602-852-9503 (fax)

www.bullpublishing.com

PAGE 2: I found keeping a notebook of a car's performance during practice runs to be very useful. Here I am with Robert Yates Racing in the mid 1990s making detailed notes on a practice day. That notebook was my bible on race day.

PAGE 6: It's a delicate balancing act to find the correct amount of body roll a race car should exhibit as it powers through a turn. Because many teams are working with increasingly softer front springs to maximize front tire grip, manipulating roll centers is becoming more important when it comes to controlling roll.

Acknowledgments

The authors would like to thank the many people who provided assistance in producing *How to Become a Winning Crew Chief*. There is no way we can thank everyone who assisted us, but we would especially like to name some of those who particularly gave of their time and talents: Denis Hambucken for transforming rough sketches into effective illustrations, Rick Ren, Colby Crooks, Derek Vaughn, Jeff Shinn, Mark Tudor and his crew at BACE Motorsports, Bradley Auto Parts, Jason Enders and RE Suspension Technology, Billy Hess and Hess Race Cars, Rudy and Ryan Zeck for all their help with their Late Model race cars, CLR Racing, Joe Cudmore, Tommy Baldwin, Frank Kerr, and Michael "Fatback" McSwain.

FROM LARRY McREYNOLDS

This book is based on my experience gained from years of racing. I'd like to take this opportunity to thank the people who have played a huge part in my career. If it weren't for these people, there is no way I would have had a fraction of the success I've enjoyed. When I first started working on race cars back in Birmingham, Alabama, it was my aunt Noreen Mears and her husband Butch who gave me my first shot. I didn't know the difference between a brake rotor and a hubcap, but Butch got me started out on the right foot. And then Bobby Ray Jones took me under his wing with his Late Model team and showed me the ins and outs of racing. I can still remember winning that first race in 1978—that win at an Alabama short track felt just as good as winning a Daytona 500.

Bob Rogers gave me my first chance in NASCAR Nextel Cup racing when I was just a skinny kid with big dreams, and I will always be grateful for his willingness to take a chance with me. Bill Terry and Bobby Hawkins gave me opportunities early in my career when I was basically out of a job and very close to being forced to give up on my dream.

Then I'd particularly like to thank Kenny Bernstein who stuck his neck out in 1985 and gave me my first big-time crew chief position. Kenny took a chance on a guy without much experience and who had never even sniffed a Nextel Cup victory lane, but we worked well together and got three wins in three years. Robert Yates taught me so much about life beyond race cars. We did a lot of winning together, but even better than that, we became good friends. And last but certainly not least, I'd like to thank Richard Childress for giving me the opportunity to work with one of the greatest race car drivers who ever lived—Dale Earnhardt. We didn't achieve all the things together on the track that we had hoped to, but I will always treasure being a part of the team that was able to help Dale get that magic win in the Daytona 500 in 1998.

And then there are the drivers. A crew chief depends on his driver to make him successful, and I've worked with some of the best. I won my first race with Ricky Rudd in 1988 at Watkins Glen. Then there were also Joe Ruttman, Morgan Shepherd, Brett Bodine, David Pearson, Davey Allison, Ernie Irvan, Dale Jarrett, Earnhardt, and Mike Skinner. All of these guys were a pleasure to work with and each taught me valuable lessons about racing. Even before I had a chance to race with these drivers at the Nextel Cup level, I had the opportunity to work with some some of the best Late Model race car drivers around, Mike Alexander and Dave Mader, who gave me my first short track win.

Finally, I'd like to thank all the many crew members who have worked with me over the years. The list is much too long to name every one, but you know who you are. You stood behind me through thick and thin, and I appreciate every one of you. I treasure every race—whether we won or lost—that we've raced together.

Most of all, I'd like to thank my wife, Linda, and my three kids, Brooke, Brandon, and Kendall, for their patience and support throughout my career. There have been a lot of ball games, dance recitals, and dinners without Dad, and I appreciate your understanding. Linda, I want you to know I especially appreciate your support through our 22 years of marriage.
Thank you.

FROM JEFF HUNEYCUTT

This is dedicated to my wife, Jennifer, and my daughters Meri, Bailey, and Allison. Thank you for your patience and encouragement throughout this project. Thank you.

Table of Contents

ABOVE: A welder is critical for any race shop. If money is tight, you can get a small one very inexpensively that can handle most of the tasks you'll face, but you still will need to send the car out when you need work done to either the chassis or the roll cage.

chapter 1

The Foundation: Shop and Crew

I believe the basis for any success you are going to have at the racetrack has very little to do with how much you spend or even what kind of equipment you own. You can own a brand-new car with all the best of everything, but if you aren't organized, if your team doesn't know how to do its job properly, and if you don't come to the track prepared, then you don't stand a chance to win.

Of course, the responsibility for making sure that a team is organized and everyone is competent in their roles falls to one person: the crew chief. And if you are reading this book, I'm assuming that's you. Back in '79 when I first got into racing, a crew chief could get by with just superior mechanical skills, but the role of the crew chief has changed since then. Today, it isn't enough to be just a good mechanic. Whether your goal is to run a Nextel Cup team or simply to win your track championship, you also have to be an organizer, a motivator, a teacher, and an all-around people person. You might think that because your race team is small, these skills aren't important—but the opposite is true. If a small team hopes to be competitive, it must work even more efficiently than a large team.

WRENCHES DON'T BUILD CARS, PEOPLE DO

The most important part of any racing organization is its people. In Nextel Cup racing, every team's equipment is fairly equal. For proof of that, just look at how close the qualifying is each week. The major difference is the people!

Most of us race simply because we love it and think it's fun. And that's the way it should be, especially since few people are fortunate enough to make a living at it. On a local level, the thrill of going racing is often the only carrot that team owners and crew chiefs can offer someone to work on

a car, because the racing budget rarely has room for salaried positions. But just because you depend on volunteer labor doesn't mean you have to accept any offer for help you receive.

Your race car is only as good as the people working on it. I don't care if you have only one guy coming in to help you and he doesn't charge a dime for doing it; if he's leaving bolts loose on your car or otherwise doing a poor job, he's hurting your program. It doesn't matter if he's your best friend or your brother-in-law; you have to honestly evaluate everyone who spends time in your shop and determine how, where, and if they can be an effective part of your team. I know asking someone not to help out is a mighty tough task, but you've got to ask yourself, "What's more important to me here, being a good old guy or being a successful racer?"

That doesn't mean you have to give the boot right away to anyone you think isn't up to par. It's the crew chief's job to develop the talent of not just the driver, but also the crew. This is where leadership comes in. I've always used the approach of treating people the way you would like to be treated. Don't give me too much credit for coming up with

BELOW: It may seem odd to start a book about racing with an entire chapter on organizing your team and shop, but this is the foundation that will allow you to have more fun—and more wins—on race day.

this one; it's also called the Golden Rule, and it has stood up well against the test of time. I made it a point even in the later stages of my career as a Nextel Cup crew chief that I wouldn't ask anyone to do anything that I wasn't willing to do myself. My role as crew chief didn't make me any more important as a person than the kid we had just hired to clean the lug nuts on the pit stop practice car. God put us all on this earth as equals, and I believe we should treat each other that way. If you lead by example, then your crew will be more willing to believe in you and to listen to what you have to say. If you are going to ask your crew members to put everything into their work—and you will have to if you hope to win—then they will expect to see you doing the same.

One way I have found to keep everybody motivatıed and working to the best of their abilities is to let them know I appreciate their ideas as much as their sweat. This can also be helpful when people notice things that you might overlook simply because they are looking from a different perspective. Maybe they notice something other winning teams are doing and suggest your team give it a try. Whatever it is, make sure to take advantage of your crew members' minds as well as their bodies; it will make them happier and more productive.

AS EASY AS INITIALS ON A CHECKLIST

Most local racers don't have the luxury of time at the track like the Nextel Cup teams have. Make sure every i is dotted and every t is crossed before

you leave the shop, because the track is no place to discover that you've forgotten a critical step. If the track opens at noon, practice begins at three, heat races start at five, and the green flag for the feature drops at seven thirty, then you don't have a minute to waste, and you don't have a lot of time to do any extra wrenching on the car. The best way to make sure your preparation is complete before you load that car and head to the track is to develop a comprehensive checklist system and adhere to it for everything you do.

Using a checklist doesn't reduce your flexibility or ability to adjust on the fly. Rather, it should provide more time for fine-tuning. A race car is a complex piece of equipment, and a certain level of organization in your maintenance and setup routines is necessary to make sure that you or someone on your team doesn't neglect a critical component. When I was working as a crew chief, I had a checklist that

had to be completed on every car before it left the shop. It was on a fairly long piece of paper that stayed on a clipboard near the car. At the top of the list were 20 or 25 maintenance items that had to be done to the car every week—clean the filter screen on the oil tank, change the gears, clean the radiator fins, etc. These were all things that had to be done every week whether you won or ran terribly.

After the car was cleaned and put up on jack stands—but usually before the first 25 items on the checklist were complete—I did a thorough visual inspection on the car. Anything I or anyone else on the team found that needed attention was added to the bottom of the list. Maybe the rear window was cracking and needed to be replaced. Maybe, at the last race, we had trouble getting through inspection because of something on the car. I'd put that problem on the list to ensure it was taken care of before it was time to load up for the next race. Those extra tasks have to be added to the checklist as soon as possible so that your guys have a chance to get to them.

Even though it's called a "checklist," don't allow guys to simply put a check beside an item once they've completed that task. Even if it's just two of you, use your initials or a mark that identifies who completed each task. This isn't so you know who to blame if something goes wrong. Pointing fingers won't help, but understanding who did what on the car can help you figure out your weaknesses. Maybe you blew a water line off the engine. Now, instead of chalking up a DNF at the track to another one of them racing things, you can track down the cause.

LEFT: In lower-level racing the competition is just as stiff but the budgets are considerably smaller. Crews are almost always all-volunteer and consist mainly of family and friends. In this situation you cannot expect everyone to be an experienced mechanic or racer. You have to be willing to teach your guys what they need to know in order to become a great support crew.

Don't Overdo It

Checklists are important to make sure you don't forget things, but they can also be dangerous if you have new or overzealous mechanics. There are some things on a race car that, over the course of a year, you may not loosen or take apart if you don't wreck. With threaded fasteners, there is such a thing as too tight, just like there is too loose. For example, if for 10 straight race mornings a guy has gone through the car and checked all the brake lines by tightening down on the fittings another quarter turn, that means those fittings are two and a half rounds tighter than when you first installed them. You can tighten a brake line only so much before it starts leaking.

Make sure you teach your mechanics that checking if a part is tight doesn't mean tightening it further. Instead of making sure it is tight, each mechanic should just be making sure it isn't loose.

OPPOSITE: A race shop is filled with flammable chemicals. Keep a metal bin for storing your dirty rags. The last thing you want is to have your shop burn down because some rag soaked with a flammable chemical was tossed somewhere it shouldn't have been.

By looking at the checklist, you can find out who tightened all the hoses. Then ask him to tell you exactly how he performed the task. Maybe he forgot to double-clamp it, or maybe he initialed the item before he actually did it. Whatever the reason, this gives you a chance to isolate the problem and fix it before it happens again.

Another benefit of checklists is that they make your crew work more efficiently. Even at the top levels of racing, if you set shop hours from 7 a.m. until 7 p.m., guys unconsciously pace themselves so that the work they have to do lasts all the way until quitting time. Instead of setting hours, if you have a paid crew, say, "OK, boys, the car has to be loaded on the truck by Wednesday night, and everything on this list has to be done before we can do that."

Now they have a goal, and they have a deadline. Your crew members can see what they are working toward and the progress they are making, and I've found that this greatly improves results. Both production and quality are better.

Over time, as your checklist becomes a routine, you will find that your team members will develop a feel for what they do best, and they will attack that part of the checklist. Help steer your guys to their strengths, and your racing effort will be better off. Just don't forget the two biggest rules when using a checklist: Everyone must sign off with his initials or some mark identifying himself, and nothing on the checklist can be marked off until that task is completed. Give it a try—I promise it will help you eliminate mistakes and get you out of the shop a little earlier.

RACE SHOP BUDGETING AND ORGANIZATION

I know there's the temptation, no matter the level at which you are racing, to believe that if you only had that next piece of shop equipment, it would put you on the road to a perfect season. Unfortunately, we all know that's not true. Few of us are blessed with more money than the law allows, and even though we may dream of racing out of a shop that would put the Nextel Cup guys to shame, that's probably not going to happen. I know that feeling myself.

My son Brandon races a Bandolero, and we have a small shop for his car. We are pretty limited in our resources, too, and often simply have to make do with what we've got.

One of the most critical decisions that you will make regularly in racing is where to spend your money. If you ask me, those decisions are right up there with ride heights, cross weights, and gear selection. You have to spend your money where it's going to have the most impact on your program— whether that's on shop equipment, new parts for the car, or even a nice meal for your crew while you are on the road.

TOOLS FOR THE SHOP

Fortunately, having the best of everything isn't critical when it comes to outfitting your shop. Instead, organization, knowing how to master the equipment you have, and a little ingenuity can get you by quite well.

For example, a sheet metal brake, which is used to make a sharp, straight bend in a piece of sheet metal, is a nice piece of equipment that's often found in race shops. However it's pretty expensive, and if you simply cannot afford one yet, it's not the end of the world. If you have a nice steel workbench, a good straight piece of angle iron, and a few C-clamps, you can make a bend in a piece of sheet metal just as straight as any brake. The tradeoff, of course, is your time. What takes you five minutes with makeshift tools might require only 15 seconds with a sheet metal brake, but if the angle iron and clamps are all you have to work with, it's still better than nothing.

A shear is another nice piece of equipment when it comes to cutting sheet metal. A pair of snips isn't the solution when you are doing a lot of cutting, because snips will wear you out, and you still won't get the nice smooth cut you are looking for. But a nice set of electric shears is a good compromise that will do excellent work on sheet aluminum and light steel.

A welder is something I recommend for every shop. That doesn't mean you have to have a big,

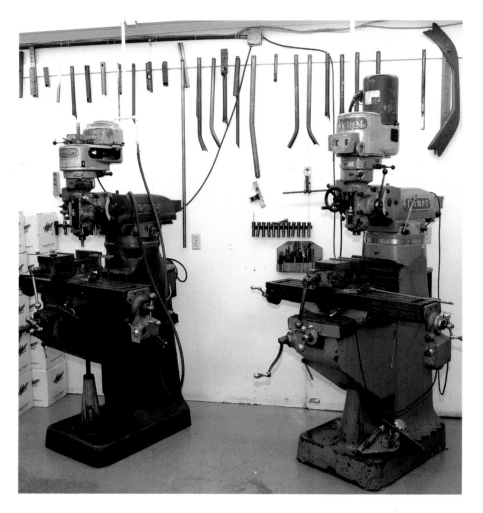

ABOVE: Machinery like mills and lathes can be big-ticket items, but you will be surprised how often you find you need them. One option is to find a machine shop that can help you out; another idea is to shop around for some older, used equipment. If you do buy used, just make sure that it isn't worn out and can still hold decent tolerances.

high-powered beast that can weld up oil rigs. You can buy one of the little 110-volt wire welders relatively cheaply, and it can meet 90 percent of your needs. I don't recommend welding frames and roll bars with it; for that you will need to find someone who has a more powerful welder to help you out. But I have found that in many industrial businesses—welding shops, machine shops, and other places—you are probably going to find at least one or two race fans who would love to be involved with a race team. If you approach them the right way and make them feel like a part of your racing effort, they might just be willing to help you out.

The same goes for machine work. A nice Bridgeport mill or a lathe is a luxury most of us cannot afford. Everybody has stuff on a race car they occasionally need to get machined, but rarely is it enough to justify the cost of a piece of milling equipment. Instead, if you can find a machine shop that's willing to work with you, you probably will be better off. You will save money over the long run and probably get a better piece from them than you can make yourself. It's simply a matter of getting the greatest return for your dollar.

The tools you *really* need in your shop are the ones you will use every day: a couple sets of well-made hand tools, a vise, cutting tools, diagnostic tools, select setup tools. This is the area where you simply aren't served by trying to get out on the cheap. You can buy a vise for $10 at the flea market, but it's going to be a cheap import that isn't going to be worth what you paid in scrap. If it is always working its way loose after you clamp down on something, you aren't going to be able to do the quality work you need to produce. I recommend you invest in tools that won't let you down and you can use for years.

If you happen to have a set of tools that are used just at the shop, I'd much rather see them hung on a simple pegboard than kept in a drawer of a toolbox. If you have a set of wrenches in a drawer, it's hard to see if one of them is missing. But if they are hung up on a pegboard and your $9/16$ isn't in its usual spot, you can see that right away. At the end of the day when you are cleaning up, it's easy to see if all of your wrenches are accounted for. Now, when you are thrashing at the last minute before loading up for the track, missing tools won't slow you down.

There are a lot of other little things you can do in your shop that will either save you time or money—and maybe both. A lot of that has to do with organization. For example, keep a bucket by your bolt bin for your old nuts and bolts. If you are a Late Model team running 25 races over a season, you probably will want to set points at one-third and two-thirds of the way through your season to replace every critical nut and bolt in the car. Those nuts and bolts aren't trash—you just don't want to take a chance on one of them breaking in a suspension component during a race. Instead of throwing these away, put them in your bolt bin for use in a less critical area, like your pit cart or workbench.

It's also a good idea to get a good fireproof rag bin. We're always using flammable chemicals in racing, and that stuff gets on your shop rags. Whether you use a rag service or plan to wash them in your washing machine (I recommend you don't do that; dirty shop rags will ruin a washing machine—believe

SHOP CHECK LIST

Here's a common checklist I used at the shop when working as a crew chief. Not every item will apply to every race team, but you can use this as a starting point for your checklist of things to be done before the race car leaves the shop.

1. Clean underneath thoroughly
2. All paint and body work complete
3. Clean radiator thoroughly
4. Clean oil cooler thoroughly
5. Check all crush panels for sealing— Front/Rear
6. Front/Rear suspension complete
7. Spot-weld all ball joints
8. Change fuel filter
9. Clean and check battery
10. Grease front end
11. Grease driveline
12. Clean all rear-end filters
13. Clean oiling system, new filter and clean screen filter
14. Install rear gear and grease
15. Rear-end pump installed
16. Let rear-end chains out
17. Motor/transmission
18. Grease in transmission
19. Oil and prime system
20. Bleed brakes (Gravity bleed)
21. New windshield and siliconed
22. All decals
23. Heat shields cleaned and installed
24. Air cleaner assembly cleaned with fresh element
25. Springs and shocks
26. Install front sway bar
27. Rear spoiler angle
28. After set-up, secure all lead
29. After set-up, set front fenders
30. After bump steer, tighten, tie-wire, and cotter key front end
31. Set cowl degrees
32. All radio wires and pouches installed
33. Weld eccentrics after set-up
34. Ignition panel installed after all welding
35. Check oil level & water after cranking
36. Check clutch, P/S fluid, and clutch fluid after cranking
37. Check charging system when cranking
38. Drain fuel and take cell loose (After set-up)
39. Check all templates before loading
40. All brake ducts installed before loading
41. Clean and vacuum inside & trunk
42. Clean all windows inside & out
43. Wax outside before loading
44. R.S. window installed before loading
45. All spare suspension parts on truck
46. Spare/crash R.S. window in pit cart

me, I know), don't just leave your dirty rags lying all over the shop. All it takes is one spark from a welder or some other piece of equipment to catch the rag on fire and burn down your shop. Even if nobody gets hurt, a fire can cause your early retirement from racing. The losses can simply be too much to bear financially. Also, hang a good fire extinguisher somewhere in the shop, and make sure that everybody who works with you knows where it is and how to use it.

Finally, give a little bit of thought to how you want your shop organized. Even if your shop is so small you barely have room to move with the car in there, it's still important to have your work areas laid out in a way that makes sense. You don't want your parts washer right next to the welder or the bench grinder. If you do, pieces of metal will get in the parts washer, and the next time you go to clean your bearings, you are going to do more harm than good. Likewise, you don't want your workbench where you pack your bearings to be across the shop from your parts washer. Every time you have to walk across the shop and back, you are wasting time and energy.

I cannot tell you the perfect layout for every shop, as every situation and working environment are different. I'm just recommending you give it a little thought. Spend a week working in your shop and keep a mental record of all your movements. Try to spot the areas where you are spending more time walking from one spot to another or moving things around than you are actually working. Those are your problem areas.

LEFT: The best way to make sure nothing gets forgotten is to keep a checklist. You can see the checklist for this NASCAR Craftsman Truck Series truck lying on the dash. In order for this to work effectively, you have to make it an absolute rule that nobody can check anything off the list until it is *completely* done, and only the person that performed the task can check that item off the list.

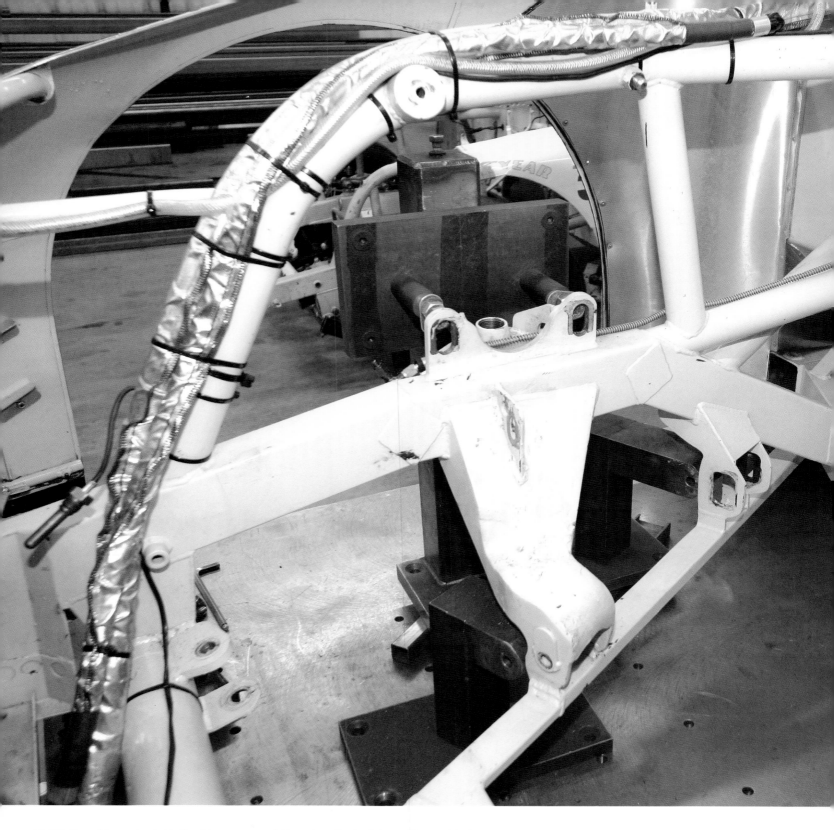

ABOVE: By making a simple jig like this, you can quickly and easily check to see if any critical suspension points have moved after a wreck. Build a jig so that it bolts to a specific location on your surface plate and fits into a certain set of suspension points (such as the upper and lower A-arm mounts in this case). Any time you worry that the frame might be bent, simply put the car on the surface plate and see if your jig fits like it is supposed to.

chapter 2

Evaluating Race Cars

Part of the crew chief's role, especially on smaller teams, is to serve as the general manager. A team's biggest investment is usually its race car, and it can be tricky trying to determine when it's time to retire a car and build or buy a new one. Most teams are one- or two-car operations, and bringing a new car into the stable is a big commitment, in terms of both money and manpower, to get it ready to race. Even on top-flight professional teams, it's critical to make sure any new equipment you acquire is capable of helping you produce wins. If you aren't always getting better, then you're probably getting passed.

BUYING NEW

If you are fortunate enough to have the budget to buy a new race car, I recommend you spend a little time looking at your needs. It is rare for a team to be able to afford a fleet of specialized cars like a Nextel Cup team. Instead, most teams rely on a single car to get them through much of the season. If you are in the situation of racing a touring series, then you need an all-around car. Road courses probably aren't part of your schedule, but you likely will need a chassis that can race well on both smooth and rough racetracks, both flat and high-banked...you get the idea. If you race at your home track every weekend, then you can work with your chassis builder to maximize your car for that track. For example, if you are racing a smooth, relatively flat track, you can really get that right frame rail down low. That lets you get the rocker down there to help the aerodynamics and also brings down the whole car's center of gravity. You can't get away with that at a rough track or at one with high banks—especially if you run your exhaust pipes out the right side of the car—because you are going to have problems bottoming out.

When purchasing a new chassis, don't allow yourself to get caught up in a design that is too far away from what you are used to working with just because somebody tells you it is the next big thing. If you get too far away from what you are used to in terms of chassis design, you may find yourself lost at the racetrack. Your old notes aren't any good because your new car is so different, and you'll find yourself experimenting more than racing. Remember, chassis development is evolutionary, not revolutionary. So if somebody tries to sell you something that is a radical departure from what you are used to, I'd be skeptical. Instead, work with your previous chassis builder to see if, together, you can make a few key improvements over your old chassis. Don't try to change a lot of things until you have a good, solid baseline.

The same thing goes for anyone who comes along and offers to build you a chassis at significantly less than the going rate. Chances are he's just getting started in the business and is desperate for a few orders. There is nothing wrong with that except this person probably doesn't have much of a track record for you to judge the quality of his work. If

ABOVE: Bumping and banging are part of the game in stock car racing, so some minor damage shouldn't scare you off when looking at a used race car. But if you find out the driver wrecks regularly or that the car has taken an exceptionally hard lick, you might want to keep on looking.

you have enough money for only one car, do you want to take a gamble with someone new? Maybe you need to go with the guy who is building the winning cars so that you know you are getting first-rate equipment. Then you can depend on your talents as a crew chief and your driver's abilities behind the wheel to beat the people who are racing the same cars you are.

BUYING USED

I've been running the INEX Bandolero Series with my son Brandon formore than five years now, so I have a little history with the cars and the people racing in my area. People come up to me all the time asking about cars they want to buy. Typically, they'll ask what I think of a particular car, and my response is usually not to look at the car, but the

driver instead. If little Joey is trying to knock down the wall every other week, then you probably want to stay away from his car. On the other hand, if you can't remember little Joey ever getting into a wreck, his car might be a good candidate. The same rule of thumb holds true for full-size cars. Even if the driver isn't a regular winner, if he doesn't wreck often, then it's a good bet that the car is still in good shape.

So you've checked out the driver and he passed the wreck test—now what? You want to find out who built the car originally. Does this builder produce winning cars? Also, almost every chassis has a serial number on it. Using that, the builder should be able to tell you when the chassis was built, if the builder has made many updates to his design since then, and whether the car has been in for significant repairs. Any concrete information you can gather is helpful. Too often I see guys try to make purchasing decisions based on how many times a car has won. Well, unless you can document the answer, the number of wins can be whatever number the owner thinks you want to hear. Besides, even if the number is true, if all the wins came before the car was wadded up in a wreck and had to have a new front clip installed, that number is irrelevant. If the car hasn't won since that new front clip was put on, then that tells you a lot more.

But no matter how much information you gather, you still want to take a good look at the car yourself. The most important pieces on the car are the sus-

A Couple of Dents? No Big Deal

We've put a lot of emphasis on discovering wreck damage as a determining factor when deciding whether to buy a used race car. A little wreck damage, however, doesn't mean that a car is ruined. As I mentioned, the only thing that matters is the suspension pickup points; everything else is essentially just along for the ride. Even a bent frame rail isn't the end of the world if the suspension is right.

One of the first Late Model cars I ever worked on was like that. It was a Camaro, and we built it sometime around 1975 or '76. Neil Bonnett was the first to drive it, and he banged it up pretty bad in the first race out at Birmingham (Alabama) International Raceway. We fixed the car with new front and tail clips, but one of the frame rails—I can't remember which one anymore—was bent so badly you could only get the lead out the back of the tube. We raced and won with that car a lot after that, including the 1978 Snowball Derby in Pensacola, Florida, so it obviously was still good despite some pretty ugly wreck damage. Just goes to show you the only thing in racing that really matters is how the car drives on the track.

LEFT: If you are having a new chassis built, make sure to communicate with your builder exactly what you need from this chassis and the types of tracks you plan to race it on. Sometimes you are forced to make compromises, but whenever you can build a car to take advantage of the specific conditions you will be racing under, you will be that much more ahead.

BELOW LEFT: Here's a jig to locate the front sway bar tube. It uses an aluminum insert to locate the center of the tube and a steel piece to find the location on the plate.

pension and steering mounts: the upper and lower A-arms, the idler arm, the steering box, the panhard bar, and the rear suspension. It's hard to tell by just looking if everything is located correctly, but you can look for cracks in the welds and bends in the metal. Both are warning signs.

Damage in other areas can also tip you off to signs of trouble. The trailing arm cross member and sometimes even the frame rails are used to locate everything on the car, so check those areas carefully. The firewall is also a great place to look. When the fabricator installs all the interior sheet metal, it's usually nice and straight; if it is bent or buckled up, you can bet the car has been banged up at some point. Now, a buckled rear firewall isn't going to harm how the car handles, but it can tip you off to take a closer look at the more important areas.

If you think the car is a good candidate, see if you can get it to the chassis builder and have him check it out. Ask if you can haul the car back to its builder if you agree that you will purchase the car if it checks out. If the seller agrees, you can have the builder put the car up on his jig to make sure all the suspension points still line up, as well as check for updates that might need to be done. If the seller doesn't agree to the idea, that might be a sign he's hiding something.

MEASURE AND RECORD

Once you have your new car in your shop, it is time to start taking some measurements. This is also a good idea if you have just joined a team and don't have any records on the car your new team is racing. First, place the car on a surface plate or a good flat surface. An even better idea is to put the car on a jig. It doesn't have to be anything fancy—many are as simple as two heavy I beams—as long as it is level and makes it easy to attach locating fixtures.

With the car either on a flat surface or a chassis jig, remove all the suspension components, making sure you are supporting the frame so that it is level. Now, start taking measurements of all the car's criti-cal dimensions. First, measure your frame height (it doesn't necessarily have to be ride height, just something you can repeat later), then follow that up with things like the upper and lower A-arm heights and their relationship to each other, panhard bar mount location and height, things like that.

Once you measure the locations of every important piece you can think of, record it with plenty of notes explaining how you made each measurement. How you measure isn't nearly as important as being able to do it again later on. If the car gets wrecked or banged up, you want to be able to set up everything just like you did the first time and take those measurements to see if anything has moved.

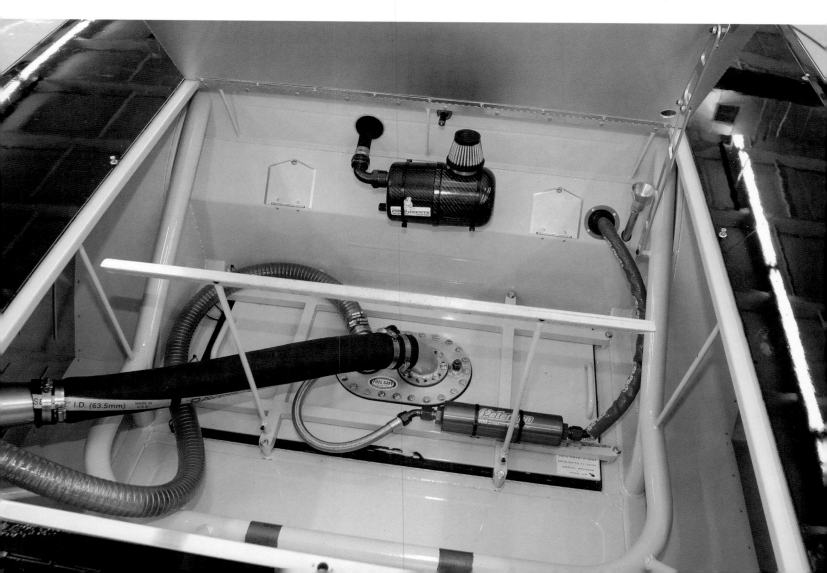

An even better way to do this is to place the car on a jig and build fixtures to all these critical points that I've talked about. It's a little more time intensive to do this, but it can really pay off later on. Even if you take all the fixtures back off the jig and store them in a corner, you now have a permanent locator for all the critical locations on your car. Say you get the front of the car reclipped—now you can put the car up on the jig as soon as you get it back from the chassis shop and check to make sure the work was done right. The fixtures can also save you a little money and time. If the car bumps the wall and you are concerned the frame might be bent but it's not obvious, those fixtures can save you a trip and the expense of carrying it back to the chassis builder. Plus, even if you have the money for the builder to check it out, it may be two weeks before he has time to put the car back on

his jig. But if you have that I beam jig with your fixtures already made up, you can check it out yourself and maybe even make some minor repairs.

I just want to stress that no matter if you are using an I beam–type jig, a surface plate, or simply a level area on your shop floor, the most important thing isn't whether you use fixtures or a measuring tape. Likewise, it doesn't matter if you set the car on jack stands or have a special set of blocks fabricated to hold the frame at ride height. The things that matter most are that you place the car in a good, flat area and you keep detailed notes so that you can repeat processes exactly the same way every time. The better you can repeat your processes, the more reliable your measurements are going to be.

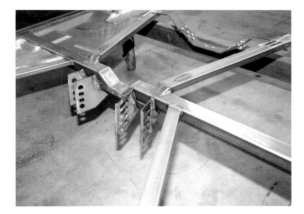

LEFT: Racers often put too much importance on the frame rails. Remember, the only purpose for the frame rails is to connect the front of the car to the rear. Even if a frame rail is bent like a banana, it's OK as long as the suspension pickup points are still where they are supposed to be.

BELOW: Nearly every chassis builder I am familiar with uses the trailing-arm cross member as the starting point and builds the reast of the car around that. If this piece is bent, it is going to be nearly impossible to know if anything else on the car is right.

Measure It

The following list contains the most common chassis measurements when baselining a chassis. All measurements should be from the center of the pivot point on the chassis mount—not the actual suspension component. Also, the car should be sitting at ride height.

Location	Measure To
Upper A-arm	Ground
	Between the two pivot points
Lower A-arm	Ground
	Between the two pivot points
Idler arm mounts	Between idler arm and steering box mounts, and to ground
Steering box mounts	To ground
Trailing arm mounts (at the car)	To ground
Panhard bar mount on right frame rail	To ground
	To trailing arm mounts

ABOVE: To maximize the protection for your driver, all the different pieces of equipment have to be able to work together as a whole. Notice how all the components of the seat form a "cocoon" around Mike Skinner to keep him contained in the event of a collision. Also, the head supports are designed to work together with a head and neck support system, like the HANS device.

chapter 3

Safety Systems: Because Racing Is Cheap When You Compare It to Hospital Bills

In stock car racing, everything is constantly evolving. Horsepower levels are always improving, chassis setups change, bodies are changing to improve aerodynamics, and anything else you can think of. But the one area that has changed the most recently—and I'm talking improvements by leaps and bounds—is the safety precautions we take for drivers.

Even though I think teams, manufacturers, and NASCAR were all headed in the right direction, there is no question in my mind that when Dale Earnhardt—the icon of our sport and a man everybody thought was invincible—was killed, it really accelerated the process. We've had a lot of improvements since then in the ways we can protect drivers in their race cars, and the good news is it doesn't apply only to Nextel Cup teams. Anyone can take advantage of these developments, and I encourage you to do just that.

PERSONAL EQUIPMENT

Let's start with the basics: the driver's personal safety equipment. This is everything worn on the body. First off, make sure your driver has a good fire-resistant Nomex driving suit. I recommend at least two Nomex layers in its construction. Then go ahead with the fireproof socks, long underwear, shoes, and gloves. I know all that stuff gets hot, but it's a lot cooler than getting burned in a fire.

Helmets are also a major consideration when it comes to personal safety equipment. Full-face racing helmets aren't required in Nextel Cup racing yet, but I think they offer a lot more protection than the open-face style. First, they offer better protection in the event of fire. And second, if your face happens to make contact with the steering wheel, instead of getting a broken nose or jaw, you will probably walk away with nothing worse than a scuff on the front of your helmet.

Don't assume that all helmets are created equal and try to get by with one designed for riding a motorcycle on the highway. Racing helmets need to be fire-resistant, including a Kevlar chinstrap and self-extinguishing rubber. Check to make sure your helmet meets the most current Snell requirements. The Snell Memorial Foundation issues increasingly better guidelines for helmet construction approximately every five years, and reputable manufacturers work with the foundation to make sure their helmets meet or exceed those guidelines. This is a great program for the racer because it is easy to know when you are getting a good helmet. All you have to do is look for the approval sticker. For more information, contact the Snell Memorial Foundation at P.O. Box 493, St. James, NY 11780. The organization's Web site is www.smf.org.

THE COCOON

If you compare the inside of a race car today to the interior of a car from 10 years ago, you would wonder where all the room went. A decade ago, a stock car had so much room inside the cockpit that you

RIGHT: Compare the photo on page 23 with this shot of the interior of a Craftsman race truck. It's a much tighter squeeze in here, but everything works together to protect the driver.

would think you could lease some of it out to tenants. Now with all the equipment we have to keep the driver safe, it's a wonder that he even has a place to sit.

I call the area where the driver sits the "cocoon," and its purpose is to keep the driver contained. When it comes to protecting a driver inside the car, the main thing is that when the car hits something and there is a sudden deceleration, the driver moves as little as possible. The biggest part of that cocoon is the seat.

Aluminum racing seats have come a long way in the last few years. They are more supportive to all areas of the body, especially the head. That protection extends all the way down to the legs, where leg supports and "knee knockers" keep the driver's legs in place in the event of a wreck.

A racing seat isn't absolutely stable. If you take a hard lick, it will give and flex a bit. Over time, if you have a couple of wrecks, that seat will open up and the metal will fatigue. Make sure you check it out periodically for cracks or bending, and check it any time you make contact with the wall or another car. That's also why you never want to buy a used seat if you don't know its history. They don't last forever, and you don't want to take a chance installing a seat that's seen better days.

Carbon fiber seats are coming on the scene in the Nextel Cup Series, but I don't think they are going to take over stock car racing in general. Carbon fiber seats work well but are expensive, and most designs won't fit in a car without serious modifications to the roll cage, seat hoop, and driveshaft tunnel. Aluminum seats are much more affordable, and when built right they provide the driver excellent protection.

BELTS

A five-point harness system is still the standard. The five anchor points are one for the crotch belt, two for the lap belts, and two for the shoulder belts. The most critical belts to me are the two lap belts. They should run at a 45-degree angle across the driver's hips. The slider locks that adjust the length of the belt should always be perpendicular to the belt. If they're not, it can cause a phenomenon called "dumping" if there is a hard pull on the belts (like in a wreck), and the belt can actually be severed.

It's also critical how the shoulder belts fit the driver. They should be anchored to a bar just behind the driver's seat that runs horizontally at about the same level as the top of the shoulder blades. This shortens the overall length of the shoulder belts, which is important because, believe it or not, those belts will stretch. Keeping the belts short limits the amount they will stretch in a wreck and improves their ability to hold the driver in place. Also, make sure the belts run perpendicular from the anchor point on the bar behind the driver's back, straight over his shoulders,

Do It Yourself

A collapsible steering shaft is a great safety feature in a race car. In the event of a wreck in which the front of the car gets crushed, the idea is that the shaft will collapse instead of turning into a spear aimed at the driver's chest. A lot of drivers like the steering wheel right up against their chest; it gives them better leverage on the wheel, but it also puts the wheel real close to their chin and makes a collapsible steering shaft even more important.

A lot of manufacturers make very good collapsible shafts for racing, but the old-fashioned way still works. When I first got started racing with a Late Model team in the '70s, we had to make almost all of our own stuff. We would hunt down a collapsible steering shaft out of a street car in the junkyard and modify it to fit our needs. All we had to do was drill a hole through the shaft and insert a small cotter pin. The pin was enough to keep the shaft from sliding in and out during normal driving conditions, but if there was a wreck, the pin was small enough to shear into two pieces and allow the shaft to collapse.

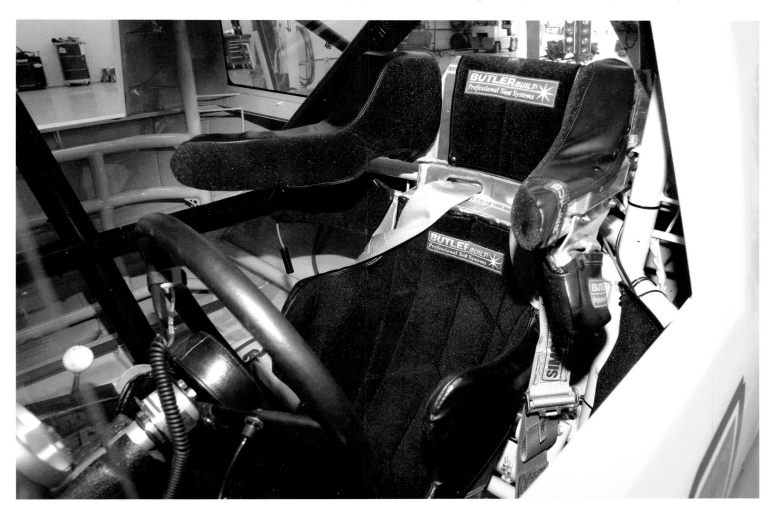

and down to the buckle. If the belts run either up or down to his shoulders, it raises the possibility of an injury in the event of a wreck.

Both the belts and the seat should be anchored using at least 7/16-inch bolts that are grade 8 in quality. Also, make sure nothing attaches directly to the floor pan. Everything that holds the driver in place must be anchored to the roll cage structure. This is easy enough to achieve with a seat hoop, which is simply tubing of the same quality of the roll cage that is welded into the structure of the cage. By attaching the seat and belt anchors to this, you are protecting your driver in a couple of different ways. First, your anchors are now a lot stronger than if you bolted them directly to the floor pan. The sheet metal in the floor pan is very thin, and I don't care how many fender washers you use, you stand a chance of pulling those bolts out on impact. Also, in the event another car spears your car right in the driver's-side door, you don't want those door bars folding in and making contact with your driver. If the seat and belts are bolted to the seat hoop and if the

roll cage is shoved inside the car, the driver and the seat will move right along with it.

Seat belts have a limited lifespan. Most of the time that useable lifespan will be set by the manufacturer, but you also want to make sure you don't do anything to weaken the belts unnecessarily. Be careful when you are washing your car not to get your belts wet. When the belts get wet and then dry out again, that weathers them and causes them to weaken. That's going to happen some no matter what, especially during a race. A driver who is really working hard on a hot night can soak both his driving suit and his belts in sweat before the night is over. If you run that same car 20 or more times in a season, you might want to consider changing out those belts before the new season starts, just to have a fresh set in there.

HEAD AND NECK RESTRAINTS

Technically, head and neck restraints belong in the same category as personal equipment, but they are so new and innovative I think they deserve special

ABOVE: One area of seat design that has been lacking until recently is a good, solid head support. A head and neck restraint will keep the head from moving forward too rapidly, but good head supports are required to keep the head steady in the event of a side impact.

RIGHT: Notice how the sheet metal of this fuel cell completely covers the bladder and has no dents or other signs of damage.

OPPOSITE: It's cheap and easy to fabricate, so I think every gas pedal should have a toe strap the driver can use to pull the throttle closed if the throttle hangs up.

attention. At the time this book went to press, there were several different devices on the market. They include the HANS device, the Hutchens device, and Simpson's new restraint. They all work, but NASCAR's testing has shown that the HANS device performs best overall.

In my opinion, head and neck restraints have become one of the final big pieces of the safety puzzle when it comes to protecting a driver. What we've learned is when there is an impact, the best way to protect the driver is to hold him stationary in that cocoon we've created. We've got the belts so that his body isn't moving, but the driver's head is encased in a heavy old helmet, and it is supported by just a skinny little neck. So when there is an impact and a sudden deceleration, the inertia from the weight of the driver's head and his helmet can be just too much for the neck to overcome. A good head and neck restraint system helps hold the head and helmet stationary so that the whiplash effect doesn't injure the driver.

Now that we've realized how important restraining the head is, I don't think any driver should make another lap without this critical piece of equipment. That includes practice laps! Even if you are scuffing tires or doing a plug check, don't make another lap without your full complement of safety equipment. I'll never forget that Ernie Irvan was injured during a practice session. Treat every lap like you are driving the final lap of the most important race of your life.

THE COCKPIT

Take the time to sit down in the car and look around for potential problems. Look for sharp edges that can cut your driver—these usually show up under the dash—and cover them with a strip of rubber. Make sure all the exposed bars that are close to the driver are covered with roll cage padding. Once the steering shaft location is set, go ahead and pad that so the driver can't crack the inside of his knees against it.

When you are mounting your fire bottle, go ahead and mount it as low and to the left as possible. That bottle is heavy, and it's OK to make its location a performance consideration. The only thing you need

to make sure of is that you can check the gauge relatively easily to make sure the bottle hasn't lost its charge. The biggest consideration is mounting the spray nozzles. A good three-nozzle system has one nozzle spraying on the engine, one on the driver, and one on the fuel cell. You don't want the nozzle that sprays the driver to be pointed directly at his head; it needs to be shooting on his legs and torso. There are two things that can hurt a driver in the event of a cockpit fire: the heat and smoke from the fire itself, and the stuff that's in those fire bottles. So don't point it directly at the driver's face. If he's smart, he will be wearing a full-face helmet anyway, and that will provide a big measure of fire protection.

Every cockpit should have a main power cutoff switch mounted so that it is in easy reach of both the driver when he is belted tightly in his seat and a safety worker if he's leaning through either window. The main power cutoff switch should be wired to the negative side of the battery cable so that when you hit it, it cuts off the power to everything in the car. That way, whether you have an electrical fire or a throttle hung open after a wreck, that switch will kill everything dead.

THE FUEL CELL

Other than hitting a wall head on, I think every racer's biggest fear is a fire. Thankfully, fuel cell technology has done a lot to reduce the potential for fire. Make sure that the date on the fuel cell bladder is current; NASCAR requires replacing it every five years. Also, you want to make sure that the can is good and rigid and has no cracks or bends.

Don't just bolt the cell directly to the car's frame. You should build a rack out of at least one-inch square tubing that completely surrounds the cell on all six sides. Now bolt that to your frame using bolts that are at least grade 8 and are at least $5/16$ inch at the shank, although I prefer three-eighth-inch

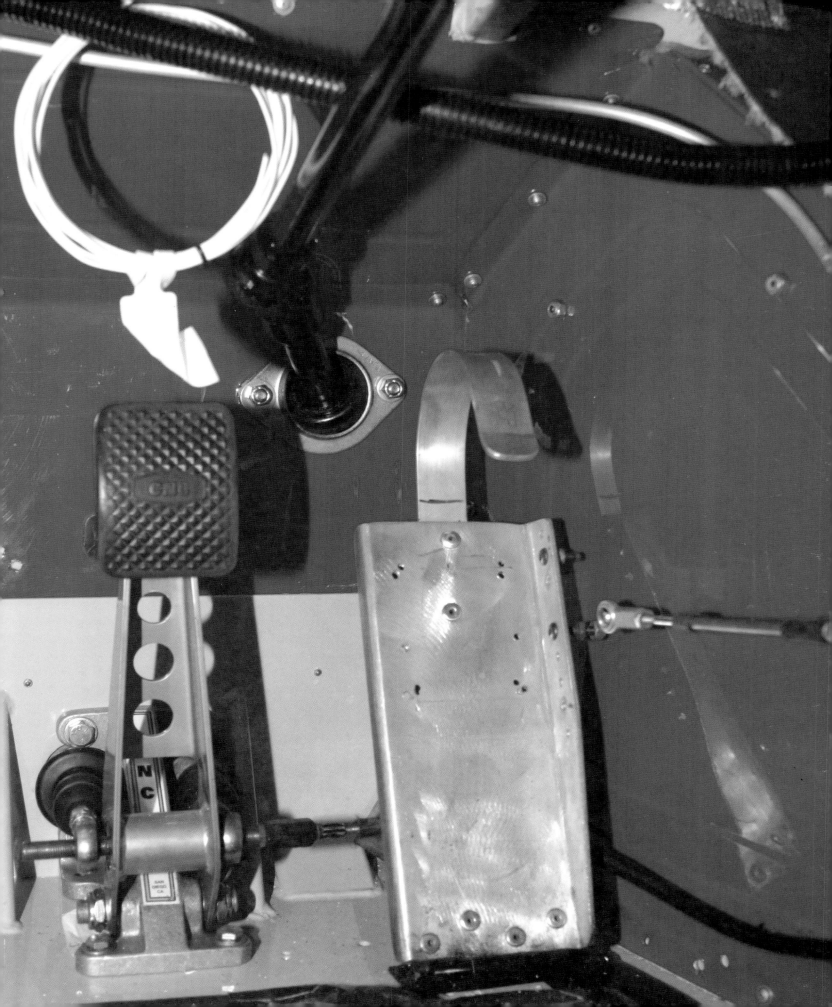

bolts. I know that this location is the worst place in the world to be adding weight—it's up high and behind the rear axle—but it's important that the cell is properly protected. Finally, inspect the fuel cell regularly just like you do the driver's seat. Keep an eye out for stress fractures in the cage and the mounting hardware, especially if the car takes a hit on the track.

In the event the car is involved in a wreck, there are a few specific additional checks you need to make on your fuel cell. First, inspect the check valve—the part inside the cell that seals off the main fill hole when it is turned upside down. That steel ball in the check valve is heavy, and I've seen that ball's inertia actually bend the cage in the event of a hard lick. So make sure it still seals up properly. Also, check to make sure the pickup line is still in the correct location. The pickup should be in the bottom of the cell in the right rear corner. Sometimes when things get shoved around in a wreck, the fuel lines pull tight and pull the pickup out of location. Next thing you know, you aren't getting the fuel mileage you expect, and it's because the pickup isn't getting all the fuel out of the cell.

BRAKES

I don't know how many people actually think about it, but I consider running two master cylinders on the braking system a valuable safety feature. The main reason racers do it is so that they can bias the braking power to either the front or rear to help the car's performance, but it also protects against a complete brake failure on the track.

Let's say you are involved in a high-speed crash that knocks the whole right front wheel assembly off, and the brake lines are ripped from the caliper. If you have a single master cylinder providing line pressure to all four wheels, your braking system will be totally disabled. But if you run two master cylinders with separate circuits for the front and rear wheels, in the same scenario you will still have brakes to the rear wheels, which can help you get stopped before you hit anything else. So even though you are just using one brake pedal, the two separate brake circuits give you a measure of braking power even if one fails on you.

Any time you are running your brake lines, keep in mind the need to allow for suspension travel. You don't want to run too much flex line because it will make the pedal feel spongy, but make sure you allow enough for the front wheels to turn all the way to the left and the right. Also run your suspension all the way up and down. I've seen people build their car without doing that, and then when they go to jack it up, the suspension extends all the way out and the flex hose gets pulled as tight as a banjo string. Finally, when you are running your hard lines, try to run them in areas that will be protected from debris flying up off the track, which can cut the lines.

DRIVER COOLING

This may not fit strictly in the category of safety, but in my experience a comfortable driver is a better driver, and that makes him a safer driver, too. The

biggest factor for keeping your driver comfortable is adequate ventilation and cooling. I've yet to hear a driver say he could use a little more heat in the cockpit.

The two most important things you can do to keep your driver cool are to insulate him from the heat sources and pump plenty of cool air on him. You might not be able to afford a $7,000 cool box, and I don't blame you, but that doesn't mean there isn't anything you can do. When it comes to insulation, the feet and the bottom of the seat are the two most critical areas. Usually, the exhaust pipes run directly under the driver, and they can make the floor pan feel like a frying pan. With today's technology, there are a lot of good insulators out there that take up a minimum amount of space, so there is really no reason your driver should get burned.

Just remember that the best insulator is an air gap. Whether it's a false floor to keep the driver's feet up off the floorboard or an air gap between the bottom of the seat and the car, that's your best insulation. If you mount the seat right on the floor of the car and the exhaust pipes are right under there, you might as well be sitting your driver right on the exhaust pipes.

One thing that we try to do is use a phenolic spacer between the seat and the seat rails at all the mounting points. Phenolic is an excellent insulator

and keeps the car's heat from radiating directly into the seat. You could use a piece of metal or a bunch of washers for spacers, but that doesn't provide any insulation. Don't, however, try to use wood as a spacer, because it will shatter in a wreck.

Also, don't be afraid to run a few hoses outside of the window to direct cool air on your driver. I know it doesn't look good, but racing isn't a beauty contest. It's about who is fastest, and a driver who can't get comfortable because his backside is burning can't concentrate fully on his driving. Give your driver a constant flow of fresh outside air. If his feet or his back is burning in a long race, run another hose from the window and point it at his feet or the back of his seat. The bottom line is if your driver is more comfortable than the next guy at the end of a 150-lap race—even if the cars and their abilities are equal—your guy has the advantage and will be more likely to prevail.

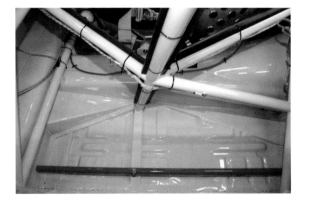

LEFT: A scatter shield isn't always required, but your driver does need protection in case of a clutch failure. In addition to a steel bell housing, we use a piece of thick rubber (like a piece of conveyor belt or the mud flap from a tractor-trailer rig) riveted to the bottom of the transmission tunnel. You'd be surprised how strong that stuff is.

BELOW: In most race cars, the fuel line is routed through the cockpit to protect it. I also recommend running it through a steel tube to protect it and painting that tube red. That way, if anybody—like a track safety crew—starts cutting the car apart, they will recognize that the fuel line housing isn't a regular part of the frame and will leave it alone.

For the Crew Chief

One thing I always practiced as a crew chief was to remind my driver to tighten his belts. No matter how hard he pulled on them at the start of a race, they would always loosen up a little. My standard deal during every caution was to come on the radio with one lap to go and tell my driver, "One to go. Clean your tires and pull on your belts." Then it became a habit for both my driver and me, and we wouldn't forget.

Also, one of the worst things that can happen to a driver is a stuck throttle. As a crew chief, you never want to put your driver in a piece of equipment in which he can get hurt, so any time you work with either the air cleaner or carburetor, take the time to check and make sure nothing moved that can potentially cause the throttle to hang up. Have your driver or someone blip the throttle a few times to make sure it returns to idle on its own and doesn't hang open.

ABOVE: Some teams use a raised "table" to get their race cars up off the ground, but a set of "elephant stands" under the wheels works just as well. All you need is something to make working under your race car easier. First, run a string weighted with plumb bobs off both the left and right sides of the rear cross member. Then, run a straightedge along the line created between the points of the plumb bobs. This replicates a parallel line to the rear cross member on the ground.

chapter 4

Stringing Your Race Car

I believe the secret to a fast race car is as simple as getting all four tires pointed in the right direction. There is a lot involved with that—camber, caster, bump steer, and so on—but before you can do that, you have to have a baseline. Stringing a car provides that baseline, and it is surprisingly simple and easy.

Stringing a car requires nothing more elaborate than a ball of string, four plumb bobs, a straight-edge, a couple of tape measures, and four aluminum "elephant stands," which are just raised stands to put under the wheels and raise the car. Stringing a car was one of the first things I learned when I was racing Late Models in Alabama, and I've been doing it just about the same way ever since. In recent years, there have been plenty of new, more techno-logically advanced laser systems for stringing a car. They all do the job, but none that I have seen is any simpler or quicker than good old string. I may be old-fashioned, but the day I ran my last race as a crew chief in November 2000, that car left the shop and I was sure the rear end was dead straight using nothing but string. So, yes, there are other ways to do it, but no method is better. After all, you can be sure that a piece of string will never lie to you.

START AT THE BACK

When stringing a car, I always start at the rear wheels and make sure those are straight. That's because I prefer to use the trailing arm cross mem-ber as my primary reference point for everything else on the car. Chassis builder Mike Laughlin taught me years ago that the trailing arm cross member is the first piece of tubing that goes in when building a new chassis, and that's been the case with every Cup, Truck, or Busch chassis I've worked with since then. A lot of people prefer to base their measure-ments on the frame rails, but I don't think that's

the best idea. The only purpose of the frame rails is to connect the front of the car to the back. One or both of them can be bent like a banana, and the car may still be capable of running great. The only problem is that if you are trying to measure off the frame rails, you will never know it.

So we work off the trailing arm cross member because we know everything is based off of it, and the first thing we begin working on is the rear end. We want to make sure the rear end is straight with the car, or "steered" correctly. The rear wheels need to be pointed straight ahead in line with the car so that it won't crabwalk down the track. Once that is done, we'll use the rear wheels to make sure the front is in line.

RIGHT: After you have set the plumb bobs and the straightedge at the rear cross member, move to the rear-end housing. Using tape, string two plumb bobs off the axle housing an equal distance and as far outboard as you can get. The plumb bobs on the rear axle don't have to be in line with the two on the cross member—that's what the straightedge is for.

BELOW: Knowing the rear end is square and steering straight ahead (A) is critical when baselining and setting up a race car. If the distance from the rear cross member to the axle housing is longer on the right side (B), the car will always be too loose. If it is longer on the left (C), the car will feel tight.

When you begin, it's easiest if the car is sitting on elephant stands or otherwise up off the ground at ride height. I've always just used four large aluminum stands that are all the same height and strong enough to hold up the car. With one under each wheel, the suspension is kept at ride height and you can work comfortably underneath the car. Just make sure the car—and stands, if you are using them—is sitting on a level surface.

As I mentioned before, you will need four plumb bobs on string, a long straightedge, and two measuring tapes. You will also need a roll of tape. Begin by taping two plumb bobs to the trailing arm cross member. One is on the right side and the other is on the left, and both are pretty far outboard (toward the frame rails of the car). Exactly where isn't critical; just make sure that both are on the same side of the cross member. In other words, don't tape one to the front of the cross member and the other to the back. Extend them down on the string until they are nearly touching the shop floor, but not quite. Make sure the plumb bobs are still, and place your straightedge so that one side lines up with the tips of the plumb bobs. This establishes the line of your cross member on the floor so that you can measure off it.

Next, fix your other two plumb bobs on string off the rear axle housing as far outboard as you can get. Again, front or back isn't important as long as you are consistent. Extend them so that the tips

are almost touching the ground but not quite. Now, using your measuring tapes, measure from the straightedge (being very careful not to nudge it out of position) to each point directly underneath the plumb bobs hanging off the rear-end housing. Be careful that your tapes aren't running at angles to each other, which will give you a false measurement. Both need to be perpendicular to the straightedge.

If both measurements are the same, then you know your rear axle is parallel to the trailing arm cross member. If that is the case, your rear wheels should be pointed straight ahead. If the measurements are different, then your alignment is off. The rear end is steered to the side with the longest measurement, so if the measurement is longer on the right side, that means the rear of the car is going to want to drift to the right and the car will feel loose in the turns. On a trailing arm car, one arm normally has an eccentric in the pivot that allows the length of the arm to be adjusted. You can work with this eccentric to steer or straighten the rear end.

BACK TO THE FRONT
With that done, we can get out from underneath the car and start working on the front wheels. This is

↑ Front of Car ↑

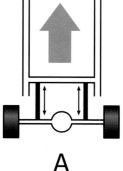

A

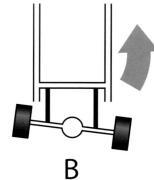

B

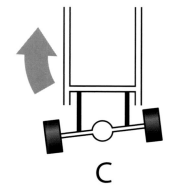

C

done by basing the front wheel location and direction off the rear wheels. You do this by stringing your car, but first it's always a good idea to "high spot" your wheels. This is simply checking to make sure that variations in the sidewall of the tire don't throw off your measurements. To do this have someone spin the tire while you hold a piece of chalk against something sturdy like a jackstand. While the tire is spinning, slowly slide the jackstand toward the tire until the chalk just comes into contact with the sidewall (avoid raised areas like letters). The area of the tire the chalk marks first is the high spot. Make sure you keep this spot or spots at the top and bottom of the tire and away from your string.

Now you are ready to run your strings. All you need to do is tie each end of the string to a jack stand; a jack stand has enough weight to keep good tension on the string but is still light enough so that you can move it and make adjustments.

Run two strings, one down each side of the car and just a few inches off the ground. First, make sure both strings are the same distance off the ground, both at the front and at the back. Next, you can start locating the string to the car.

Move to the left rear wheel and take two measurements. Measure the distance from the edge of the rim to the string at the back of the rim and at the front. Now move the jack stands until that measurement is the same at both the front and the back of the rim. The distance between the rim and the string isn't important—it can be two inches or it can be eight inches—but what is important is that the measurement is the same. Once it is, you know that the string is parallel to the direction of the rear wheel, and the line created by the string runs all the way past the front wheel.

A couple of words of caution here: I like to keep the string down low on the wheel, because all we are worried about when stringing a car is the contact patch, or the part of the tire that is making

ABOVE: Using two tape measures, mark the distance from the straightedge to the point just underneath each plumb bob. Make sure your measurement is a good 90-degree angle to the straightedge. If these two measurements are equal, then your rear end is straight. If they are not equal, then you know your rear end is out of alignment.

LEFT: On most truck-arm cars, the arm on the right side is mounted with an eccentric that allows adjustments to the angle of the rear end. The eccentric is the egg-shaped washer welded to the bolt. As the bolt is turned, the eccentric rides against the rail on the mount, pushing the bolt forward or backward. This in turn pulls the right side of the axle—and the right rear wheel—forward or backward.

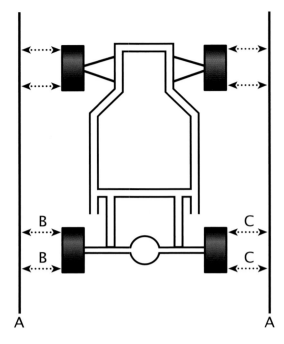

TOP RIGHT: Once the rear end is squared, string-ing the front wheels is straightforward. Run two strings along both sides of the car a few inches off the ground (A). It is best if the strings are tied on each end to jack stands or some other object with some weight that's still easy to move. Adjust the strings until the measurements on both the front and rear of the rims are the same (B and C). Now, make the same measurements at the front wheels. If you measure a front wheel and get different measurements at the front and back of the rim, that shows your amount of toe in or out. If your measurements are the same at the front wheel but differ from the mea-surements you have at the rear wheel, then your wheels aren't tracking in a straight line. Track can be adjusted individually at the front wheels by installing different length control arms or wheel spacers. Track can also be adjusted individu-ally at the rear end with wheel spacers, or you can shift the entire rear end from side to side by adjusting the length of the track bar.

BOTTOM RIGHT: Once the rear end is straight, it's time to move to the outside of the race car. Pull a string between two movable anchors—jack stands usually work the best—on both sides of the car about six inches away from the wheels.

contact with the track. We don't care what the top of the tire is doing, so it makes little sense to run the string up at the top of the wheel. Also, making camber changes at the front wheels can move the contact patch in or out. If the string is run at the center of the wheel, you might not notice how cam-ber changes are affecting track width, because the front wheels tend to pivot around the hub. Also, I prefer taking my measurements from the rim to the string and not use the tire, because I feel the rim is more precise than the sidewall of the tire. Just make sure you are using a nice, straight set of rims that aren't bent up. We'll talk about this more in chap-ter 10 on setting up your car, but it's a good idea to keep a new set of tires mounted on new rims in your shop and use them for nothing except setting up your car. It just eliminates a potential variable from the equation.

Adjusting the string at the front and the back can be a bit aggravating. It's really a two-man job, but just keep at it until you get both measurements exactly the same. When you get it right, move to the front wheel and measure at the same locations.

As an example, let's pretend that you've strung the car and gotten measurements of 6 inches on both sides of the left rear wheel. You move to the front and get 5 7/16 at the rear of the front rim and 5 9/16 at the front of the rim. Now you know that the front wheel is toed in 1/8 of an inch. You can straighten this out by adjusting the tie rod out until both sides

measure 5 1/2 inches. This just gets your front wheel pointed straight ahead—we'll worry about setting toe later. Also, notice that this isn't the same mea-surement that you got at the rear, but because both measurements at the front wheel are the same, you know that the front wheel is now pointed straight ahead. The difference in the 6 inches between the rim and the string at the rear wheel and the 5 1/2 inches at the front means that the front wheel is outboard of the rear by 1/2 inch. In other words, the track left by the rear wheel is going to be inside the track left by the front wheel by 1/2 inch.

Now move over to the right side of the car and repeat the process. Once you have the right front wheel pointed straight ahead, check the track between the right front and right rear wheels. We'll discuss this further in chapter 10, but I always want my front tread width a little bit wider than the rear tread width. That just helps the stability of the race

LEFT: Here is where stringing a car becomes a two-man job. While measuring at the front and back of the wheel, move the two jack stands until you get the same distance to the string. Now you know the string is parallel to the wheel and you can move to the front wheel to check toe in or out and how the wheels are tracking.

BELOW: Although it isn't absolutely critical, I recommend that the string be at the same height at the front and rear wheels and that both strings on the left and right sides of the race car be at equal heights.

car. In a perfect world, my rear is one-eighth to one-quarter inch narrower than the front. But that difference isn't split. The left side of the car is lined up perfectly, and the difference is between the right-side tires. I hate the right front being less than one-eighth inch outboard of the right rear, but I don't really want it to be any more than a quarter inch outboard, either. If the right front is inboard of the right rear, however, you can't put enough spring on that right front wheel to make it feel secure getting into the corner.

If you need to make adjustments to the car's track, you have a couple of options. First, you can locate the rear end from side to side by adjusting the length of the track bar. One end of the track bar normally mounts to the right side of the frame, and the other end mounts to the left side of the rear-end housing. Lengthening the track bar shifts both rear wheels to the left, while shortening it does the opposite. Changing the track bar length, however, also affects the alignment of the rear end. So an adjustment will also require realigning the rear end with

ABOVE: Elephant stands are useful because they allow you to raise the car up off the ground—which makes it a lot easier to work under—while keeping it level and the suspension at ride height.

OPPOSITE: By taking an "X measurement" of the steering components, you can easily determine if your steering is centered. An X measurement is simply measuring from the four pivot points between the steering box and the drag links (A, B, C, and D in this photo).

the trailing arm cross member.

A second option is wheel spacers. Obviously, spacers move the wheels out. I don't mind using wheel spacers on the rear end because steering isn't involved, but I hate to use more than a half inch of spacer on either of the front wheels. More than that just creates too much tire scrub.

CENTER THE STEERING

When you are aligning the front wheels, you need to make sure the steering is locked down on center. It doesn't do any good to try to get the front wheels lined up straight ahead if the steering wheel is off to one side. On a race car with a rack-and-pinion front end, all you have to do is turn the wheel from lock to lock and then halve that to find the approximate center, but on a car with a drag link steering system like most stock cars use, this is pretty important to get exactly right.

The way we do it on a conventional drag link steering system is by finding what we call the *X measurement*. This is done simply by measuring from the center of the pitman arm pivot to the center of the drag link pivot on the opposite side

and measuring from the center of the idler arm pivot to the center of the opposite drag link pivot. The imaginary lines created by the two measurements create an X. (It's hard to be accurate if you are leaning over the car and trying to reach past the radiator. The best way is to take the measurements from underneath the car.) If the measurements are the same, then you know the steering is centered. If not, turn the steering wheel until the measurements are equal. This should happen at the same time the steering box centers up.

You can tell when the steering box is centered because there is a flat spot on the input shaft (connecting the steering wheel to the box). That flat spot should be pointed straight up when the box is centered. Most boxes will have a "hard spot" that you can feel in the steering wheel. When you feel that hard spot, you also know that the steering box is centered. Still, don't depend on the steering box to tell you if your steering is centered. If you have banged wheels with another car or scrubbed the wall, you might have bent a tie rod or the pitman arm and thrown off your steering. The only way to know that is by checking the X measurement.

Driver Considerations

Modern race-built steering boxes still have a hard spot to mark when the box is centered, but in most cases it's hardly noticeable. Still, you may have a driver who doesn't like the feel of going across that hard spot. I've always worked hard to make sure that the steering box is favored just a little bit to the left after my final setup so that the driver won't have to steer across that hard spot every time he enters a turn. Donnie Allison got me started doing this. He would always tell us, after we had centered the steering and set the toe: "OK, now do me this favor. Lengthen the right-side tie rod a quarter round and shorten the left side tie rod a quarter round." What that would do is require the steering wheel to be turned to the left a little bit to center the steering back up. It didn't affect the toe or anything, but it did favor the steering to the left so that he wouldn't have to feel that hard spot.

ABOVE: When checking camber and caster gain, you need to be able to make measurements at different levels of suspension compression. To do this, make a measurement from a specific point on either the upper or lower A-arm to a point on the upper frame tube (make sure both points are clearly marked) while the car is at ride height. Pull the spring and use a floor jack to compress the suspension. Remeasure your points to determine your specific suspension travel.

chapter 5

Understanding Camber, Caster, and Kingpin Angle

Camber, caster, and kingpin angle are grouped together in this chapter because they all have to do with the front wheels and suspension. Camber is used to maximize the tire's "footprint," or that part of the rubber that is actually making contact with the asphalt at any given time, while caster and kingpin angle affect steering and how the car feels to the driver.

CAMBER

Camber is the angle of the tires relative to a line perpendicular to level ground. Positive camber is when the top of the wheel is leaned away from the car, and negative camber is when the top of the wheel is leaned in toward the engine. So, if the wheel is leaned toward the engine one degree from vertical, that's one-degree negative camber.

When we use camber as a tuning tool, the goal is to keep as much of the four tires in contact with the track as we can. As the car goes through a turn, the right-side tires will try to roll up on the outside side-wall while the left-side tires will want to roll on the inside sidewall. That is why in oval track racing, you will always want negative camber in your right-side wheels and positive in the left side (but in different amounts in the front versus the rear). The banking on a racetrack can dictate how much camber you want to run; a flatter racetrack will respond well to more negative in the right front and more positive in the left front.

The best way to adjust camber is with the upper control arm, which is also called the upper A-arm. On most cars, you can use shims to move the inner pivot point of the upper A-arm in or out. Moving the pivot point in toward the center of the car will cause the upper A-arm to pull the top of the spindle in and add negative camber. Moving the pivot point

out (usually by removing shims) will do the opposite and add positive camber.

Measuring camber is pretty straightforward. First, you need to make sure that your steering is centered and the wheels are pointed straight ahead. It doesn't have to be absolutely perfect, but center the steering by taking an X measurement between the idler arm, the pitman arm, and the drag link pivot points (as discussed in chapter 4). Also, make sure the tie rods are adjusted so that the wheels are pointed straight ahead with the steering centered. Unless the car is brand-new or has just been crashed, these settings should already be right. Don't worry about toe out as long as you are running one-eighth inch or less.

Several companies make and sell dedicated caster/camber gauges for racing. These gauges are the best—and just about the only—way of getting a good reading when it comes to measuring either camber or caster. If you are serious about racing, go ahead and invest in a caster/camber gauge. I've always preferred a digital gauge because it makes it a lot easier to be precise, but the bubble gauges are also good, and plenty of crew chiefs have won

BELOW: Camber is defined as the angle of lean of the wheel and tire relative to vertical. If the top of the tire is leaning away from the center of the car, that is positive camber. If it is leaning toward the center of the car, that is negative camber. The amount is measured in degrees from vertical. Moving the inner pivot point of the upper A-arm in or out influences camber (A), and adding shims to move it in adds negative camber (B), while removing shims to move the pivot point out adds positive camber (C).

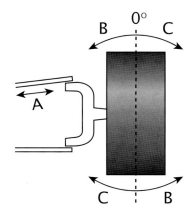

RIGHT: Caster is the angle of the spindle as viewed from the side of the car. Positive caster leans the top of the spindle back toward the driver, and positive caster in both front wheels makes the car easier to drive straight. Opening up the caster split, especially less in the left front, makes the car easier to turn, but the result can be a car that feels squirrelly or loose getting in the corner.

races with them. The gauge typically mounts to the wheel hub. Whether it is a digital or a bubble-style gauge, both depend on the gauge being level when checking both camber and caster. With the wheels pointed straight ahead and the gauge leveled, take your camber reading and you are all set.

CASTER

If you are looking at the car from the side, *caster* is the angle of the line between the upper and lower ball joints relative to vertical. In everyday terms, it is how much the spindle is angled back or forward. If the spindle—or to be more precise, the line between the ball joints—is angled so that the top of the line points toward the back of the car, that's positive caster. If the top of the line points toward the front of the car, that's negative caster.

Caster angle is important because it affects how easy it is to steer the car. Positive caster makes the car want to steer straight and resist turning. If you are turning a car with positive caster in the wheels and you let go of the steering wheel, the car will straighten itself up until it is going straight again. If you let go of the steering wheel when the car is going straight, it will keep going straight ahead. Negative caster is the opposite. It makes a car feel squirrelly, and if you let go of the steering wheel with it going straight ahead, there is no telling what it will do. We never run a car with negative caster in both wheels, and only rarely have I ever run any negative caster in any wheel.

Since most cars run positive caster in both of the front wheels, tuning is done with the caster split, or the difference in caster angle from the right front to the left front. For the most part, you always want to have a little more caster in the right front than the left front. The greater the caster split, the more the race car is going to want to turn left. A good start-

Camber Considerations

Be careful with your air pressures, because they can affect your camber. This is especially true at short tracks where the pressures are low anyhow, down in the 18 to 25 psi range for the Nextel Cup cars. If you are running 15 pounds of pressure versus 25, that can make a big difference in the camber. What the sanctioning body normally does these days is check your rear camber at what we call inspection air pressures. The limit in the Nextel Cup Series is 1.9 degrees per wheel at the rear wheels. That's because we try to optimize our rear camber at flat tracks like Martinsville, Virginia, where you really want a lot of camber in the car. I think the recommended air pressures were 18 in the left-side tires and 25 in the right, but we would sneak the right-side pressure up a bit higher than that, which would bring some of the negative camber out of it and bring it back in line. Afterward, we'd let the pressure back out and the negative camber would go up. Of course, NASCAR realized what was going on after a while, so now they check the air pressure before they check the camber. Stagger changes can also affect your rear camber, so remember to keep an eye on that, too.

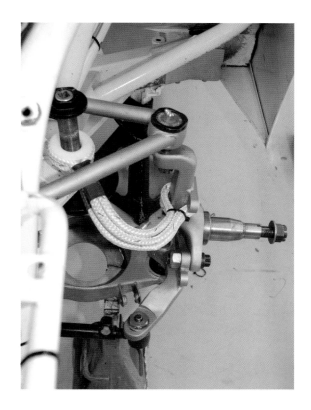

ing point in a modern race car with power steering is four degrees positive in the right front and two degrees positive in the left front.

Remember, when it comes to caster, there are two factors you have to balance: caster and caster split. Adding positive caster in both wheels will make a car easier to steer, but a lot in both wheels also results in tire scrub when turning, so you want to limit it. On the other hand, too much caster split will make the car too loose. It will want to turn left all the time and make it difficult for the driver to turn back to the right. If you get loose and try to correct for it by turning the wheels to the right, too much caster split can make your life hard. Overall, it will make the car difficult to race.

Measuring caster is straightforward, just like camber. With the caster/camber gauge on the wheel hub while the wheel is straight ahead, turn the wheel 15 degrees and zero the gauge. Whether you begin by turning the wheel in or out depends on the gauge. Now turn the wheel until it is pointed 15 degrees in the other direction. Make sure you have leveled the gauge at both points. Now you are ready to take your caster reading.

The easiest way to adjust caster is with shims on the upper A-arms. Unlike camber, where you use equal shims on both sides to move the pivot point in or out, now you add or remove shims from one side in order to angle the upper A-arm and move the upper ball joint forward or backward. Generally, I don't like to have more than a quarter-inch difference worth of shims between the front and the rear pivot points because it can cause the A-arm to bind up. If it becomes more than that, you need to get a different upper A-arm. Also, you never want more shims in the rear of the A-arm than you have in the front because it adversely affects anti-dive and caster gain. Some newer cars have slugs in the upper A-arms that allow you to slide them forward or backward without using shims, which can make your life a lot easier. Either way, be aware that changing the caster settings will also change your camber, so once you make a caster change, you will need to go back and recheck your camber.

DYNAMIC CHANGES

We've talked about what camber and caster are and

LEFT: Camber and kingpin angle can sometimes be confusing. Camber is used to control the tilt of the wheel either toward the center of the car or away from it. It is adjusted by changing the upper A-arm length or using shims at the inner pivot point. Kingpin angle is built into the spindle. The farther inboard the hole is on the shoulder at the top of the spindle, the greater the kingpin angle.

BELOW: Caster is the angle of lean of the spindle. You can see the positive caster in this left front spindle.

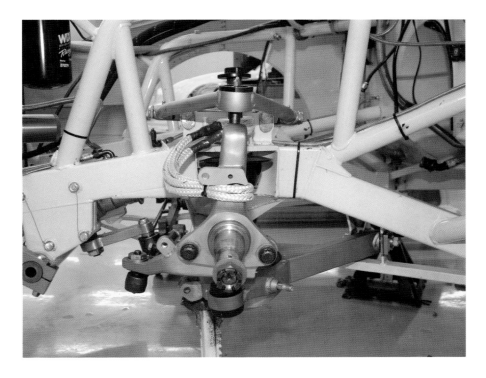

ABOVE: A caster/camber gauge is a relatively simple device, but it is critical for setting up your car. This gauge is the one I use to set up my son Brandon's Bandolero, and it uses a bubble level. It works well, but I actually prefer the digital gauges because the readout allows you to be just a little more precise.

how to measure them at ride height, but it's important to remember that a race car isn't always at ride height. Suspension settings, including camber and caster, when the car is sitting still are considered static. But as the suspension moves when the car accelerates, decelerates, or rolls as it goes through a turn, your suspension settings are in a continuous state of change. Caster, camber, and many other suspension settings can be one thing at ride height, but they are something else at one inch of suspension compression, and even something else at two inches of compression. Settings that change

because of suspension movement are known as *dynamic changes*, and you need to be able to chart them to know what is happening to your car on the track.

Checking camber and caster change is done with the help of a bump steer gauge. We'll get into bump steer in more detail later, but it must be checked at different increments of front suspension travel, so the gauge is designed to make it easy to measure suspension travel in fractions of an inch. Check both camber and caster at ride height, and at one, two, and three inches of compression travel. If you

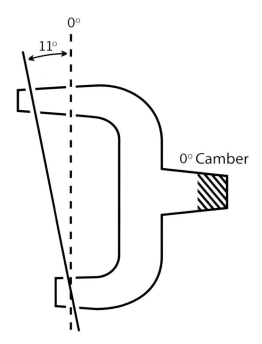

0°

11°

0° Camber

suspect your setup has the left front suspension in extension as the car exits a turn under power, check your settings at extension, too. Creating a quick chart of your findings can help you visualize what you are getting.

Camber change is controlled by the length of the upper A-arm. A longer arm will slow down the rate of change, while a shorter arm will speed it up. Typically, for a moderately banked racetrack, you want something in the range of 1.25 degrees of negative camber gain in the first inch of suspension travel, 1.5 degrees at 2 inches, and 1.75 degrees at 3 inches. These are cumulative totals; you want 1.5

degrees of total negative camber gain at 2 inches of travel, not 1.5 inches gained between 1 and 2 inches. If you check and find you have too much negative camber gain, going with a longer upper A-arm will help in this situation. Whenever you change the arm length, you will need to adjust the shims to move the inner pivot point and correct the static camber.

Also, in a race car you always want your camber change to be a negative gain. You do this by making sure the upper A-arm is angled slightly up from the inner pivot point to the ball joint while sitting at ride height. If it is angled down, that means the camber change will move toward positive until the upper A-arm is level and then go negative as the suspension continues to compress. This will create strange handling characteristics that you don't want. Check your shock travels when you test at each track. If you find your right front is only traveling two inches, then there is no need to worry about camber gain at three inches of travel.

You adjust caster gain by changing the angle between the two pivot points on the inside of the upper A-arm. With caster change, you want it to gain toward positive as the suspension travels. Generally, one degree of caster gain from ride height to full

LEFT: Kingpin angle is the angle of a line drawn between the upper and lower ball joint holes when the spindle is at true vertical (zero camber). Typical setups in modern race cars include an 11-degree kingpin angle in the left front spindle coupled with an eight-degree angle in the right front spindle. The result: Wedge is taken out of the car when the driver turns left. For slower tracks with less entrance speed, like Martinsville and Richmond, teams will normally switch to a right front spindle with a five-degree kingpin angle.

There Was Only One Earnhardt

One of the interesting things about working as Dale Earnhardt's crew chief for a year and a half was he often liked to race certain setups that most other drivers wouldn't even consider. He definitely had his share of success, so you couldn't argue with him.

One of those things was caster split. Earnhardt wanted the feel that comes from a lot of caster split. There were certain racetracks—Bristol, Dover, Darlington, and Rockingham—where he didn't want to have to turn the car into the corner. He wanted the car to do it on its own. To get enough caster split into the car, we had to put negative caster in the left front. That was something almost no one else would run—or *could* run.

With that setup in the car, he could be going down the straight and let go of the wheel, and that car would turn dead left. Most drivers, if we had gotten them to try that, would have gotten right back out of the car and said, "No way. It feels like it wants to spin out on the straightaway." It doesn't mean that those other drivers were bad drivers; Earnhardt just had his own way of driving a car.

One place where negative caster worked well for us was when we won the '98 Daytona 500 with Earnhardt. We had negative caster in the left front, and that's helpful with a restrictor-plate car because it doesn't have a lot of power. That caster split makes the car want to turn by itself and doesn't seem to bog down the engine as badly, because the driver doesn't have to turn the wheel as much. I run negative caster in my son Brandon's Bandolero for the same reason: There isn't any horsepower in that little engine to waste. If you are in the same situation, you might want to consider it. I won't say to go negative on the left front, but maybe try it at half a degree of positive caster and see how that works.

compression is good. To force the caster to gain as the suspension compresses, you want the upper A-arm to angle down slightly from front to back. (This also controls anti-dive.) For more caster gain, move the front of the upper A-arm up a little; for less, move it down. Be aware that changing caster gain can also affect camber gain.

KINGPIN ANGLE

Imagine the spindle is positioned so that it is perfectly vertical (if a wheel were attached, the camber would be zero). Now draw an imaginary line between the centers of the upper and lower ball joint holes. How much this line varies from vertical (in terms of degrees) is called the *kingpin angle*, sometimes also referred to as the *kingpin inclination*.

Generally, the shoulder on top of the spindle into which the ball joint hole is cut is larger than the corresponding hole at the bottom of the spindle, which creates the angle. For years we ran a standard kingpin angle on both sides. Some people called it seven degrees, some people called it eight, but it ended up being 7.6 or something like that. When we started playing with kingpin angle, we found that we could improve how the car turned by adding kingpin angle to the left front spindle. In the Nextel Cup Series, most teams found they could go as far as an 11-degree kingpin angle in the left front.

There is a chassis-tuning reason for this: When the driver turns the steering wheel, the spindle with the greater kingpin angle jacks extra weight into that wheel—as well as the wheel to its diago-

nal. Because it's the left front with the greater kingpin angle, it's the same as taking wedge, or cross weight (which we discuss in chapter 8), out of the car when you turn the wheel. The result is that it helps the car turn in the center, and it doesn't harm the entrance or exit.

Next, some people started getting creative and played with taking kingpin angle out of the right-

Rear Camber

Camber in the rear wheels can be just as helpful as in the front. The only problem is making it work with a solid rear axle. There are companies today that produce rear-end housings with a specific amount of camber built in, but in the early days in Nextel Cup racing, we did it ourselves.

In the early '90s, Junior Johnson with Bill Elliott and Andy Petree with Harry Gant were the first teams to figure this out, and they used camber in the rear ends to whip the rest of us pretty good until we caught on. When we first started running cambered rear ends, we'd put camber in them by heating up the tubes with a torch and then throwing a wet rag on one side to draw it up. We put the rag on the top to create negative camber or on the bottom of the tube to create positive. But the components weren't designed to be run on angles, and we started stripping axles and drive plates. We had to go to crowned axle flanges and do a lot of other things to get a cambered rear end to live. Still, you can't run nearly as much camber in the rear as you can in the front of the car.

side spindle. But that magnifies the effect, and it's easy to overdo it. You have to be careful when taking kingpin angle out of the right front because it can really make the car loose getting into the turn, since it is taking weight off the right front and left rear wheels. What most teams have settled on is an 11-degree spindle in the left front and eight degrees in the right front.

Finally, remember that kingpin and camber aren't the same thing, but changing the kingpin angle can affect camber. If you pop a different spindle on there, you will need to readjust your camber, and you might even need to change the length of your upper A-arm to get your camber gain back.

ABOVE: Running a front sway bar with a chain or a slider on the left side can be helpful, because if you clip the curb in a turn, it won't upset the right front tire. But if your car gets loose or you are trying to correct a slide by turning to the right, like Jeremy Mayfield is here, a sway bar with that setup becomes useless.

chapter 6

Tuning with Springs, Shocks, and Sway Bars

There are a lot of adjustable pieces on a race car, but when it comes to setup, it's the shocks, springs, and sway bars that get most of the attention. And that makes sense, because they are easy to change at the track and can make a big difference in the way a race car handles.

SPRINGS

Whether you run big springs like in the Nextel Cup Series or coilovers, in which the shock and spring are integrated into one package, springs work the same way. The only job we have for the spring is to hold the car up off the ground. Of course, it's not quite that simple, because a race car almost always has multiple forces acting on it. Some of these are internal: Acceleration, deceleration, and turning are the big ones. Some are external: How rough or broken the track surface is, the degree of banking in the turns, and the force of the air on the car are just a few.

For years, the thinking in Nextel Cup racing was to use the right front spring to hold up the car in the turns. We didn't use much of a sway bar at all, so we ended up needing a pretty heavy spring in there. Then, to keep the rest of the car balanced, we ended up with big springs all the way around. That also seemed to be common in short track racing, too, but now all that is changing.

Surprisingly, it was the two biggest tracks that we go to that brought about this shift in thinking. Contrary to popular belief, Daytona and Talladega are two of the roughest track surfaces we race on. Back before we started running the soft spring packages, we would put tons of rebound into the shocks (rebound keeps the springs from raising the car back up when the suspension is compressed) in order to hold the car down against the track and

improve the aerodynamics. But that made the ride so rough that you could hardly understand drivers when they came over the radio, because their voices were vibrating so badly.

Using lots of rebound in the shocks worked to a degree; it pulled the car low to the ground, which helped the speeds down the straights. But aggressive shocks are hard on the tires, making them wear out and lose their grip sooner. So we started softening up the springs so less rebound was needed. That worked great down the straights, but now in the turns the car just about wanted to roll over on its side.

To level the car back out and keep the left front corner on the ground, we had to go with a bigger

BELOW: The sway bar doesn't have to extend beyond the frame rails, but bends in the arms that move the links to the control arms as far outboard as possible provide a better feel for the driver. Notice also the full rubber that's in the spring.

BELOW: Here is a sway bar mounted to the rear axle of a NASCAR Craftsman Truck.

front sway bar. The sway bar influences the roll in the front of the car. Our engineers at Richard Childress Racing (RCR), where I was working with Dale Earnhardt and Mike Skinner at the time, started working to figure out what size sway bar would be required with our softer front springs to get the same roll in the front we had with our old setup packages. This change to softer springs and a bigger front sway bar works best at the big, flat tracks like Michigan. In the old days, teams would run a 1,200-pound left front spring and an 1,800-pound right front, and package that with a sway bar that was only 1 ⅛ to 1 ¼ inches in diameter at the most. If you walked through the garage at Michigan today, you'd see most teams running springs in the range of 500 to 600 pounds on the left front and 600 to 800 on the right front. The difference is they have a sway bar up front that may be two inches or bigger in diameter. Just remember that this example is

specific to high-speed racetracks. If you race a ⅜-mile track, more conventional setup packages that aren't concerned with aero will proabaly work better for you.

No matter if you are still racing the more traditional package or working on a soft spring/big sway bar setup, springs play a major role in tuning your car for the track. As a general rule, a softer spring increases grip. If your car is pushing, that means the front wheels are losing traction before the rear wheels. Switching to softer front springs (commonly just called "softening" the spring) is a standard fix for a pushing car. Switching the rear springs for ones with a higher rate (called "stiffening" the springs) can also help, but that isn't usually the best solution. Stiffening a spring, or using a spring with a higher weight rating, will generally reduce the amount of traction available at that tire. Although stiffening the rear springs on a car that is pushing

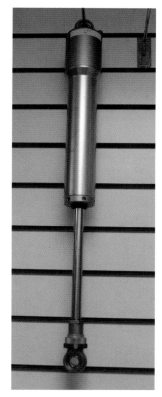

may help take care of the push, all you are doing is balancing the car by taking away traction. And that's really not the direction you want to go, because you never want to give up grip if you can help it. So when the front end is pushing first, try to fit softer springs in the front to solve the problem before changing to stiffer rear springs. In other words, if the front tires are sliding—which is what happens when you have a tight car—fix the front tires. Don't make the rear tires start sliding, too, as a way to correct for it.

HOW LOW CAN YOU GO?

So then, if a softer spring can improve traction, the obvious question is, how soft can you go? The answer is until the car starts bottoming out on the track or the suspension begins binding uncontrollably. Excessive body roll is a consideration, but as I've already mentioned, a lot of that can be countered with a larger sway bar.

When teams started going to the soft spring/ big sway bar packages in the Nextel Cup Series, many got themselves into trouble because they didn't think through all the repercussions a drastic spring change can make. They missed the fact that the race car is a package deal; it all has to work together. That's the reason I never had a problem telling anyone what springs I had on the front of the car when I was a crew chief, because you could screw people up more than you could help them if you didn't give them the whole setup sheet. You had to use a completely new package or else it didn't work. Teams that just changed springs without making the other necessary adjustments—like switching to a larger sway bar or slowing down the camber gain—usually found that the car was actually worse than before, not faster.

In addition to softening up the front springs, we also began making some pretty significant spring changes in the rear. *Spring split* is a term used to describe the difference in rates between corresponding springs on the left and right sides of the car. For example, if you had an 800-pound spring on the left rear and a 1,000-pound spring on the right rear, the spring split is 200 pounds. That amount of spring split can often be as important as the actual weights of the springs you have on the rear end.

Before moving to the softer spring packages, teams rarely ran much rear spring split. Chassis-wise, increasing the rear spring split makes a car's handling looser. But as we were experimenting with springs, the race cars were also becoming more aerodynamically efficient. If you have a race car with a big rear spoiler, you know anything you can do to keep that spoiler up in the air will help the car feel better getting into the corner. We figured out that a good, strong spring on the right rear of the car will help keep that corner of the rear spoiler up in the air. There is also a second advantage: Once the car gets into the middle of the corner and the speed slows down, that big spring kicks in from a chassis standpoint and helps the car turn from the center of the turn through the exit (commonly called "from the center off").

But like the soft springs on the front, this change required additional changes to keep the car under control. In this case, it is the panhard bar, which is also called the track bar. On a real aggressive setup, we may have run a 300-pound left rear spring along with an 800- or 1,000-pound right rear. But to make that work, we had to bring the track bar down and take some rake out of it. That helped tighten the car back up a little bit and kept things from getting out of control. We'll get more in depth on the track bar and how it works a little bit later.

What we've also found with the softer springs is we have to run much more wedge than before. It used to be pretty common to race a Nextel Cup car with 47 to 48 percent wedge. But once we started getting these soft springs and a lot of spring split

LEFT: Modern racing shocks are designed to be rebuildable and allow more adjustability than ever, which opens up a lot more tuning options. I recommend double-adjustable shocks because you can adjust both compression and rebound without having to take the shocks off the car. Notice the orange line on the bottom of this shock; it gives you a quick visual reference to find your beginning point in case you made a valving change that didn't work and you want to set the adjuster back where you started.

ABOVE: In the Nextel Cup Series, we use big springs that are separate from the shock absorber, but many racing series use the coilover shock design, which mounts the spring on the shock body (shown here). Fortunately, tuning rules remain basically the same no matter which type you use. There are even spring rubbers made for coilovers. A "full rubber" (to the left of the coilover shock) forms a full circle. A "half rubber," as you might expect, is a half circle.

in the rear, we had to get that wedge number up. Fifty percent wedge is a lot more common today, which is a really big change. This may not sound like much, but a 2 percent change on a Nextel Cup car is actually huge. By dropping the wedge on a 3,400-pound car from 50 to 48 percent, you are cutting the weight on the right front and left rear wheels 68 pounds! Normally, changes on Nextel Cup cars are less than half a percent.

Another important factor to remember is that inflated tires also have a spring rate. At one point, Nextel Cup teams were spending a lot of money developing devices that would help them determine the spring rate of their tires, but NASCAR has outlawed their use at the track. Goodyear, however, does

mark the spring rate at a given pressure on the sidewall of the tires. They probably aren't going to do that for the guy racing on Saturday night at the local racetrack, but a good rule of thumb to remember is a tire with a softer compound will usually require a stiffer spring. But if you are racing on harder tires, you can usually get by with a softer spring.

SPRING RUBBERS

So far we've talked only about single-rate suspension springs. Spring manufacturers can produce progressive-rate springs, where the rate goes up as the spring compresses, but NASCAR's rules requiring the coils in the spring to be evenly spaced and to have a constant diameter (not barrel shaped) pretty much rule out progressive springs. Fortunately, spring rubbers, which have been used in racing for years, do much the same thing and provide an extra measure of tunability.

Spring rubbers are simply rubber doughnuts that slide in between the coils of a suspension spring. Once the spring compresses to a certain point, the rubber between the coils ups the spring rate substantially. Rubbers are made with different hardness levels and in different sizes. A harder rubber, for example, will have a greater effect on the spring rate. Likewise, a full spring rubber will cause the spring to increase its rate more progressively than a half rubber.

Add In Adjustability

Ernie Irvan earned a reputation as a very aggressive driver, but he's also one of the smartest drivers I've ever worked with. I credit him with teaching me to think ahead about putting as much adjustability into the car as you can. It always seemed that near the end of practice, just when we were getting the car where we wanted it, Ernie would start asking to make changes. Or he'd even come to me on Sunday morning and ask if we had any spring rubbers in the car.

Maybe there was one in the right front, but he always wanted more. He'd ask me to soften up the rear springs 25 pounds each and put a half or quarter of a spring rubber in there to make up for it. He wanted to build more adjustability into the car in case we needed it later in the race. Remember, it's always easier to take out a rubber than it is to put it in. So adding two pieces of spring rubber is simply two more adjustment options that you have at your disposal.

These days, NASCAR won't allow us to start a race with any spring rubbers in the front springs, but if your racing series allows it, then it's worth giving it a try. Regardless, keeping as much adjustability in the car as possible is a philosophy that has served me well since my days of racing with Ernie.

SHOCK ABSORBERS

When you are working with a spring, there are only two ways you can change it: You can go softer, and you can go stiffer. A shock absorber is just about the opposite. Because of the different ways you can adjust a racing shock absorber's compression and rebound, you can come up with a nearly endless range of characteristics.

Everything about a shock absorber boils down to two factors: compression and rebound. Compression is the shock absorber's resistance to pushing forces that act on a car. When the wheel hits a bump or when the car rolls on its right side through a turn are both times the shock absorber is put into compression. Rebound is the opposite; it's how strongly the shock absorber resists a pulling force. When we talk about rebound, it's important to remember that rebound is not a function of how much the suspension travels or even how much the car rolls over. It controls how quickly the springs can return the car to ride

height after the suspension has been compressed.

Consider two cars with identical springs on the right front corner of the suspension. One has a shock with more rebound than the other. If you compress the suspension on both cars, the one with the shock that has less rebound will return to ride height first.

Understanding the two movements of a shock absorber (compression and rebound) is easy; it's when you start getting into how the shock controls those two movements that things can get confusing. By changing the piston inside the shock, you can change the piston speed for a given force (usually measured in inches per second). The two most common types of pistons are linear and digressive. A linear shock steadily increases the amount of piston movement as the force increases. If you dyno that shock, the graph will show a straight line with both speed and force increasing. A digressive shock does not exhibit a linear relationship between force

BELOW: This chart graphs two 650-pound springs, one with a spring rubber and one without. Both springs have been pre-loaded to 1,300 pounds. You can see how the spring with the rubber starts out behaving a lot like the standard spring but then increases its rate significantly around the two-inch mark.

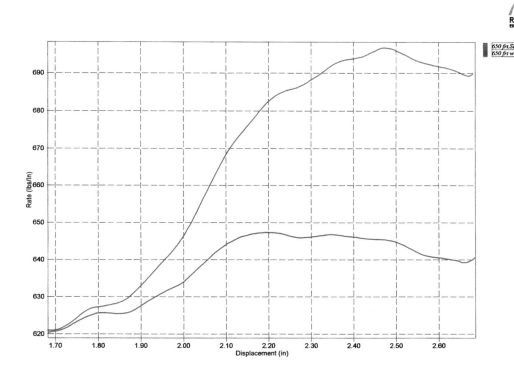

BELOW: RE Suspension Technologies charted a popular racing shock for us, which you see here. It is built to be linear on compression (the top line) and digressive on rebound (the bottom line). In compression, as the force on the shock increases, the piston speed increases at an approximately equal rate. The digressive rebound is quite different; as force increases, the rate of resistance doesn't climb at an equal rate. This allows the shock piston to behave more like a linear piston at lower force levels but move much more quickly than a linear piston at higher force levels. This is called a linear/digressive shock. A digressive/linear shock would be the opposite: digressive on compression and linear on rebound.

exerted on the shock and the resulting piston speed. Instead, the piston offers resistance at lower force levels and, after a certain point, quickly levels out.

The type of shock chosen often has as much to do with driver feel as it does lap times. When I was at RCR, Dale Earnhardt and Mike Skinner often raced setup packages that were quite similar—except for the shocks. They simply had different preferences. There are times, however, when the track you are racing demands a certain shock package. For example, Pocono and Indy are two very similar tracks. Both have long straights and tight turns, but they require very different shocks. At Pocono, you cannot be very aggressive with the rebound because the track is so rough. Indy is much smoother, so you can go with much more rebound, which helps increase grip at the tires.

With all these options, shock tuning can be a little intimidating at first. I would recommend you be careful with your shock selections. A good shock package won't make a 10th-place car a winner, but poor shock choices can take a top-five car and send it to the back of the field. For that reason, I think you should work on making sure all of your other chassis adjust-

ments are about as good as you can get them before turning to your shocks for fine-tuning.

If you are just starting out with a shock program, don't use the hour before a race to start experimenting. Instead, invest the time and effort into a test session just for shocks. A lot of the shock absorber's characteristics are predictable, but some aren't, so you need to have experience with how different shock packages will react with different chassis setups. Most shock manufacturers will gladly offer advice of have recommended starting points for different types of tracks. They are probably very conservative, but they are a good place to start. The first thing to do is to figure out which family of shocks you want to run, and the best way to do that is to have the same family on all four corners. That's the reason you will see Cup teams changing four shocks at a time during a test session—they are changing the whole package.

It's hard to give hard-and-fast guidelines for what works best when it comes to shock absorbers. As much as any other part on a race car, shocks are a lot about driver feel. My experience at RCR emphasized that. So keep that in mind when doing your tests.

One of the best things about modern shocks is that you can get them with plenty of adjustability built in. Single-adjustable shocks for either compression or rebound and even double-adjustable shocks that allow adjustments for both compression and rebound at the same time are now readily available. I've always liked the adjustable shocks because when you are late in the practice session and still working on the handling, you can make adjustments right on the shocks without taking them off the car. Just remember that adjustable shocks are for fine-tuning only. If you need big changes, you probably will still have to change the shocks on the car.

BUILDING YOUR OWN SHOCKS

Building your own shocks isn't impossible, but it does require some training. Fortunately, most racing shock manufacturers, such as Penske, Bilstein, and others, are more than willing to help out. It also can

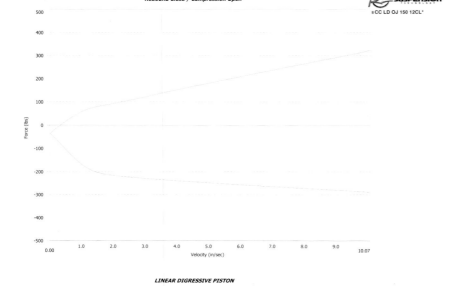

be tough to see exactly what your shocks are doing on a car; the only way to know exactly how changes affect shock performance is to run the shock on a dyno and have it graph out the results. Even if you aren't building your own shocks, it's a good idea to get your inventory dynoed once or twice a year just to make sure nothing has been damaged or that the shocks' characteristics haven't somehow changed.

After you determine the type of piston that works best for both your car and driver (and track testing is just about the only way to do this), the second biggest factor when building a shock is the gas pressure. Gas is used in the shock to keep the oil from getting tiny air bubbles in it (which is called *cavitating*) as it is pushed through the piston. You have to be careful with gas pressure because it acts a lot like the air in a tire. As the shock heats up, so will the gas, raising the gas pressure. Higher gas pressure in a shock tends to make the shock drive that tire into the track harder. The result is a higher rate of wear and increased tire temps.

If you are building a shock for qualifying, then higher gas pressure can be beneficial because it helps get heat into the tire more quickly. But if you build a shock for a race—or if you aren't allowed to change shocks between qualifying and the race— then consider running the least gas pressure you can without cavitating the oil. Using a shock dyno, bring the gas pressure down in steps until you reach the brink of cavitation, and then knock it back up a couple of pounds for a safety margin. If you do, you can expect longer tire life and lower temps after long runs. If they are allowed, base-valve shocks, which limit oil cavitation by using shims to create a small high-pressure zone between the oil and gas, allow you to run even less gas pressure without foaming up the shock oil.

A lot of shock builders think there is a magic oil

out there that will allow them to do things nobody else is doing. Some people may even tell you they have tried running water instead of oil. Don't listen. Instead, find yourself a good-quality oil from a reputable shock manufacturer and stick with it. A lot of the stuff out there is just snake oil and will hurt you a lot more than it can help you.

Finally, when building shocks, remember that it's a lot like building a race engine. Good shock builders are meticulous about keeping their assembly area clean so they do not get any foreign contaminants inside the shocks. They always measure every shim when assembling shim stacks—even if they are coming straight out of the box.

Any time you open a shock and notice that the oil is aerated, go ahead and change it—that shock oil will never be good again. Any time you are pushing a mixture of oil and air through the piston, it isn't going to work right. Also, strain the oil. If you notice any shavings or dirt in there, it's best to go ahead and change it. Finally, keep a thin film of lubricant on the O-rings to protect them from tears or rips. They take a lot of abuse, so they need to be changed out at least once a year. If you are racing the same set of shocks every race, I recommend changing them out every six races if you can afford it.

SHOCK TUNING

In most cases, shock changes affect handling much like spring changes. If your car is tight from the center off, adding compression to the right rear shock will work a lot like beefing up the right rear spring, making the car turn better from the center off. Likewise, more compression on the right front shock will help with a car that's loose getting in. It's not 100 percent of the time, but you can almost always count on compression changes on a shock making the car react the same way a spring change will.

ABOVE: The secret to a shock's adjustability is the valving. These valves may look nearly the same, but they control whether a shock is linear, digressive, or double digressive. Shim stacks, which are thin disks, stack above and below the valves and control the shock's stiffness.

BELOW: The front sway bar is normally housed in a protective tube in front of the wheels. The sway bar arms connect it to the lower control arms. This unit uses a slider on the right side to protect the right front wheel from getting upset if the driver clips a curb with the left front.

Rebound, on the other hand, can be more tricky, but it is often more useful for making a handling change. Taking rebound out of the right rear shock, or staggering the rebound in the rear shocks with more in the left rear will make a car turn better from the center out. But you have to be careful: Too much left rear rebound will make a car loose getting into the corner.

Many times, putting more rebound in the right front shock holds that corner down, which can make a car loose getting into the corner. The benefit is it can make a car turn better from the center off. Just remember that more rebound is harder on the tires, and it doesn't matter which corner we are talking about.

There is one part of the shock absorber package that is very difficult to predict, and that's the left front rebound. Normally, you want as much rebound in the left front as the driver can stand, especially at flat tracks, because it helps keep that corner down. However, the left front tire sometimes seems to do different things depending on the rest of the handling package. But that doesn't mean you shouldn't worry about it. In fact, I put more emphasis on

getting the left front to work than any other corner. Anybody can get the most out of the other three corners, but when you get the left front sharing the load, then you've got a car that handles.

SWAY BARS

The way teams used sway bars changed dramatically when they started going to the soft spring packages. For years and years, it was easy to predict what a sway bar change would do. I had no problem making a sway bar change on race morning and going out to race without testing it. If the car had been a little bit free anywhere through the corner, I could put a bigger sway bar in there and it would tighten up. If my car had been tight and pushing the wheels, I knew a sway bar $\frac{1}{16}$ inch smaller would help that.

But as we've gone to softer springs, bigger sway bars, and more aerodynamic bodies, we've learned that a sway bar's effect on handling is no longer predictable. We've talked about how vital it is aerodynamically to keep that left front corner of the car planted through the turns so that air cannot get under the car. Well, a bigger front sway bar helps

keep that corner planted. Instead of the car rolling over on its right side, a big front sway bar will compress the suspension on the left front, too, and suck the whole front of the car down against the track. In this situation, when you put in a big front sway bar along with softer springs, instead of tightening up the car, that sway bar helps take advantage of the aerodynamics and makes the car turn better. There were plenty of times when we were trying to figure out this stuff that I got fooled. We'd try to tighten up a loose car by putting in a bigger sway bar, and the thing would just get looser.

When running a sway bar, there are a couple of things you can do mechanically to get the most out of it. One, run the ends as big as you can get them. The ends of the sway bar aren't supposed to flex; they are there for mounting the arms. If the ends are flexing, the sway bar is a lot less consistent, so make sure the ends are the beefiest you can find. Also, attach the sway bar to the suspension as far out on the edges as you can. That improves the leverage and smooths everything outboard. Finally, one of the problems with running a big front sway bar is that if you clip a curb or an apron in a turn with the left front, you aren't going to upset just the left front. That big sway bar means both front wheels are going to be upset. You can solve that by putting a three-segment length of chain between the sway bar arm and the suspension on the left side; then if the left front hits a curb, the chain will absorb that motion without transmitting it to the right front. I recommend using only three lengths because that's just enough to do what you need without it getting tangled or caught on something. The only downside to running a chain on a sway bar is if the car gets sideways and the driver has to turn the wheel back to the right to correct it, the chain makes the car act as if it has no front sway bar at all, and you lose that stability.

While front sway bars are very important in the soft spring/big sway bar packages, the rear sway bar is becoming less common. Just like in the front, the effect of adding a rear sway bar is to increase the overall spring rate and equalize the split between the left and right sides. As spring splits in the rear have become more important, rear sway bars have fallen out of favor. It can be hard to get a consistent feel with a rear sway bar. You can drive off into the corner, and the rear sway bar won't feel like it's having any effect at all, and then all of a sudden, boom! It kicks in all at once. Still, there may be situations when a rear sway bar may be beneficial to you, and you never want to ignore a possible tuning option if it can make you faster.

Often, what the driver can't stand is the way a rear sway bar feels getting into the corner because it increases that rear spring rate quickly and makes the car too loose. What we did to help that is run a chain on the right side. (If you have the rear sway bar mounted to the bottom of the suspension, the chain should be on the right. If the sway bar is mounted to the top, then the chain should be on the left.) That way, when the car went off into the corner, the rear sway bar didn't have any effect until the suspension traveled enough to take the slack out of the chain. That was usually about the middle of the corner when we needed the sway bar to increase the rear spring rate from the center off. The result is that the springs are nice and soft to keep the rear end grippy getting into the corner so that the driver feels secure. Then, when the sway bar engages from the center off, it raises the rear spring rate and helps the car turn better mechanically.

There have been plenty of times when we've been racing that conditions changed and the rear sway bar was no longer helping. To make it easy to simply take the rear bar out of the equation, I've always attached one end with a quick-release pin instead of a nut and bolt. That way, if you decide in the middle of a race that you don't want that rear sway bar anymore, you can just have a guy pull out that pin. The bar will still be there, but it won't have any effect on the car.

LEFT: If you are going to test and plan to try a bunch of different shock options, go ahead and build your shim stacks. Just zip-tie them together like this, and you will be ready to quickly rebuild your shocks to different specifications while minimizing the risk of making a mistake.

ABOVE: Checking toe is essentially a two-man job because you need a set of hands at each wheel.

chapter 7

Understanding Wheelbase, Track, Toe, and Ackerman

There is a large range of chassis adjustments available in your search to make your race car handle and drive well. Being able to measure your race car's wheelbase, track, and toe is not difficult, but all three are critical because they are the building blocks upon which many other chassis adjustments are based.

WHEELBASE

Wheelbase is simply the distance between the center of the front and rear tires. In terms of setting up a race car, all we care about is the distance between the contact patches. But that is difficult to measure, so we go by the hubs. Since the hub is the center of the wheel, we know that it's always going to be in the middle of the contact patch.

There are several ways to measure wheelbase. If you have help, you can simply use a measuring tape. Most hubcaps are marked to make it easy to find the center. Another option is to measure between the rims. For example, measuring from the rear of the rim on the rear wheel to the rear of the rim on the front will give you the same measurement and can be easier if your hubcaps are banged up or not marked on the centers. If you are working alone, there are also special tools to help you measure between the wheels without an extra set of hands.

In Nextel Cup racing, the wheelbase is 110 inches. NASCAR looks for that wheelbase to be pretty much right on either the left or right side, and then it will give you a half-inch tolerance on the other side. Now, most everywhere we went—the exceptions were Daytona and Talladega—we ran the wheelbase a little longer on the left side. In other words, if we were at 110 on the right side, we would be at 110.25 on the left. You keep the rear end squared and make the wheelbase a little longer at the left front wheel. A longer wheelbase on the left side will make a car turn better. It even works that way on my son's Bandolero.

Remember, however, that wheelbase changes at the front wheels are done by moving the lower control arm. That will also change the caster, so you have to watch your caster when making wheelbase changes. If you move the lower control arm forward to increase the wheelbase, you are also adding positive caster to that spindle.

TRACK

Track or tread width is the distance between the wheels on the left and right sides. A wide track on a race car is an advantage because it reduces the leverage that the car's center of gravity has as it tries to roll the chassis over on its side in the turns. Picture your race car as a table, and the four legs are the four tires on the car. If the table is 12 inches tall and 12 inches wide, when you push on the side, the table won't be difficult to tip over. But given the same situation, if the table is 12 inches tall and 36 inches wide, it's going to be a lot more resistant to tipping over.

BELOW: You can make asymmetrical changes to both the wheelbase and track width to help a car feel more stable on the track. Increasing the wheelbase on the left side (so that distance A is a quarter inch greater than distance B) helps a car turn through the center of the corner. Also, moving the right front an additional quarter inch outboard of the right rear (C greater than D) helps the car feel more stable on the entrance of a corner.

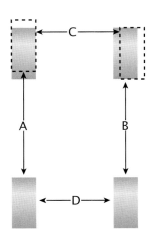

RIGHT: Ackerman is dictated by the distance between the spindle pivot point (the imaginary line between the upper and lower ball joints) and the point where the tie rod attaches to the spindle's steering arm. If the distance is shortened, the turning rate for that particular wheel will be faster. In order for there to be positive ackerman on the left front wheel, that distance must be shorter than on the right front.

BELOW: There are different methods for checking toe, but I recommend a toe plate because the process is simple and the results are precise and repeatable.

Most sanctioning bodies have a tread-width rule, and it's a maximum, not a minimum. Normally, tread width is measured from the inside of the left front to the outside of the right front. True tread width is from center to center, but that gives you the same number. Either way, I encourage you to take full advantage of what your sanctioning body will allow. That will definitely make the car handle better.

I've always been a big believer in running my front tread width just a little bit wider than the rear. It seems to make the car more stable. If the front is narrower, it makes the car unstable. Remember, as you apply brakes going into the corner, the front end of the car travels down, and because the front suspension is independent, it will lose tread width. The rear end never changes width because it's one solid piece; it just travels up and down. So you always want to start out with the front tread width just a little bit wider as a precaution.

My teams always ran our stuff about a quarter inch wider in the front than the rear. And like wheel base, we didn't split that extra quarter between the two sides. It's that right front that really needs to be out there, because it sees the most loading. If you ever get the right front inboard of the right rear, you cannot put enough spring in the right front to make the car feel stable. So we always had the left-side wheels track right in line with each other and then pushed the right front a quarter inch outboard of the right rear.

The easiest way to make tread-width adjustments is with wheel spacers. Of course, you never want to have too much spacer on the front wheels because that leads to excessive tire scrub. If you are way off on the front, you can try different length A-arms, but be careful that you don't screw up other settings,

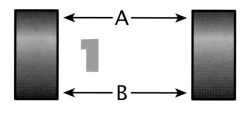

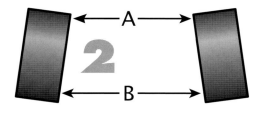

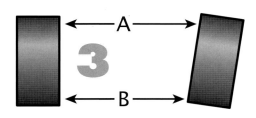

especially static camber and camber gain. Wheel spacers are no big deal on the rear end because the wheels aren't used to turn the car. If you do add wheel spacers, make sure you still have enough threads on the lugs to cover the full depth of the lug nut. On the flip side, if you remove spacers, you may need to consider switching to shorter lug studs. Too much length will slow down your pit stops.

TOE

Toe is the amount that the left- and right-side tires (either the front or rear) vary from parallel. Toe is normally a tuning factor with the front wheels, but you can buy a rear end with a small amount of toe built in. This, however, isn't adjustable like it is on the front.

On the front wheels, you always want to run toe out. That means that the tires are angled out—the distance between the front of the left front and right front tires is greater than the distance at the back of the same tires. Toe in is the opposite. For asphalt racing, a good rule of thumb for toe out is one-eighth inch. I think that works pretty well across the board. Too much will create excessive tire scrub going down the straightaways, and too little makes the car unstable. If you are running a car with limited horsepower, you might, however, want to cut back even further on the toe out to minimize scrub.

The easiest method for measuring toe is simply with a set of toe plates. With the car on level ground, the plates are pressed upright against the wheels. Notches are cut into the plates that allow for

LEFT: Toe is the direction of a set of wheels in relation to each other. If the direction the tires are rolling creates parallel lines as in example 1, that's zero toe. Measurements taken between the front of the two wheels (A) and the rear (B) are equal. Toe in, as seen in example 2, is when distance A is smaller than B; this condition will make a car feel unstable on turn entry. Example 3 is a unique example of toe out. Notice that the left wheel is pointing straight ahead, while the right is turned outward. This is still toe out, since distance A is greater than B. Toe out is preferable on the front wheels of a race car, and I've found that setting all the toe out (one-eighth to one-sixteenth inch, usually) in the right front makes the car more stable than splitting it between the two wheels.

Wheelbase as a Tuning Tool

Normally, people check to make sure their wheelbase is within the rules and then forget about it, but you can use it as a tuning tool in certain situations. A good example is what happened to us in the fall of 1993 at Lowe's Motor Speedway. That was the time that NASCAR had the bright idea to make the "five and five" rule, that mandated the rear spoiler could be only five inches tall and the front valance had to be five inches off the ground.

Ernie Irvan was the driver, and we ran well in practice, but he said the car always felt like it was getting loose in the corners. We had only five inches of rear spoiler so it was obvious why, but since everybody else was fighting the same problem, we were OK. We were all trying to tighten things up mechanically by doing things like running bigger right front springs and a bigger front sway bar. But no matter what, we couldn't fix the loose condition on turn entrance. No matter what we tried, it seemed the only thing we could do was make the car push more from the center off.

Finally, on Friday night, I sat down to think about the problem some more. As a crew chief, I always kept a list of every element on the race car I could adjust, and whenever I ran into a problem, I always went over that list to see if I was missing anything. When I went over that list on Friday night, I read the word *wheelbase* and realized, "Hey! That thing is a quarter inch longer on the left side to help it turn!"

So when we went to the garage Saturday morning, I had the guys shorten the wheelbase on the left side until it was equal to or maybe even a little shorter than the right. That change fixed the problem of getting into the corner without making it push from the center of the corner through the exit.

Well, we must have been one of the only teams to figure that out, because we spanked the competition. It was a 334-lap race, and Ernie led 328 laps. Wheelbase isn't normally used for tuning a car, but it sure paid off for us then.

RIGHT: Toe, along with tread width, can be checked while stringing the car. For more information on the particulars of how to string a car, check Chapter 4. Tread-width changes at the rear end can be done with spacers or wheel offset. But if you need to make large changes at the front, control arm changes may be necessary in order to keep tire scrub to a minimum.

BELOW: Ackerman is the relationship of the front wheels when turned. Normally, we want the left front to turn more than the right front, which improves driver feedback and reduces scrub through the turns. As a general rule, if the right front turns in a 15-degree arc, you want the left front to gain an additional half degree of swing. In other words, when the right front turns 15 degrees, the left front should turn 15.5. This is accomplished by making the distance from the tie rod connection point to the wheel's pivot point shorter on the left (A) than on the right (B). The easiest way to do this is by modifying the steering arms on the spindles.

precise and repeatable measurements with two tape measures. It can be tempting to try to measure the toe by placing the end of a tape measure in a groove in the tire or hooking the end against the shoulder of the tire, but when you are trying to keep tolerances less than $1/32$ inch, this method is just too haphazard. It is simply too hard to get consistent, precise toe measurements without some type of fixture, and a set of toe plates is the simplest out there.

Once you've determined what toe setting you are looking for, it's easy to make adjustments. Loosen the nuts on the tie rod and screw the tie rod sleeve in or out to get the setting you need. When setting the toe out, I've always held the left front straight and put all the toe in the right front. A lot of people prefer to split the toe between the two wheels, but when I've tried that, the driver has usually complained that the car feels a little loose getting into the corner. That may sound a little odd, and I don't have a good reason for it, but I've tested it both ways back-to-back (all the toe out in the right front versus splitting the toe between the front wheels), and the driver has always preferred it that way, so I've stuck with it.

The same theory applies to the rear end. Toe has to be built into the rear-end housing, so you have to choose a number that you can live with just about wherever you go. I think a good number is $1/32$ inch of toe in, with all of it in the right rear wheel. This means the left rear is pointed dead straight ahead. Just like with toe in on the right front, I've always found if the right rear has any toe out, the car will

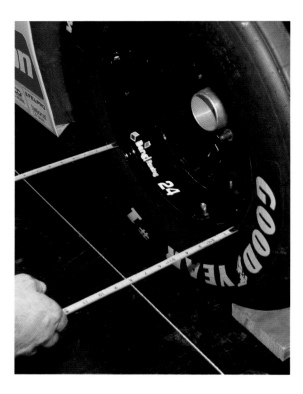

always feel loose. Putting a small amount of toe in at the right rear isn't just to make the car more stable, it's also to make sure nothing happens to give the right rear any toe out.

ACKERMAN

When a car goes through a turn, the wheels are actually following two different radii. The inside wheels are trying to turn sharper than the outside wheels. In the case of oval track stock car racing, we know that the left-side wheels are always going to be on the inside. If the steering system is set up so that the wheels turn the same amount, then the inside tires are going to scrub a small amount through the turns. The sharper the turn, the more the inside tires are going to scrub. It isn't much, but it can be enough to harm speeds and heat the tires.

At first, it would seem that the answer to reducing tire scrub on the left front is to put more toe out in the front end, but that creates scrub down the straights. What we want is for the tires to be pointed straight ahead when the driver has the steering wheel straight, and when he turns, we want the left front to turn slightly more than the right front. This can be done by adjusting the geometry of the steering system, and the effect is known as *ackerman*.

Simply put, ackerman is the difference in movement between the front wheels when you turn the steering wheel. Ackerman gain is simply a func-

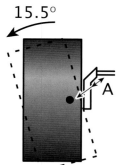

15.5°

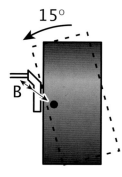

15°

tion of the tie rod location. The length of the tie rod affects bump steer, but where it connects to the spindle affects ackerman. If you move the tie rod end out on the spindle away from the ball joint pivot location, that's going to slow down the steering. If you move it in toward the pivot, that's going to speed up the steering. Positive ackerman means the tie rod on the left front is closer to the ball joint than the corresponding tie rod end on the right front. If you are racing stock components, you must switch to a different spindle with either longer or shorter steering arms or you can drill holes in the arms if there is room. Some racing spindles allow greater adjustability; they have slots in the arms and use slugs that locate the attachment holes exactly where you want them.

The best way to check ackerman is to start with the front wheels pointing straight ahead while sitting on a set of turn plates. Turn the wheel to the left until the right front turn plate reads 15 degrees. Now look at the left front wheel: If it is turned more than 15 degrees, that's positive ackerman. If it is turned less, that's negative ackerman. With a big, heavy Cup car, we normally ran positive ackerman. On tight, short tracks, you usually want to run a little more than on the big tracks like Daytona.

Just as important as positive ackerman is knowing how quickly the car gains ackerman. The left front tire doesn't just jump out an extra degree once the right front gets to 15 degrees; it slowly gains on the right front as the driver turns the wheel. So when you check ackerman, make sure to check it at several points and chart your findings. We normally checked it in 5-degree increments—stopping at 5 degrees, 10, and 15. If your target is ` degree of positive ackerman at 15 degrees, you want to see steady and consistent gain from straight ahead all the way to when the right front is pointed 15 degrees to the left.

Of course, when I say to check the ackerman at 15 degrees, it's important to remember that's not a magic number. If your driver ever turns the wheel 15 degrees to the left, he's as good as wrecked. But when you are talking about such small ackerman

gains, you have to go that far before you can really see what you are getting. So the 15 degrees is just my guideline for setting up the car. And that isn't just for checking the ackerman—it's for everything you will do when setting up a race car for the track. If you find a number or other guideline that works well for you, that's fine. Just make sure you are consistent and know what those numbers will translate to the racetrack.

Besides wheel scrub, ackerman also affects how a car feels to a driver. You don't need much to minimize wheel scrub, but the driver will often want more to make the car feel stable. Too much ackerman also causes wheel scrub, so to keep that down, I always tried to keep it to a minimum. Our normal range was along the lines of three-quarters of a degree for a track like Martinsville, three-eighths to one-half degree for a midsize track like Lowe's Motor Speedway, and one-eighth to one-quarter degree for Daytona. All of those figures are in terms of ackerman gain when the right front is turned 15 degrees to the left.

BELOW: Many lower control arms are adjustable using slugs. If your chassis does not allow slugs, you can order different control arms to move the lower ball joint forward or backward to control the wheelbase. Just be careful, because wheelbase changes also affect caster.

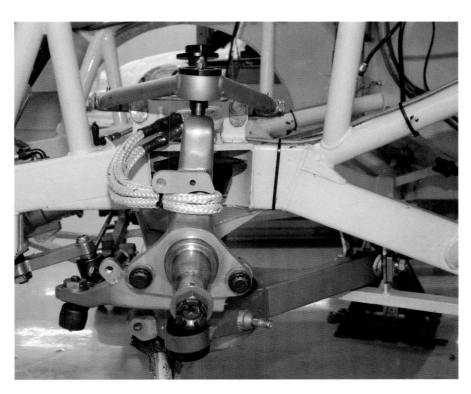

ABOVE: Don't forget what's in the fuel cell. Fuel weighs approximately 5.75 pounds per gallon, and a little fuel can make a big difference in your weight distribution. Here, a crewman pumps weight from a fuel cell as he prepares to scale this car in qualifying trim.

chapter 8

Understanding Ride Height, Weight, and Cross Weight

The title of this chapter sounds like pretty simple stuff, and in some ways it is. Weighing your race car is easy, but placing that weight so that your percentages are right, your frame is at the correct height, and you are still at the minimum weight allowed by the rules can be a bit trickier. In one way or another, frame height, weight, and cross weight all affect each other, which is why we discuss them as a group.

RIDE HEIGHT

Because it is easy to adjust a car's ride height by adjusting the jack bolts (or the adjusters if you have coil-overs), it's easy to think that you can adjust your height at the last minute with no problems. Unfortunately, that's just not true. You actually need to be thinking about ride heights while the car is still being built.

Before I explain why, I want to stress that no matter what division you run, you need to keep track of your frame heights. There are several different ways of measuring the heights. You can do it to the bottom of the frame or to the top, and you can measure at different specific points on the frame. It doesn't matter how you do it—the most important things are that you know how your chassis builder measures it and that you do it the same way every time. If your chassis builder tells you that you need four inches between the bottom of the frame rail and the ground on the right front corner, that sounds simple enough. But if he's measuring to the bottom of the frame rail and you are measuring to the top, then that's going to cause problems with your setup. Also, always measure your heights on a nice, level surface.

I mentioned that it's important to know your heights while the car is being built. That's because most sanctioning bodies will have minimum body

heights in addition to minimum frame heights. Those minimum heights are there for a reason—mostly because going below those numbers will make you faster—so you want to make sure you are legal at all the reference points without giving anything away. This means that if your minimum frame height is four inches and the rules also say that the rear quarter panel must also be 36 inches at the base of the rear spoiler, you want to be legal at both points without being too tall, or too low, at either one.

What this means is that whoever hangs your body—whether you do it yourself or you have it sent out—has to have the car sitting at the correct ride height when he hangs the panels. If he doesn't and he's off either way, that's bad news for you because most Saturday-night racers simply cannot afford to cut off a body and start over. For example, imagine your body hanger had the frame too low and then hung the body at the correct height from the floor. But once you take the car to the track, you have to raise the frame to meet the rules. This means your body is now too high, leaving you at a distinct disadvantage with the rest of the competitors.

When I was working with Nextel Cup teams, body

BELOW: On a big-spring car, ride height is adjusted by the jack bolts. These bolts thread through a point in the frame and control the height of the upper spring cup. Screwing down on this bolt raises that corner of the car.

location was critical to whether you were capable of winning or barely making the top 10. The body was normally hung right after the chassis was completed, and I knew a lot of teams that would just throw any old rear end under the car and use any front suspension pieces they could find. They just wanted to get it rolling so they could get it to the body shop and get a body on it. But I've always felt that you are setting yourself up for mistakes if you do that. I wanted my guys to put the pieces on the car that we actually would be racing. That way we knew we wouldn't have any surprises when we started setting up the car for real.

WEIGHT

Most racing divisions have a minimum weight rule that includes total weight and right-side weight. If you are over that weight, you are OK as far as the rules are concerned. But overweight cars aren't normally competitive. Also, the rule book may say how much the car has to weigh, but it doesn't say how high off the ground it has to be located. What you want to do is build your car as light as possible so you can use lead ballast to meet your minimum weights. You can secure your lead in the very bottom of the car to lower the vehicle's center of gravity. One word of caution here: Reducing weight is a good thing, but only to a point. Don't cut so much that you sacrifice your chassis rigidity or your driver's safety.

We also know that when racing on asphalt oval tracks, the best location for weight is low and to the left. That way, the weight keeps the car from rolling over on the right side so badly in the turns, and the weight on all four wheels is more balanced. Racing series normally make a minimum right-side weight rule to keep racers from spending a fortune in order to get all the weight they can to the left side of the car. Still, you want to make sure you maximize what's allowed.

Finally, you also want to make sure you have the correct weight split from front to back. In racing, you generally want more weight on the rear wheels

The Driver Weighs Something, Too

I was watching the crew for Sterling Marlin's 40 car one weekend at a track and saw something I've always thought was a pretty good idea. The crew was getting ready to weigh the car and Sterling wasn't around, but that wasn't a problem for them. They had six or eight sandbags that they carried around with them, and the total weight of those sandbags equaled Sterling's weight with his suit and gear on. That allowed them to get their weights on the scale without having to wait for Sterling to show up, and if you've been around Nextel Cup drivers and the demands on their schedules, you never know when they are going to show up.

Even if your rules don't require you to weigh your car with the driver in place, there are several good reasons to check your total weight (car and driver) during your setups. Setting the sway bars is a good example. If you set up the sway bar without the driver in it, the change in weight when he gets in will preload the sway bar and cause handling problems. Usually, a team can get by using a crew member who is approximately the same size and weight as the driver, but sandbags allow you to be even more precise.

Changing Wedge at the Track

A cross weight change is one of the easiest ways to make a handling adjustment during a pit stop, but you have to be careful not to mess yourself up in other ways. We ran into that one time with Mike Skinner's Craftsman Truck team at Atlanta.

Mike was racing the truck and said it was loose. The crew chief, Rick Ren, made the call that I, too, thought was right. He told the team to put two rounds of wedge into the left rear on the next pit stop. But the car chief remembered that the truck was already at its maximum allowed height at the rear. He told Rick that two rounds of wedge in the left rear would raise that corner of the truck too high to get through inspection after the race. The car chief was doing his job, and that helped Rick do his job. As much as he hated to do it, he had to find another way to help Mike out, and he ended up taking two rounds out of the right rear instead.

so that the weight will shift forward under braking and balance the load evenly over all four wheels. It's usually not much. In the Nextel Cup Series, the front weight percentage will be 50 to 51 at a short track like Martinsville. At the higher-speed tracks with a fair amount of banking, like Lowe's Motor Speedway at Charlotte, the front percentage will be between 52 and 53 percent. At Daytona and Talladega, braking isn't a factor, but the split is usually 52.5 percent in the front and 47.5 percent in the rear because that seems to help tighten up the cars on entrance.

Total weight, right-side weight, and rear weight are easy enough to adjust: Just check your scales. If your total weight is too high or too low, just add or remove weight. (Of course, this is assuming your car is below the minimum weight required before adding lead. If your car is over the minimum weight limit before lead, you've got a problem.) If your right-side weight is off, just shift lead between the left and right frame rails.

CROSS WEIGHT

Frame height and weight are about as straightforward as it gets. Now we'll throw a curveball into the mix by adding cross weight. Also called wedge, cross weight is simply the percentage you get when you divide the total weight on the right front and left rear tires by the total weight of the car.

Adding cross weight makes the right front and left rear wheels handle more of the load through the turns. Normally, increasing wedge will tighten up a car. You never want too much wedge in a car, as that can make it unbalanced.

There are two ways to change the cross weight numbers in your race car. The first is by simply

Math Class

Here are the formulas for calculating front percentage and wedge.
LF—Left front
RF—Right front
LR—Left rear
RR—Right rear
TW—Total weight
FP—Front percentage
W—Wedge (cross weight)

Front Percentage
FP = (LF + RF) / TW
For example, if the left front wheel weight is 925 pounds, the right front is 800, and the total weight is 3,400 pounds, the equation would look like this:
FP = (925 + 800) / 3,400
FP = 1,725 / 3,400
FP = .507, or 50.7 percent

Wedge
W = (RF + LR) / TW
Keeping the same example, our left rear wheel weight is 875 pounds, so the equation works out like this:
W = (800 + 875) / 3,400
W = 1,675 / 3,400
W = .493, or 49.3 percent

moving weight around, but this can upset your left/right and front/rear percentages. The other way is by adjusting your jack bolts on each of the wheels. This allows you to change the wedge percentage without affecting your splits, and it makes life a lot simpler. The only thing you have to be careful of here is using the jack bolts to adjust cross weight, which will also affect the car's ride height.

Screwing down on the jack bolts at either the right front or left rear wheel will increase the cross weight; the same thing happens if you go up on the left front or right rear. Likewise, going up on the right front or left rear, or down on the left front or right rear, will decrease cross weight. Knowing this can help you keep your chassis heights in check if you are making wedge adjustments. If you need to add a round of wedge into the right front wheel but cannot because it raises the frame too high, you can accomplish the same thing by putting a quarter round into both the right front and left rear wheels and taking a quarter round out of both the left front and right rear wheels.

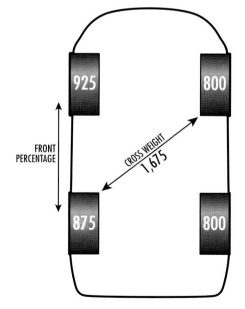

MARTINSVILLE 2000

925		800
FRONT PERCENTAGE	CROSS WEIGHT 1,675	
875		800

TOTAL WEIGHT = 3,400
LEFT SIDE %   = 52.9
FRONT %   = 50.7
WEDGE   = 49.3

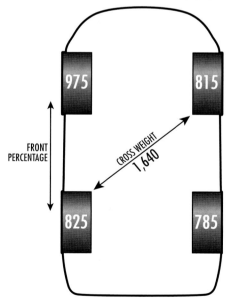

CHARLOTTE 2000

975		815
FRONT PERCENTAGE	CROSS WEIGHT 1,640	
825		785

TOTAL WEIGHT = 3,400
LEFT SIDE %   = 52.9
FRONT %   = 52.6
WEDGE   = 48.2

OPPOSITE: A coilover car uses a different method for height adjustments. Here, the spring is mounted over the body of the shock, and an adjusting collar actually threads up and down the shock body to control the height of the top of the spring.

LEFT: It is easy to track your weight placement whenever you compete. Over time, this will help you build a database of what works best at different tracks. My last year as a Nextel Cup crew chief was the 2000 season. Here are my weight charts from the fall of that year, showing how we ran the cars at two very different tracks, Martinsville and Charlotte. Today, teams have made advancements in the soft spring setups, so their wedge numbers will be closer to 50 percent.

ABOVE: It's a delicate balancing act to find the correct amount of body roll a race car should exhibit as it powers through a turn. Because many teams are working with increasingly softer front springs to maximize front tire grip, manipulating roll centers is becoming more important when it comes to controlling roll.

Chassis Geometry

Entire books have been written about understanding roll centers and other aspects of chassis geometry. Race teams hire engineers whose only job is to solve chassis geometry problems. Obviously, a single chapter in this book isn't enough to cover everything, so the purpose here is to explain the basics of chassis geometry—namely, how to calculate front and rear roll centers—so that you can be aware of what is going on.

My personal philosophy is that it's good to understand how to determine your roll centers so you can know if something is way off. But I have seen too many racers get themselves in trouble when they give roll centers priority over things like camber gain and bump steer. Unless you have an engineer on your staff, I suggest that you calculate your roll centers to make sure you have consistency from car to car, but don't spend too much time trying to manipulate it to adjust a car's handling. Any change you make to a race car to adjust roll center will affect something else. Although the change you make can put the roll center where you want it, that change can also throw something else completely off and leave your car worse than before.

ROLL CENTERS

A race car's *roll center* is literally the point about which the body rotates as it goes through a turn. As the car turns, the tires pull the car to the left while centrifugal force tries to make it continue in a straight line. The result is the body and chassis—the portion of the car that is held up by the springs—roll to the right. By controlling the axis of that roll, called the roll center, you can influence how much of the energy in that roll is exerted in the form of downforce on the outer wheels.

Because the front and rear suspensions are

mechanically different, front and rear roll centers are calculated differently. As you might expect, since the front suspension is more complex, roll center calculations for the front are more complex, too. Although the rear is simpler to calculate, the simpler mechanism of the rear end makes it secondary in importance to other tuning options.

One important thing to remember is that neither the front nor the rear roll center is constant. Roll centers are dynamic, moving points, and their locations are dictated by numerous suspension points, all of which move as the suspension moves. This means that when the suspension compresses as you brake and roll through a turn, the roll center is also moving around. Calculating your roll centers with the race car sitting at inspection height is a good starting point, but it's not necessarily realistic for racing conditions. If you are running a soft spring front setup, your car may never even be at inspection ride height during a race. Even Nextel Cup engineers are still working to understand all the complexities involved in roll centers, so don't feel that you have to know everything there is to know about roll centers before you can be successful.

BELOW: The distance between the car's roll center (A) and its center of gravity (B) is called the moment arm. The longer this arm, the more leverage the center of gravity has on the sprung mass of the vehicle. As the car rolls through a turn, inertia tries to force the car's mass to roll the body over on its right side. The greater the moment arm, the more pronounced the tendency to roll.

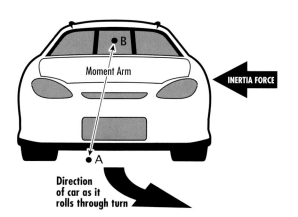

Moment Arm

INERTIA FORCE

Direction of car as it rolls through turn

RIGHT: Finding the front roll center is relatively simple after you have determined the instant center for each wheel. Using the center of the ball joints (A) and the A-arm inner pivot locations (B) to find the two instant center points (C), draw a line from the center of each wheel's contact patch (D) to the instant center location for the same wheel. The point where those two lines intersect is the front roll center.

BELOW: The instant center location is determined by extending lines from the ball joints (A) through their corresponding A-arm inner pivot points (B). The point at which those two lines intersect is the instant center (C). The instant center can help you determine camber gain because it represents the center of the arc around which the wheel travels as the suspension moves. The greater the distance from the instant center to the wheel, the slower the rate of camber gain.

CALCULATING FRONT ROLL CENTER

Calculating your front roll center doesn't require much more than graph paper, a good measuring tape, and a pocket calculator. Using your graph paper, find a ratio that works for you so that you can keep everything in proportion (for example, a common practice is to make each block on the graph paper equal five inches, which is easy to convert), and then graph the major suspension points. For calculating the front roll center, these are the upper and lower ball joints, upper and the lower A-arm pivot points, and the center of both tires' contact patches. A good place to start is the inner pivot

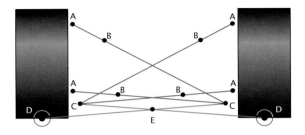

locations for the lower A-arms, since those locations are critical. Find their heights from the ground and the distance from each other, and then mark them in the center of your graph paper. Using those two points as the basis for the rest of your measurements, locate the upper A-arm inner pivot points and the center of the ball joints.

On your race car, it is relatively easy to find the center of the pivot points for the A-arms, but it can be more difficult to find the center of the pivot for the ball joints. There is no scientific method for doing this that doesn't involve unreasonable cost and effort. My recommendation is to get a spare ball joint that's the same size you use in your car. Hold the thing and make it swivel in its socket until you get a feel for where the center of the rotation comes from.

Once you have those points marked on your graph paper and you are sure everything is correct, it's time to start playing connect the dots. First, pick one side of the car and draw a line extending from the upper ball joint through the upper A-arm inner pivot point. Do the same thing with the lower ball joint and the lower A-arm inner pivot point, and extend both lines until they intersect. That intersection point is the instant center for that wheel. The instant center is the point around which the wheel rotates as the suspension moves. The closer the instant center is to the wheel, the greater your camber gain will be. For most race cars, the instant center falls just inside the wheelbase on the opposite side of the car. After you have done that, determine your instant center for the other wheel. It is important to remember that for chassis specifically built for oval track racing, the pivot points and corresponding instant centers will not usually be mirror images.

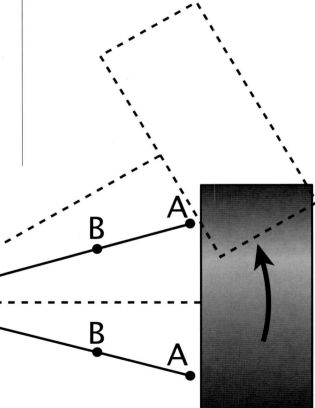

With your two instant center locations marked on the graph paper, draw a line from the center of the contact patch of one tire to its corresponding instant center point. Do the same with the other side of the car. The point where those two lines cross is your roll center. On most race cars, it is at ground level or just a few inches above and slightly to the right of the car's centerline.

CALCULATING REAR ROLL CENTER

Calculating the rear roll center is much simpler. In fact, about all you need is a tape measure. Because a stock car features a solid rear end, the roll center is dictated entirely by the placement of the track

bar. Roll center height is determined by measuring the heights of the right of the track bar where it attaches to the chassis and the left side where it attaches to either the rear-end housing or the end of the truck arm. If the left side of the track bar is 9 inches high and the right side is 12 inches, the roll center height is 10.5 inches high. The lateral location is basically the midpoint of the length of the track bar—pretty simple compared to the front end.

Unfortunately, the simplicity of the rear roll center also makes it difficult to take advantage of. Because changing the track bar height can make such drastic changes to how the race car handles, few racers bother with the rear roll center location. Instead, the

ABOVE: Tracking all the variables involved in suspension geometry is a tricky task. That's why many upper-level racing teams employ engineers just for tackling suspension problems. Even if you cannot afford an engineer, it's not the end of the world; concentrate on more important issues like caster, camber, and toe, and just keep an eye on your roll centers to make sure nothing is getting way off base.

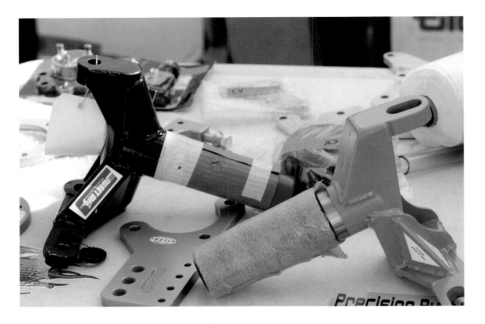

ABOVE: Some spindles, such as the gray one in the foreground, use adjustable slugs to locate the distance between the ball joint and the spindle shaft. These can be used to make many adjustments—including camber, kingpin angle, and the front roll center—without having to buy new spindles.

RIGHT: There is no scientific way to determine the center of the ball joint pivot location when you are plotting your roll centers. The best solution is to hold a ball joint in your hand and rotate the joint inside its casing until you get a good feel for where the center of the pivot is. Then, use your best judgement when measuring to the pivot locations on a fully assembled suspension.

track bar is located where it makes the car handle best, and the roll center is left to fall where it may.

CENTER OF GRAVITY AND THE MOMENT ARM

A race car's center of gravity is a lot harder to calculate. Manufacturers like Ford and GM have specially built test machines that move a car around and can calculate its center of gravity, but that is way beyond the means of most race teams. If your chassis builder is on the ball, he can help you find the general location, but actually locating your car's center of gravity isn't as important as knowing your front roll center. All you really need to know is that the center of gravity is above the roll center, and the distance between the two affects how much body roll your car will exhibit as it turns. This is why you want to keep as much of the car's weight as low as you can get it.

The only time you have any influence on the car's center of gravity is when it is being built. Concentrate on mounting all the components as low (and to the left) as you can. The higher up something has to be, the more thought you should give to how you can make it as light as possible without breaking the rules or putting your driver in any danger. The lower the car's center of gravity, the less effect it will have on body roll.

The vertical distance between the roll center, either front or rear, and the center of gravity is

known as the *moment arm*. The longer the moment arm, the greater the leverage the car's center of gravity exerts. In other words, if everything else is equal (track, speed, spring package, etc.), the longer the moment arm is, the more pronounced the car's body roll will be. Once your car is built, its center of gravity really won't change, so even though you may not know exactly where it is, you know you can control the moment arm by raising or lowering the roll centers.

TUNING WITH THE FRONT ROLL CENTER

Understanding and harnessing your front roll center is important because it helps increase the mechanical downforce on the right front wheel. The energy that isn't converted to downforce as the car rolls through a turn remains as lateral force that tries to push the car to the outside wall.

As I mentioned earlier, the amount of roll is determined by the length of the moment arm, the mass of the car, and the car's speed. The length of the moment arm is determined by the height of the

roll center. Lowering the roll center increases roll because it increases the length of the moment arm, which increases the force that the mass of the car exerts trying to "roll the chassis over." Raising the roll center moves it closer to the center of gravity and reduces the leverage. This is normally done by switching to taller spindles. "Taller" spindles simply have a greater distance between the two ball joints. You have to be careful raising it too much, however, because the front suspension's design will create something called a *jacking effect*. If the roll center is too high, it will create lift and reduce friction between the right front tire and the track. Still, it can sometimes be useful to raise or lower the roll centers because that allows you to tune the amount of body roll without having to go to stronger or softer springs. This way, you can have a nice soft spring on the right front in order to get the tire to really bite the track but still keep the car nice and level through the corners.

The roll center's lateral location is also important. In most cases, you want the roll center to be just to the right of the centerline of the race car. This increases the downforce on the right front tire. You don't want the roll center too far to the right, however, because the excessive downforce created will cause the right front tire to wear out while the left front is underutilized. Moving the roll center to the left of the centerline cuts down on the downforce and increases the lateral loading on the tire. Obviously, this is not what you want.

Because there are so many variables, it's impossible to say, "Do this and this, and you will have the correct roll centers." There are just too many options, and different things work for different people. My recommendation is simply to understand what is going on with roll centers, find a setup that works for you, and then find and document the roll centers for that setup. When you are tuning your race car at the track, concentrate on the more

BELOW: Determining the roll center at the rear of the car is much easier than at the front. Simply find the height from the ground of the two pivot locations on the track bar (A and B). The average of those two numbers is the roll center height. Lateral location is normally said to be the midpoint between those two pivot points (C).

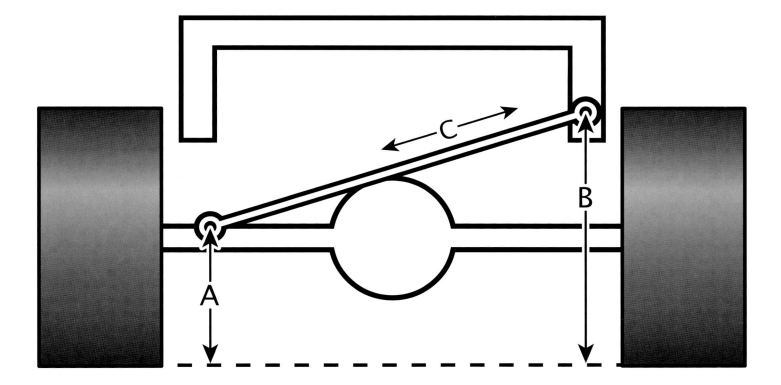

OPPOSITE: Over time both the upper and lower ball joint holes in your spindles will wear. The holes usually become oblong with the long end pointing toward the hub. Checking for this is easily done with a dial caliper. A common fix for this is simply to ream out the hole a little larger and make it round again. Be careful doing this, though; because the hole is cone shaped, making it larger will mean the ball joints will seat deeper in the spindle. This will change your front roll center location.

BELOW: When charting points to determine your roll centers, it is important to remember that the point you are trying to determine isn't just the pivot location, it's the *center* of the pivot location. For ball joints (A), this means the center of the ball joint. For hinged pivot points, such as the inner A-arm pivot (B), this is the center of the bolt. Although it is impossible to stick your measuring tape in the center of a ball joint to get a perfect reading, it is important to try to be as exact as possible.

immediate things like caster, camber, bump steer, and caster and camber gains. Don't worry about your roll center until you have everything else like you want it, and then check to see where it is. If you are racing two cars and are having trouble getting them to handle the same—even though you are using the same spring/shock/sway bar package—it's always a good idea to compare the roll centers. If the roll centers are in different locations, it can be difficult to get repeatability from car to car.

Often, you will get two chassis that, although the builder tells you they are the same, don't perform the same. You will get one car running great with a particular package, then throw that same package on the other car and it will run like a sick dog. It can leave you scratching your head because you know you put the same A-arms and spindles on both cars. But the roll centers aren't the same because the chassis builder didn't get the A-arm inner pivot locations in the same place. I've found that making sure those pickup points are identical is critical in building two cars that handle the same. We talked before about building jigs on a surface plate to make sure critical points on the chassis don't move in the event of a wreck, and the inner pivot points of the lower A-arms are definitely two of those points

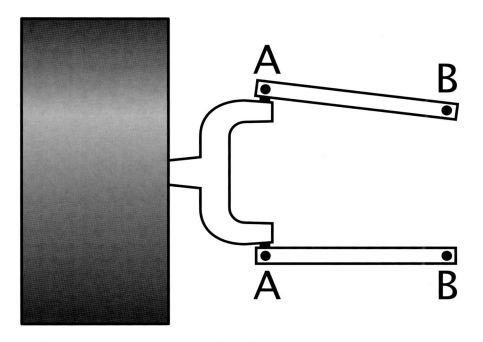

worth keeping an eye on. If you know the roll centers are the same, the other difference could be the bodies are hung differently and, thus, are giving you different aerodynamic characteristics.

Bob Riley, a Race Engineering Groundbreaker

I was working as the crew chief for Kenny Bernstein in 1987 when he told me he was hiring an engineer to help with our race team. At the time, I couldn't imagine what use an engineer could be at our tiny operation in Travelers Rest, South Carolina, but I have to give Bernstein credit for thinking ahead of the game.

The man he brought in to help us was Bob Riley (of Riley & Scott Race Car Engineering), an old-school engineer and a true racer. Bob taught me a lot, and one of the most important lessons he taught me was never to get caught up in the details so much that you lose sight of the blind obvious.

I'd watch Bob use some of the crudest tools you have ever seen, but they got the job done. He would be on his knees on a surface plate with the car and a sheet of graph paper. He'd track caster change by putting a framing square against the spindle and marking the spot on the graph paper. Then he'd jack up the suspension one inch and do it again. That's the way he did caster change, bump steer, camber gain, and everything you can imagine. He lived and died by those graphs.

Bob made me realize the importance of being specific about these things and that it really doesn't matter how you get the information as long as you get it. Even all those years later when I was at Richard Childress Racing, every once in a while out of curiosity I would take a car and put it on a surface plate in the back of the shop, and then do those same graphs again just to see what the patterns were. Of course, by 2000 at RCR we had four to five full-time engineers on staff with some very sophisticated equipment at their disposal. In a very short time, they could tell us where all the suspension points on any car in the inventory were.

ABOVE: Before beginning the setup process, go ahead and put everything on the car just like you plan to race it. This includes fuel and even water in the radiator—anything that can have an effect on weight distribution.

chapter 10

The Setup: Preparing Your Car for the Track

We've finally gotten to the crux of this entire book: setting up your race car. As a crew chief, you have two jobs that are absolutely crucial to the success of your race team. The first is to put the best-handling chassis package on your race car for the track and conditions you are going to race, and the second is to provide solid leadership on race day. We'll handle race day activities in chapters 14 through 16. Right now, let's get down to business on setting up your race car.

In previous chapters, we've discussed a lot of concepts that will come into play when setting up your car—everything from caster to weight splits to stringing a rear end. Those are all tools for understanding how to make a race car fast, and it's time to use them. Please be sure to look back at those chapters if you need to refresh yourself on how to perform specific tasks—like measuring camber—when you get to those steps in our setup procedure.

STEP 1: SETUP PREP

Everything we are doing in this chapter is to try to make the tires grip the racetrack as effectively as possible. This may sound odd at first, but the most important part of any race car is the tires. That's what connects the whole mass of the car to the asphalt, and the goal is to keep those four tires on the ground and working as equally as possible. That is true whether we are talking about one qualifying lap or a 500-mile race. If you are overworking one tire or not using one to its full potential, you are leaving speed on the track.

With that in mind, the first thing you need to do is make sure you have the right size tires on the car. Compounds are not that critical, but you have to make sure the tire is the right height and width, because that can change the height of the car or the

tread width. If you run an inner liner, make sure you have those in your tires. Inner liners can add a lot of weight—around 10 to 12 pounds in the case of the Nextel Cup Series—so you have to make sure you take that into account. Also, make sure the tires are at inspection pressure (that's the pressure you plan to go through the inspection line at, not necessarily the pressure you plan to race at). If you run one track and you can afford it, I suggest you get one set of tires mounted on a set of good rims and save them just for doing your setups. They aren't even to leave the shop.

If you cannot keep a new set of tires set aside just for setting up the car, at least make sure the tires you use are clean. Maybe you run the same track every week, so you know the tires you came home with last Saturday night are correct. But if you have a bunch of rubber caked up on them when your driver came off the track with the tires hot, that can affect the height and throw off several critical measurements. It's small, but it does make a difference.

Next, make sure your car is as complete as possible. It doesn't make sense to go to the trouble of setting up your car without fuel in it. The same thing

RIGHT: Before you start checking frame heights and cross weight (wedge), go ahead and rough in your lead placement. It doesn't have to be perfect before you get the car on the scales, but if you can get it close, it will save you a lot of trouble later on.

goes for water in the radiator or oil in the engine. If your rules for minimum weight include the driver, be sure to make provisions for that. You don't want to have it hooked up yet, but go ahead and have the sway bar you plan to use and the connectors in the car. I know it's not always possible, but in a perfect world you would have everything installed on the car—I'm even talking about the air cleaner and grease in the rear end—that there will be when it hits the track. For one thing, that stuff adds weight, which can affect ride heights and your wedge numbers, as discussed in chapter 8. If you add anything after you have your lead placed, you run the risk of throwing off those factors, and even running more lead than necessary. You never want to be over the minimum weight if you can help it.

While you are prepping your car, go ahead and leave it on the jack stands. It's a lot easier to put lead in the car or install the sway bar with the car on jack stands than it is on the setup plate. If you have already run this car, you should know just about what you need. If the car is new, then give it your best guess.

STEP 2: ON THE PLATE

If you have a setup plate, now is the time to put your car on it. If you don't, then find a nice level spot in your shop and dedicate that area for performing your setup tasks. Mark it off with paint or tape, including the exact areas where the tires make contact with the shop floor. Every time you set up your car, make sure the tires are in those exact spots. That will improve your consistency week after week.

With your car on the setup plate, check your air pressures again. Even a small air-pressure change can make a big difference in tire height and tread width, so if setting up takes you the better part of a day, check your tire pressures several times to make sure your tires aren't slowly bleeding off pressure.

Now you're ready to begin the steps in setting up the race car. The process is a lot like an arc. The first half of setting up a race car is mostly roughing in all your measurements. That's when you are walking up the arc. The second half is a lot of these same tasks, but in the reverse order as you dial everything in and lock it down. This is when you're walking back down the other side of the arc. You will be doing a lot of the same things you've already done, but you have to do that because nearly everything you change on a race car affects something else. If you move the wheelbase, it affects caster. If you change the height of the car, it affects camber. The list goes on and on.

Frame Heights

The first step on your setup list is to rough in the frame heights. Normally, you have different heights for all four corners because a chassis usually has rake from front to back and tip from left to right. These heights don't have to be perfect right now, but they do need to be close. There are a lot of different ways to measure your frame heights; the way you do it isn't important as long as your numbers are in line with what your chassis builder recommends. Settle on one measuring method and then stick with it. Once you have your frame heights roughed in, go ahead and check any minimum body height requirements your rules might require. If they are too low, you will either have to cut off your body and start over (not likely) or raise your frame heights more than you would like and learn to live with it. The only measured heights not to worry about right now are those that are adjustable—maybe the front valance, the rear spoiler, or the rocker skirts. If it's adjustable, you'll fix it later on the back side of the arc.

Panhard Bar Height
Now move around to the back of the car and check your panhard bar height. Again, it doesn't have to be dead on because you'll probably be moving it later, so getting it within 1/32 inch isn't necessary. Knowing exactly where you want your track bar located comes from experience—where was it the last time your raced this track?—or a best guess based on what you know. If you have raced the track before, use what worked best. If you have never raced at the track you are setting up for, call around for suggestions or just go conservative. The same holds true for a lot of the other settings you will be doing. If you don't have a specific idea of what you want, aim for a good, middle-of-the-road setup that will allow you plenty of room for adjustment once practice starts.

Cross Weight
With that done, go ahead and get the wedge roughed in. This can be tough because you are not ready to weigh the car yet, and it's hardly worth getting out the scales just for this, but you can get it close. The old-fashioned way I used to do this still works. Put a jack under the center of the rear end and jack it up. You just need to make sure you have a good pivot point under the rear end. (A one-inch socket between the jack and the rear end usually works well.) Have somebody spin the left rear tire, and slowly lower the car. The minute the left rear barely skims the ground, look and see how much daylight is under the right rear. Over time, you will get a feel for how much space under the right rear relates to your wedge number.

STEP 3: CASTER AND CAMBER
Once the wedge is close, it's time to put the car on the front-end plates—if you have them—to check the

BELOW: You need to be able to measure your toe settings within 1/16 inch. A good set of toe plates is about the only way to do this reliably.

caster and camber. But before you can do anything, you must make sure that, if your car uses a drag-link steering system, it is locked down on center. Center your steering box by either checking your X measurement or making sure the flat spot on your steering box input shaft is pointing up (or by doing both), and lock the steering shaft in that spot. If you are racing a car with a rack-and-pinion system, there isn't really a center—just turn the wheel from lock to lock to determine where the center is. You can lock the steering by using a specially made tool for the task, or save yourself a few bucks and just use two vise grips. Lock them both on the steering shaft so that they are up against a frame rail or roll bar and the shaft cannot turn in either direction.

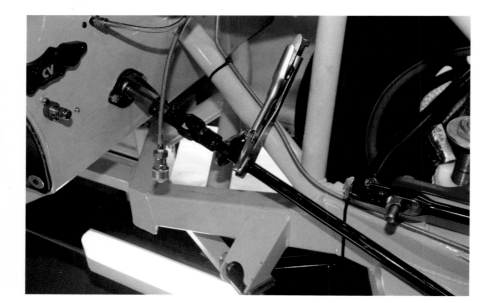

Now string up the car to make sure that the front wheels are straight with the rear wheels. It doesn't have to be perfect because you haven't squared the rear end yet; it just needs to be close. If it isn't, adjust the front wheels by threading the tie rod ends in or out.

Once you've got that, you can check the caster and camber. Check your camber first, because it can affect frame heights. If you change the camber a lot, you will need to recheck your frame heights because

when the tire rocks up on its sidewalls, it can raise the car. Exactly how much camber you want is determined by several factors, including the size and banking of the track, springs, and other things. But any time you are turning left, you know you want positive camber on the left front (the top of the tire is leaning out, away from the car) and negative camber on the right front (the top of the tire is leaning in, toward the car).

Move on to caster. Again, I can't tell you what caster numbers you need to run because that has a lot to do with driver feel. The main thing to remember is that caster split—the difference in caster from the right front to the left front—affects how the car turns. The greater the split (with more in the right front than the left front), the more the car is going to want to turn left on its own. When roughing in caster and camber, if you are within one-eighth to one-quarter of a degree, that's close enough for now.

STEP 4: TREAD WIDTH AND ALIGNMENT

Take the car back off the front-end plates and string it up again. This time around you want to check tread width, so use the strings to make sure the front and rear wheels are in line. Remember, you haven't set the toe yet, so the front wheels should be pointing straight ahead and the steering still locked down.

Normally, most sanctioning bodies will measure tread width from the inside of one front tire to the outside of the other. True tread width is center to center, but this method is easier to measure and gives you the same number. Regardless, make sure you know how your sanctioning body measures it so you can do it the same way. This is the only way you can make sure you take full advantage of the maximum limits.

Robert Yates taught me to think about a race car as a table with four legs. The four legs are the tires, and the same ways you can make a table stable will work with a race car. If your table has one of the legs tucked underneath it, it's going to be pretty wobbly and unstable. But if all four legs are pushed all the way out to the corners, then it's going to be stable. A race car is the same way; the farther you get the tires out on the corners (both in terms of tread width and wheelbase), the bigger the footprint and the better it's going to handle.

As I mentioned earlier, I've always been a big believer in running my front tread width just a little bit wider than the rear. It just seems to make the car more stable because it allows the right front tire to be out there a little farther relative to the right rear. Remember, most of the time when you go into a corner and the car travels down, the front end is going to lose tread width because it is independent. The rear isn't going to do that because it's a solid axle. Running the front about a quarter inch wider than the rear just makes sure that when the front suspension is compressed, the front end won't become narrower than the rear and make the car squirrelly.

While the car is still on the ground, now is a good time to check the toe on the rear wheels. Basically, you just want to check and make sure you don't have a rear toe problem. If you have a rear end with toe built into it, you should know what that figure is. Normally, the only time you will have a toe problem on the rear end is if you have banged the wall or bumped wheels with another car. Just check it with a toe stick or toe plates exactly like you would the front end. As a rule of thumb, you usually want $1/64$ or $1/32$ inch of toe in on the rear end. What I have found is if you push the envelope of having the rear end dead straight, you always stand the chance of it being knocked a little out. And a rear end that is toed out even a little always runs loose. So I'm willing to sacrifice a little bit of tire scrub just to make absolutely sure we don't have any toe out.

STEP 5: CHECK PINION ANGLE AND REAR CAMBER, THEN SQUARE AND CENTER THE REAR

The next step is to square the rear end. This is going to require getting underneath the car, so it's a good idea to have it up on what I call "elephant stands." These are just four aluminum stands that are the same height and are capable of holding the car's weight. The four tires rest on the stands so that the car is up off the ground but the car's weight

is still on the tires, keeping the suspension at ride height.

Since you are already underneath preparing to square the rear end, now is also a good time to check the pinion angle. The way I like to do it is simply to unhook the driveshaft, put something straight and flat against the yoke on the input shaft of the rear end, and place an angle finder against that. I think if you have 3.5 to four degrees of negative pinion angle (pointed toward the ground), you are in pretty good shape for most tracks. More negative angle tends to be more drag on the drivetrain, but the theory (which seems to be true) is that it helps forward bite. So at a high-speed track we may run no pinion angle, but at a track where acceleration is important, we may run five to six degrees of negative pinion angle. Unless you are a professional race team with full-time mechanics, pinion angle isn't something you will want to bother with every week, so 3.5 degrees negative is a good compromise that

ABOVE: Tread width requires a fixture to measure accurately. A tread-width fixture doesn't have to be complicated, and many racers make their own. Here, Rudy Zeck measures his front tread width. The other side of this fixture has a pointer that reaches around the belly of the tire and touches the rim. Zeck knows the distance from the end of the pointer to the other side of the fixture. By measuring the distance from the rim to the end of the fixture and subtracting that from the fixture's total width, he knows the tread width.

OPPOSITE: During the
setup process, you will
see me cranking up and
down on the jack bolts
numerous times. Putting
a mark on the bolt will
give you a visual aid to
help you count the turns.

should serve you well everywhere you go. To change the angle of the rear-end housing, you can use pinion angle shims or tapered lowering blocks between the trailing arms and the rear-end pads.

Another good thing to do now, especially if your sanctioning body checks it, is to document your rear camber. You check rear camber the same way as the front. The same concepts for camber that work on the front end of the car also work on the rear, but you can't run nearly as much because a solid rear axle simply can't handle it.

Once the pinion angle and rear camber are checked, document your numbers and forget about them. These settings won't change, so you don't have to worry about them anymore.

With those two tasks out of the way, it's time to get on to squaring and centering the rear end. Remember, in this book we are using a truck arm car as our example. Other rear suspension systems will have different ways of making adjustments, but on truck arm vehicles there is usually an eccentric on the right trailing arm pivot. The way you change the rear-end center (left to right) is by lengthening or shortening the panhard bar. Remember, like caster and camber on the front wheels, when you are trying to center and square the rear end, one adjustment will affect the other. So you may have the rear end squared, then find out after you have centered it by adjusting the panhard bar that it's no longer square. You just have to keep working back and forth until you have both right.

Of course, just because we call it centering the rear end, it doesn't mean that we necessarily want it exactly centered under the car. Remember, earlier I said we want the tread width of the front tires a little wider than the rear. Camber affects tread width, so that's one of the reasons we have roughed that in already. We know we want the left wheels aligned with each other. Now whatever the width difference is that you plan to run, you want the right front farther out than the right rear by that amount. If the right front is inboard of the right rear, you can't put a strong enough spring on the right front to keep it from feeling like it's going to roll underneath the car

in the turns. This situation will also cause a car to be loose. But if the right front is farther out than the right rear, that just adds to the car's stability.

Rear steer, or setting the rear end on an angle, can also be a tuning tool. When I was a crew chief, we always left the shop with the rear end squared on the car, but there were times when we just could not get the car to tighten up on corner entry. In that situation, I might turn the eccentric on the truck arm to bring the right rear wheel forward a bit to help tighten the car up. Also, there were times when the car always wanted to push on exit from the corner. If you rolled the right rear back a bit, that helped loosen it up on exit. That can help out for fine-tuning—just make it one of your last resorts.

Squaring and centering the rear end are at the top of our setup arc. Once we've got those right, we won't go back to them, so make sure you have the rear end dead on before you move on to the next step. Also, check to make sure the eccentric on the trailing arm pivot and the jam nuts on the panhard bar are tight so that those adjustments are locked down. From here on out, you are fine-tuning.

STEP 6: SCALES

It is finally time to get the car off the elephant stands and break out the scales. Most racing divisions have a minimum total weight and a minimum right-side weight. Of course, we all know the optimum location for lead is low and to the left. But a lot of rules won't allow all your lead on the left side of the car because of the minimum right-side weight rule. When we put the car on the scales, we want to look at those two weights because we have to make sure we are legal. You also want to keep an eye on the front/rear percentage and wedge. Wedge, or cross weight, is simply the weight on the right front and left rear wheels divided by the total car weight.

The only way you can change the total weight, the right-side weight, or even the front/rear percentage is by good old-fashioned lead placement. You can't change any of those by turning jack bolts. There are two ways of influencing wedge, however: by turning the jack bolts or moving lead. Since moving lead

ABOVE: A quick way to check wheelbase is simply to hook one end of a tape measure into the back of the rear rim and measure to the back of the front rim. This can be easier than finding the center of the hub, but be careful—this isn't the most exact way to measure wheelbase. First, if either wheel has toe and isn't pointed straight ahead, it can throw off your measurement. Second, if the body extends wider than the wheels, it can make it difficult to keep the tape straight between the wheels.

affects the other three factors, jack bolts are generally accepted as the best way to dial in wedge.

Find your target total weight, right-side weight, and front/rear weights first before you begin to dial in the correct wedge. But just like everything else, you have to keep checking all four factors whenever you make a change, because they all affect each other. For example, let's say we are looking for 51 percent nose weight. That means that 51 percent of the car's total weight is over the front wheels. We've got only 50 percent nose weight, but our wedge is right. If we move some weight forward to get the nose percentage right, we have to look at the other three factors again, because moving the lead will change the wedge.

Once you have the total amount of lead in the car, you've got to keep moving between your weights and percentages. But there is another factor you have to take into consideration: As you move your jack bolts to change the wedge, you are also changing your ride heights. It can get difficult to continually check frame heights while the car is on scale pads, but it has to be done because now you are dealing with total weight, right-side weight, front percentage, wedge, and frame heights all at once. And believe me, it can get confusing. One trick is to run a string between the tires and the scale pads on one side of the car from the front to the back and pull it tight. Then do the same thing on the other side of the car. This simulates the ground so you can measure ride height from the frame rail to the string.

It is easy to get your heights out of kilter if you aren't careful. A good rule of thumb is once you've got your weights placed but find you need to change wedge, try to make equal changes on the left and right sides of the car. In other words, if you need to put wedge in it and your heights are good, try to do a little bit on all four jack bolts. Remember, you can add wedge by screwing down on the jack bolts (clockwise) in either the right front or left rear or by screwing up (counterclockwise) on either the left front or right rear. So if your heights are already close and you need to add 10 pounds of wedge, instead of cranking a round into the left rear, try adding a quarter round into both the left rear and right front and removing a quarter round from both the right rear and left front.

When the wedge is where you think it should be for the track you plan to race, put the car back on the ground and recheck the frame heights. You are on step 6 now, and you want to go all the way back to the beginning and make sure you haven't done anything to get the frame heights off target. Of course, any time you touch the jack bolts, you should do a quick check of the frame heights.

STEP 7: WHEELBASE AND ACKERMAN
The next step on your list is to put the car back on the front-end plates and restring the front wheels with the steering locked straight ahead. Recheck and finalize the caster and camber settings. You've already done this one time on the rough-in side of

the arc, but now you are adding one more step. Since this time around you have the rear end where you want it to be, you can also check and adjust the wheelbase. The center of the rear wheels dictates one end of the wheelbase, and since the rear wheels are locked into place, you'll use the front wheels to make your changes.

If you remember from chapter 7, wheelbase is adjusted by moving the lower control arm forward or back. In addition to changing the wheelbase, this also affects caster. Lengthening the wheelbase will add positive caster to the spindle, while reducing the wheelbase will do the opposite.

In the case of a Cup car, the wheelbase is 110

The Setup

Here's the setup sheet that has served me for years as a Nextel Cup crew chief. I've always been a big believer in good lists and note taking. This one will help keep you from forgetting a step and show the best order for doing things, because almost every change you can make on a race car affects something else.

BEFORE STARTING
1. Make sure you have proper tires set at inspection air pressures.
2. Install inner liner in tires, if applicable.
3. Ensure that the fuel cell is filled appropriately (qualifying or race).
4. Anticipate the amount of lead ballast and location, and rough it in.

SETUP
1. Rough in all heights, including frame, roof, quarter panels, crankshaft, track bar, and wedge (using the jack-and-socket trick on the rear end).
2. Put car on front-end plates, string front wheels straight, and rough in caster and camber.
3. Restring front wheels with steering centered and locked down. Take car off plates, check front and rear tread width, and make sure rear toe in is correct.
4. Put car on aluminum wheel stands. Make sure rear end is aligned with chassis and rear-end offset is correct. Check and document panhard bar heights. String car to align front wheels with rear.
5. Put car on scales, and fine-tune weight and wedge while trying to maintain correct frame heights.
6. Return car to level ground. Recheck all heights to make sure they are the same as in step 1. If you must adjust frame heights by much, you must rescale the car and then recheck heights. Continue until measurements and percentages are correct.
7. Put car back on front-end plates, lock steering on center, and restring front wheels to rear. Check and finalize wheelbase, caster, and camber. Continue adjusting and rechecking until all three are correct (they affect each other). Check ackerman on front wheels. (Steering will need to be unlocked to check ackerman.)
8. Restring front wheels dead ahead with steering locked down. Put the car on jack stands, and check bump steer on left front and right front wheels. Check at .020, 1, 2, and 3 inches of compression. Check droop if you determine it necessary.
9. Put car back on front-end plates, and set toe out. Set fender tuck to match both wheels.
10. Return car to level ground. Recheck heights, set valance height to ground, and trim rocker panel skirts. Hook up sway bar(s).

FINAL CHECKS AFTER SETUP
1. Measure jack bolt heights and record them.
2. Make sure all lead is secured and mapped.
3. Make sure all eccentrics are tightened, marked, and secured (cotter pin or spot weld).
4. Double-check rear spoiler angle.
5. Tighten panhard bar jam nuts.
6. Check upper A-arm fasteners.
7. Tighten all bolts on front end, especially steering system, and secure using safety wire or cotter pins as necessary.
8. Lock down and secure tie rod adjusters.
9. Tighten all fender braces, and secure using lock nuts or jam nuts as necessary.

ABOVE: You can also mark the right side of the track bar and the mounting bracket at your base height. This way it is easy to return to your baseline setting.

inches. NASCAR looks for that length on either the right or left side and then allows you a half-inch tolerance on the other side. We take advantage of that by setting the wheelbase at exactly 110 inches on the right side and using the part of that extra half inch to make the left side longer. In other words, we'll go 110 inches on the right side and 110.25 on the left. A longer left-side wheelbase will make the car turn better. It works that way on every solid rear-axle car I've worked on.

Now that we've added wheelbase to the mix, we have a pretty long list of adjustments that can affect something else on the car. Sometimes it can get confusing when you try to remember what changes what.

Changing the wheelbase affects caster but not camber. Caster changes, however, affect camber as well as wheelbase. Camber does not change caster or wheelbase; it can change the height of the car only.

Now it's time to move on to ackerman, the difference in distance that one wheel turns versus the other when the steering wheel is turned a certain amount. Normally, you want a little bit of positive ackerman dialed into the steering, but how much depends on where you are racing and the driver's preference. Generally, smaller tracks require more positive ackerman to limit wheel scrub. You check ackerman last because it doesn't affect caster, camber, or wheelbase.

STEP 8: BUMP STEER, CASTER, AND CAMBER GAIN

Now it's time to check the bump steer. To check and set the ackerman, you had to unlock the steering, but now you want to lock it back up before setting up the jack and bump steer gauge on the wheel you will be checking (see photo on page 88). There is no doubt about it: Checking and setting the bump steer can be the biggest pain in the rear you will have setting up a race car, but it's a necessity. Some teams try to check the bump steer several times with the wheels turned different amounts. It is really easy to get yourself mixed up doing that. I think it's just more information than you can use. My recommendation is to track bump steer with the wheels pointed straight ahead and leave it at that.

The good news is it isn't always necessary to check bump steer every week. If you bump a front tire or change ball joints or steering box—anything that affects your steering system—then you definitely need to check your bump steer. But if you have raced without incident and not bent anything up, then it's not likely that your bump steer settings have changed.

Zero bump steer is our goal in a perfect world, but since that's not possible because of the design of the steering and front-suspension systems, minimizing it is the next-best thing. Under no circumstances do you want the bump steer to be negative so that you get toe in. Normally, you check the first 3 inches of compression travel at 1-inch increments, but there's a chance that bump steer can cause the wheels to toe in in the first few fractions of an inch of travel and then begin to toe out. So you also want to check bump at .020 inch and make sure it's beginning to toe out a little bit. I suggest aiming for .015 inch of toe out per inch of compression travel. That means by the time you get to 3 inches of travel, you have added .045 inch of toe out. That's a pretty safe number.

There are two other things you want to check while you are doing your bump steer: caster and camber gain. You are only looking to see how much the caster and camber change as the suspension compresses, not what the caster and camber measures at ride height. To check it, you simply put your caster/camber gauge on the hub and check both through full travel. Always check caster and camber gain at the same time. Normally, a good target is 3 degrees of caster gain through the full sweep. For camber gain, a good target is 1.25 degrees at 1 inch of travel, 2.75 degrees at 2 inches, and 4.5 degrees at 3 inches. The rate of camber gain increases as the wheel travels, but it shouldn't be too much. If you gain 1.25 degrees in the first inch of travel, 1.5 between 1 and 2 inches, and 1.75 between 3 and 4 inches of travel, that should be just about right. If you check camber gain and find the rate of gain to be too low, you can shorten the upper A-arm. If the gain is too fast, switch out the upper A-arm for a longer one.

After checking caster and camber gain, put the car back on the ground and put everything back together. To check bump steer, you probably had your springs out and your jack bolts turned all the way out to get the springs out. Now you see why it's important to have a measurement on those jack bolts and always to count your rounds when you are making changes. It just makes it a lot easier to get your car back to the correct settings. After getting everything put back together, check to make sure your heights are correct, and then lock the steering back down on center once again—it's time to finalize the toe.

The best way I've found for setting toe out is to make sure the left front wheel is straight by putting the string on it and making sure it's lined up with the rear wheel, and then set the toe out on the right front. In other words, if we are running fj inch of toe out—fj to $\frac{1}{16}$ inch is usually pretty safe—I want it all in the right front. I've tried splitting the toe or putting it all in the left front, but every time I have the driver has always complained that the car feels edgy or a little loose getting into the corner.

STEP 9: DOUBLE-CHECK EVERYTHING

Once the toe is set, you are done with the setup process. All that's left to do is make sure all your i's are dotted and t's are crossed. Take the car off the front-end plates and check your heights one last time. If you haven't figured it out by now, frame heights are one of the most critical measurements that can tell you if anything is off. It's also a good idea to check your body inspection heights one last time.

Also, go through and measure your jack bolts again and record those settings. Now when you are at the track, if someone is changing a jack bolt and loses count, you have something to fall back on. Or maybe you have to raise the front of the car all the

way up to get it on your trailer. Now when you get to the track, you have an easy measurement to return the car to ride height without messing up the wedge number.

Secure the Ballast

Go back through and make sure all the lead in your car is secure. If that lead moves around while the car is on the track, there are a couple of things that can happen, and none of them is good. If the lead just slides around inside the frame rails, all the percentages you worked so hard on will be off, and it likely will ruin the car's handling. And that's the best-case scenario. The last thing in the world you want is for that lead to come out of the car. If it does, you can run over it with your back tire and cut it down, which will wreck you. Or maybe you don't hit it but the guy behind you does and it wrecks him. Your worst nightmare is that lead slings out and bounces up into the stands. I saw a piece of lead come out of a car at Phoenix once during practice. It flew out of the car, bounced over the fence, and broke a window in one of the suites. I don't have to tell you what would happen if a piece of lead came out of your race car and actually hit somebody.

Map the Locations of the Weight

One trick I always used was having a map of where all the lead was in the car, and I made it right after we secured it in the car. The map told me how much lead—or in the case of Nextel Cup teams, tungsten—was in the frame rails or the lead box and exactly where each piece was. I even put down where the spacers were and how big they were. At the track, if I decided I wanted to put more front percentage in the car, I could look at that map and say, "OK, we have room to move this spacer and slide the piece up a little bit." It kept me from having to take the end caps off or from trying to remember where all the lead was. I recommend such a map for everyone, because it can give you information quickly and help you be more decisive at the racetrack.

Secure Eccentrics and Fasteners

Next, check and lock down all the eccentrics on your car, especially on the trailing arms and lower control

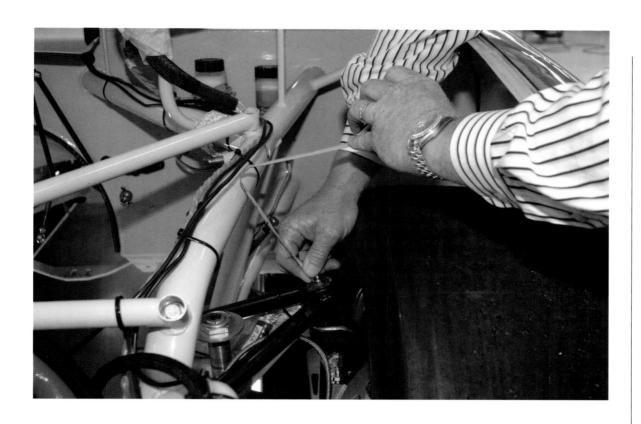

LEFT: When checking dynamic caster, camber changes, or bump steer you must be able to measure ride height as the suspension is compressed. The easiest way is to make a mark on the frame and measure from that point to the grease fitting on the upper A-arm. If the measurement is 10 inches when the car is at ride height, then you know if you get nine inches, the suspension has traveled one inch.

arms. Maybe put a spot weld on them to make absolutely sure they aren't going to vibrate loose. Then go through and double-check all the nuts and bolts on the suspension and steering systems and hook up the sway bar. I like running regular bolts on the front suspension when you are setting up the car because you are taking those nuts off and putting them back on so many times. But before you go to the race, make sure you replace them with lock nuts or put a thin jam nut on there. The same goes with the nuts securing your shocks. I don't like to run regular fasteners on any of those pieces during a race because of the likelihood that vibrations will make one of them come loose. Finally, secure your tie rods and other steering components with cotter keys or tie wire.

Make Final Adjustments

Finally, go through and set anything that's adjustable on your car before you take it off the surface plate. Maybe you have an adjustable front valance, rear spoiler, or rocker panel skirts. Go ahead and get that set and ready for inspection before you put the car on the truck. The same goes for anything else you can think of that you want to do to the car before it hits the track. If you know how much tape you want to run, go ahead and put that on. I know when you are racing in July, if you have a lot of stuff to do to that car at the track and it's 110 degrees in the shade and the asphalt feels like it's 200, then you aren't going to have a lot of fun. But if you can get there, unload the car, and have a minute to relax, then it just seems to make your whole night go better. You can spend your time thinking about the race and enjoying yourself rather than sweating the details you should have taken care of at the shop. A lot of racetracks inspect cars based on whoever gets in line first. That means if you are ready first, you are through inspection first and ready to hit the track as soon as it opens for practice. Meanwhile, those poor slobs at the back of the line are still trying to get through inspection while you are getting the jump on them with every extra practice lap you make.

ABOVE: Good brakes on a race car involve more than just the calipers and pads. You have to consider everything from the pedal all the way to the rotor as a system and make sure everything works together effectively.

chapter 11

Brakes: Going Fast Means Stopping Fast, Too

If there is one thing that's a given in racing, it's that new racers will underestimate the importance of a good braking system. And sometimes it takes veteran racers quite a while to realize it, too. Yes, racing is about going fast, but that's for complete laps and not just the straights. As a general rule, the smaller and tighter the track you race on, the more important good brakes are to your success. I recently heard Nextel Cup driver Ryan Newman make a very good observation about Martinsville Speedway that I absolutely agree with: "It's the one track we go to where braking power is more important than acceleration or horsepower." If you race on a tight, half-mile or smaller track, this is probably true for you, too. By maximizing your braking system, your driver can slow the car at the last possible moment, allow the car to settle, then get back on the accelerator early, producing the best possible lap time. A car that blasts down the straights but struggles through the center because the driver can't get it slowed down will rarely be in contention.

I am not going to suggest much in the way of specific brands or products because there are so many variables for different types of racing. Yes, the big six-piston calipers that we use in Nextel Cup racing are probably the best thing going in terms of stopping power and consistency, but they are awfully expensive, they aren't allowed in many series, and you can't fit them inside a smaller wheel. Even with limits on what you can run, a little planning will help you find the right combination that provides balanced stopping power that won't fade under extreme use (which is really just normal use in racing).

PLAN TO BE BIASED

Your brake system starts with the master cylinders. In chapter 3, I mentioned the value of dual mas-

ter cylinders when it comes to safety, but running two master cylinders has another advantage: You can control the brake bias between the front and rear tires. Bias is the difference in braking pressure applied to the front wheels versus the rear wheels. You will almost always want more braking bias on the front wheels than the rear, but you will not always want the same amount. A brake-bias adjuster is a simple mechanism that allows you to easily control the amount of bias. It does this by changing the leverage—and thus, the force—that the brake pedal applies to each of the master cylinder pistons.

If you have a driver who you trust to make the adjustments, you can mount the knob of the adjuster within his reach. A driver who knows how to dial in the right amount of brake bias and keep a car balanced can make a car run well for long green-flag runs, but I've also seen drivers dial themselves right out of contention because they were cranking on the adjuster knob too much. If this sounds like your driver, mount the adjuster out of his reach—maybe even under the hood where only the crew can adjust it during practice—until he gets a better feel for what the car needs.

BELOW: Twin master cylinders allow a measure of safety. If one fails, you still have partial braking power to get the car slowed. Tuning is also possible by using two different size pistons to push the brake fluid. Notice the delay valve mounted to the master cylinder on the left. It delays the actuation of the rear brakes by a split second to make the car more drivable when the brakes are first applied.

BELOW: Both master cylinders are actuated by the same brake pedal, but a balance bar can adjust how much braking pressure is applied to the rear versus the front. The driver can use it as an adjusting tool as fuel is burnt off or other factors affect the handling of the race car.

There are a couple of methods for properly using a bias adjuster. First of all, you can't just turn the knob and think it's set. Instruct your driver to apply slight pressure to the brake pedal when making adjustments. This will ensure the slider on the adjuster doesn't bind up the next time he stomps the pedal entering a turn. Also, the adjuster should be considered only a tool for fine-tuning your car's handling. Generally, if you are loose on turn entry, you can dial in more front brake and less rear to help reduce that. The reverse is true for a car that is pushing—more rear brake and less on the front to help the car turn better. But, if you are fighting a loose condition, dialing a ton of front brake to the adjuster is only a Band-Aid, not a cure. Now what you are doing is putting all the braking load on the front brakes and abusing them—and running the risk of losing them. Your rear brakes aren't working to capacity while the front brakes are getting cooked.

When you run dual master cylinders and a bias adjuster, it's important to make sure you start with the brakes set to a known bias. Gauges are available that screw into the bleeders. This process requires three people but is relatively simple. One person sits in the seat ready to operate the brakes, the second threads the brake pressure gauge into the bleeder on the front caliper, and the third does the same thing at the rear on the same side of the car. Then the person in the driver's seat applies the brakes firmly while the other two read the gauges. This allows you to quantify the amount of bias split between the front and rear brakes. Normally, you want to start out with 100 pounds more pressure in the front and adjust from there.

MASTER CYLINDERS

You should choose master cylinders according to the piston size. This may sound backwards at first, but a smaller piston provides more braking pressure at the caliper for the same amount of pedal travel. Normally, racers use a seven-eighths-inch piston on the master cylinder feeding the front brakes and a one inch for the rear. This automatically provides a bit of brake bias toward the front.

Piston size can also be adjusted to provide the feel a driver is looking for. A larger master cylinder piston requires more pedal effort for the same amount of stopping power. This is because you have to move more fluid. The same goes for the size of the brake line. A smaller piston and brake lines mean less effort from the driver for the same amount of stopping power. This has nothing to do with how well the car actually stops, but you can never underestimate the importance of providing your driver with a car that's comfortable for him to drive. You want to help him so he doesn't wear himself out mashing the brake pedal, but at the same time you want the pedal to require enough effort that he's aware when he's using the brakes so that he doesn't abuse them. There are no clear-cut guidelines for how stiff a driver likes a pedal—you just need to experiment. Also, just like suspension setups, the best setting is not necessarily

what makes the driver most comfortable. Whatever makes him fastest is what you have to give him.

Also, consider running the largest fluid reservoirs on the master cylinders that you can get. You can't have too much fluid in my opinion. If you are running lengthy races at tracks that use a lot of brake, a standard master cylinder reservoir won't hold enough fluid, because as the brake pads wear and the pistons extend farther out of the calipers, brake fluid is used to fill that void. Consider how much fluid is required if you have two-piston calipers on all four wheels. You can be running great, but if your reservoir runs dry and you start pumping air, your brakes are shot.

Another reason to run the larger reservoirs is that you don't want to have to fill them all the way to the top. When brake fluid heats up, it expands. If you have topped off the fluid in the reservoir and haven't left it anywhere to go, that expansion will virtually lock up the brakes. I've always left an inch to an inch and a half of room at the top to allow for the fluid to expand.

BRAKE LINES

The number one rule when it comes to running your brake lines is to use hard lines whenever possible. Flex lines contribute to a spongy-feeling brake pedal, and the more you use it, the worse it is. The only places to use flex lines are the suspension points where you have to allow for wheel movement. Also, always avoid using OEM rubber brakes lines. Use even a short length of that stuff and you will never have a nice, firm pedal.

When you are routing your brake lines, be aware of potential hazards and heat sources. Hide the lines behind chassis tubing so that debris from the wheels cannot get kicked up and cut or crimp

LEFT: This is another option for a delay valve. This one can be adjusted for the amount of delay you want.

Dealing with Drivers

You want to provide your driver with the best possible brake system so that he can use what he needs and then get off the brake pedal quickly. But you might be surprised how often drivers will use the brake pedal when they don't need to. Many aren't even aware how much they are using the brake and harming their lap times.

Several times in my career, I've worked with drivers whom I suspected were using the brake way too early but weren't noticing it. What I had to do with a couple of them was put a brake light on the dash. The light went off and caught their attention, and they were forced to notice exactly where on the track they were first applying the brake. Drivers also get into the habit of lightly resting their left foot on the brake pedal and applying slight braking pressure without realizing it. That's not only going to slow the car down, it's also going to put unnecessary heat into the brakes. Like I mentioned before, excess heat in the brakes not only hurts the brakes, but it also heats the tires and raises the air pressure unnecessarily. It's easy to rig up a brake light if you think your driver could use the visual cue. All it requires is an oil-pressure light hooked to the brake pedal so that any time pressure is applied, it turns on the light. If your driver insists on resting his foot on the brake pedal, then put a stiffer return spring on it so that it requires noticeable pressure to activate the calipers. He'll probably complain that you are wearing out his leg with the stiff brake pedal, but just tell him that when he quits using it for a footrest, you will take some spring out of it.

I've also had some drivers on the other end of the spectrum. You can actually stab the brakes in a turn to help the car take a set and get turned around. Davey Allison used to do this all the time at places like Martinsville. He was fast around that track, but he was also awfully hard on the brakes, and they just wouldn't last an entire race. We had to work real hard with him to get him to stop using the brakes as a tool to get the car turned so that they wouldn't die on him with 100 laps to go.

them. Also try to keep the lines away from radiant heat sources like headers, oil pans and tanks, and exhaust pipes. This is critical because once brake fluid boils, its usefulness is over. Heat from the pads and rotors is bad enough—you don't want to add to it from other sources.

Another area of additional heat that we didn't take into account for quite a while is the rear end. There was a time when we were building Nextel Cup cars that we would run a single flex line from the chassis to the rear-end housing, tee off of that, and run two hard lines to each of the calipers. We thought we were improving performance by limiting the amount of flex line, but we weren't accounting for the amount of heat the rear end was pumping into the brake lines that were secured against the housing. Now most teams will put up with a little extra flex line in order to keep that extra heat out of the system. They will run hard line to each side of the chassis directly above both rear calipers and then run flex line down to the calipers from there.

CALIPERS, PADS, AND ROTORS

Like the master cylinders, you can install different size calipers to help keep the car balanced. Smaller calipers and harder pads give the rear end less grip, which can help keep a car from getting loose entering a turn while braking. But be careful—you don't want to go too far and take too much rear brake from the car. If you do that, you are overworking the front brakes, and you take a chance of wearing out the pads or overheating the fluid.

It goes without saying that you want to choose the smallest and lightest calipers and rotors that you can get by with. Other than the roof of the car, the wheels are about the worst area of a race car for extra weight. That's unsprung weight, and it makes the suspension less responsive. Some pieces, as in brake rotors, are also rotating weight, which can significantly harm acceleration. Fortunately, there is a lot of technology being developed that makes rotors, calipers, and pads more effective with less mass. One of the big ones is slotted rotors. When brake pads are pressed against the rotors to create

friction, a gas is also produced as a by-product. This gas can actually reduce the frictional coefficient of the pads rubbing against the rotors. The slots in the rotors provide an escape route for this gas, which increases the stopping power of the brakes without shortening the lifespan of the pads like old-style cross-drilled rotors. Also, modern caliper designs are producing lighter calipers with greater rigidity. One of the most significant is the use of a "bridge" across the center of the caliper. A good bridge can significantly reduce caliper warping under load. A weak or flexible caliper will balloon out at the bottom under clamping load, reducing its ability to provide stopping power. Uneven pad wear can tip you off to this condition—pads will wear more at the top (away from the center of the wheel) than at the bottom because the greatest amount of flex is at the bottom of the caliper.

Also, with older or OEM-style calipers, the pads often tend to wear along the leading edge, or the edge of the pad that the spinning rotor first made contact with. This means that the caliper/pad/rotor combination was giving up braking power, since it wasn't making full use of the pads' entire surface area. Manufacturers solved this a few years back by going with multiple pistons and staggering the sizes. They've since figured out how to get consistent pad wear with the same size caliper pistons, but if you are experiencing uneven pad wear and are on a budget, you might want to consider looking around for a lightly used set of the staggered-piston calipers.

The simple rule when it comes to brake pads is, normally, the harder the pad, the longer it is going to last but the less grip it is going to have. A softer, grippier pad is just the opposite. It will provide more stopping power, but you have to be careful because it might not last in a long race with lots of braking and it will produce more heat. The opposite is true when you are qualifying. You usually can't get heat into the pads quickly enough and you aren't concerned with durability, so consider using a softer pad that will provide you plenty of braking power going into the first turn when everything is still cold.

One place where you don't want to sacrifice any

strength for weight savings is the caliper mounts. Your calipers have to be rigidly mounted if they are going to do their job. If the mounts cannot hold the calipers steady, that movement reduces the amount of friction the brakes can produce and also ruins the "feel" a driver has at the brake pedal. I've also seen caliper mounts on the rear-end housing so light that they broke off during a race. Do not take shortcuts with your caliper mounts: you need beefy stuff, especially if you are running a hard-braking track or a heavier class of car.

COOLING

On short tracks with a lot of braking, you need to provide lots of cooling to your rotors. The problem with brakes is once you boil the brake fluid, the brakes are shot. So you have to make sure not to overstress the system. Some of that comes from your driver, but a lot also comes from providing your brakes with a cool stream of fresh air. The best way to do this is through the tried-and-true brake ducts.

You don't have to go out and buy a full-bore carbon duct system; some high-temperature hose intelligently placed in your car will do the trick. Point the outlet end of the hose at the center of the rotor, and keep the length of hose as short and as straight as possible. Brake hose that's coiled like a snake through the engine compartment only serves to kill the air velocity before it reaches the rotor. It is also key that the hose points to the center of the rotor and not the edge where the brake pads make contact. The rotor's cooling vanes actually act as an air pump as the rotor turns, pulling air from the center, or eye, of the rotor and drawing it to the outside edge. This makes a steady stream of cool air to the center of the rotor more effective than trying to cool the outside edge directly.

On the other end, it's important how you fabricate

ABOVE: Small blowers such as these can help provide additional flow of cool air when you just can't seem to keep your brakes cool enough. They are also useful at tracks where you don't want to cut holes into the nose of the car because downforce is critical. In that case, you can point the blowers at the ground just behind the front valance and let them pull from the air that comes underneath the car.

RIGHT: You don't have to use high-end carbon-fiber ducts like these, but some form of cover to help force cooling air into the center of the rotor will help tremendously with keeping your brakes within proper operating temperatures.

your hose inlets on the front of the car. The locations where you cut your holes in the front bumper are critical. From my experience in the wind tunnel, the air-pressure patterns on the nose of a race car are the same no matter what the shape. The air pressure is highest in the center of the bumper and down low. The higher up you go or the farther out you go toward the corners, the more the pressure drops. You want the duct holes as close to the high-pressure areas as possible to maximize the air that gets to the brakes, so basically, you want the cooling duct inlets to be right up against the radiator box. In Nextel Cup, we were allowed only three hoses per brake, so we usually ran two to the center of the rotor and one to the caliper. Also, when you are fabricating your inlets, remember that corners kill air velocity. Keep the inlets nice and rounded like a funnel to keep the air speed up.

Of course, there is a tradeoff for cutting a lot of air holes in the front of your race car: It adds drag and hurts front downforce. On bigger tracks where you need a slick car, you might want to keep the front of your car smooth. But if you are using a lot of brake, you still need some cooling. In the Nextel Cup series, Indianapolis is the perfect example. It's a big track with high straightaway speeds, but the corners are sharp and require a lot of brake. If you have an efficient radiator system, you might consider robbing air from inside the radiator box to feed the brake ducts instead of cutting holes in the front of the car. Another option is to use small blowers under the hood. Mount them so that the inlet is just behind the front valance to pick up any air coming from underneath the car and feed it into the standard brake hose. They make fancy ones just for racing now, but when we first started doing it in the Nextel Cup Series, we just used marine blowers made to exhaust fumes from around inboard boat motors before you crank them, and they worked just fine.

You can do the same thing if you find you need to provide some cooling air to the rear brakes. Use the blowers and mount the inlet in the rear firewall so it pulls air from the cockpit. Besides cooling the brakes, it is also pulling hot air away from the driver. Just be careful if you've got four blowers feeding air to your brakes and another one blowing air on the driver—it's easy to outrun your alternator, so make sure it is capable of handling your increased need for electrical power.

Big-Track Qualifying

Even if your driver isn't applying the brakes, every time a pad touches the rotor as it spins, it causes a little bit of drag. This can mean two- to three-tenths at places like Daytona and Talladega. To combat this, we always took a screwdriver and pushed the pads back away from the rotors. This frees up a little horsepower by eliminating all friction between the brake pads and rotors. There's just two things you need to make sure of if you try this. One, when your driver gets in the car, make sure he doesn't touch the brake pedal, even to rest his foot on it. And two, the minute he takes the checkered flag after his qualifying lap, get on the radio and remind him to pump the brake pedal. You don't want him to forget and enter pit road without the brakes ready to slow him back down. I really don't recommend this except at high-speed, high-banked tracks where brakes aren't used for qualifying.

There are several ways to find out if your brakes are getting too hot. One of the easiest ways is simply to use the same infrared temp gun you use on your tires. The only problem with this method is it is difficult to determine the maximum temperature the brakes see while the brakes are being applied. If it takes your driver a while to reach you after he comes off the track, the brake temps may be significantly cooler. To record the maximum brake temperature seen during a race, you can use temperature paints or decals made specifically for the purpose. Simply apply the paint on the outside edge of the rotor and the decal on the caliper.

While we are talking about cooling air, I want to remind you there are other uses for air ducts. When I was the crew chief for Mike Skinner, he would drive a car so hard into the corner it would overwork the right front tire. The tire would heat up, the air inside it would expand and push the air pressure up, and the car would start pushing. Not only that, but we were also running the risk of the tire failing on Mike.

So we put one of those blowers under the hood and blew air right on the bead of that tire to try to keep it cool and keep the pressure down. We had to do something because once the air pressure in a tire gets too high, it's not going to go back down while the car is on the track.

BEDDING IN

Most companies that sell high-performance brake pads and rotors also offer prebedded pads and rotors as an option. This is a time-saving service, but it costs extra and you might not want to pay for it. If not, you can bed in your own pads and rotors yourself. Bedding in new pads or rotors is simple. At the track, have your driver go out and slowly and steadily build up the heat in the brakes by using the brake pedal. What you want to do is really heat up the brakes, then come in and park the car. That will heat-soak the new pads or rotors and burnish them in. Allow the car to sit until the brakes cool back down, and then you should be good to go.

BELOW: Keeping your brake fluid cool is critical for a braking system that won't fade halfway through a race. It can be tempting to run the brake lines along the rear axle housing, but that adds heat to the system. Instead, run them along the frame and use a flex line to drop straight down to the rear calipers.

ABOVE: Caliper flex is the enemy of a firm pedal. I know it's tempting to try to save weight wherever you can, but good, beefy caliper mounts are a must.

RIGHT: Poor-quality or overworked calipers will flex, reducing the stopping power available. When pressure is applied, the sides of the caliper actually flex outward. You can tell if this is happening to you because the pads will wear more at the top (where there is less movement) than at the bottom (where the excessive movement means there is less pressure pushing the pads against the rotors).

One thing you do not want to do is to try to burnish in a new set of pads and rotors at the same time. It just won't work; either the pads or the rotor needs to be used. That is why it requires a lot of time to burnish in a new set of both pads and rotors and is best done during a test session, not during practice before a race. When I first got started in Nextel Cup racing, we were still bedding in our pads and rotors ourselves, and we used to spend entire days at a track just building up an inventory of rotors and pads that were already bedded in. You need to always have spares on hand because the worst thing in the world is to discover after practice is completed that you have a cracked rotor. Now you have to start the race with a brand-new, green rotor, and that's just about guaranteed to hurt you. The rotor will act like it is glazed over, and you will never get good grip between the rotor and pads.

MAINTENANCE

One of the biggest culprits that can lead to brake fade, or failure altogether, is the brake fluid. Make sure you use a high-boiling-point fluid. Regular fluid intended for passenger cars isn't suitable. Look for a fluid with a dry boiling point of at least 600 degrees Farenheit. You will find this only in products designed for racing; it's a bit more expensive, but it's worth it because once you boil the fluid in your race car, you've lost the brakes—and they aren't coming back.

Even if you don't boil the fluid, the high heat generated by racing can break it down over time. Any time you run a 200-lap race, go ahead and replace the break fluid. Even if you are running only 20-lap features every week, it's a good idea to fully flush the system a couple of times during the season. And I don't mean just bleed the brakes—you've got to get all of that burnt-up fluid out of there and replace it with fresh brake fluid.

The problem with completely flushing the system is it can be difficult to refill all the brake lines throughout the car and get rid of any air bubbles. I used to spend two days trying to bleed the brakes on a new race car, pumping the brake pedal until I thought my leg would fall off and still not getting the air bubbles out of it. The trick is to allow the brake system to gravity feed. The process is relatively simple: Just fill the fluid reservoir, crack the bleeders on the calipers, and allow gravity to pull the fluid through the system. It may take an hour or more, but as long as the reservoir is the highest point on the circuit, it will work every time. You just have to make sure you never allow the reservoir to run out

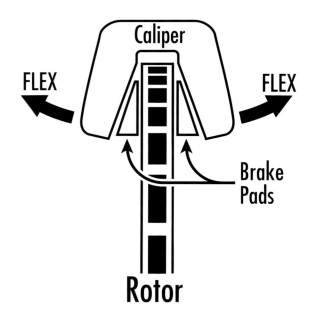

The View from the Pit Box

If you pay close attention during a pit stop, you can learn a lot about how a driver is treating his brakes without ever getting off the pit box. When the front tire changer pulls off the front wheel and tire, check to see how much brake dust falls out. If it has been a short run but a small pile of brake dust falls out of the hub, you need to let your driver know he needs to be more careful with his brakes. Likewise, if the tire changer hits the first lug nut and instantly looks like a coal miner after a hard day's work, that's another sign that the pads are getting really worn.

or you will have to start over again. Once you see a steady stream of fluid coming out of a bleeder, you can close it off. After you've closed off all four, go ahead and top off the fluid reservoir and bleed the brakes like you normally would. Before you close off the bleeders for the final time, take a rubber mallet and tap around the caliper to dislodge any air bubbles that may be clinging to the inside of the caliper and get them out of the system. If you are working alone, it can be difficult to keep up with all four calipers as well as the reservoir; just open one bleeder at a time so that it is easier to keep up with. This will take longer, but it does the same job.

Taking care of the fluid while it is still in the can is also important. Because the brake fluid absorbs moisture out of the air (which lowers its boiling point), it is possible to put bad fluid in your car that you think is brand-new. When changing fluid, always keep the cap on the can or bottle until you are ready to use it, and put the cap back on as soon as you are done. Use only one can at a time. Also, if you have had a can of fluid sitting around for six or seven months, use that stuff in your tow vehicle and get yourself a new can for the race car.

Make sure to keep an eye on the rotors. Even if you are just running short races, check your rotors every week for cracks. It is normal to get small cracks that look like pencil marks, but if those cracks get to either the inside or outside edge of the rotor, that rotor needs to be replaced. Rotors can also be turned if they need to be cleaned up a bit. You cannot turn them to the extreme that passenger-car rotors can be turned, but it can be helpful to do just enough to true the face of the rotor. Also, make sure that the bolts securing the rotor to the hat are safety wired. The temperature changes and vibrations to which rotors are subjected will cause any bolt to work itself loose over time. It's easy to eliminate that possibility with pre-drilled bolts and a little safety wire.

Brake calipers also require frequent attention. Besides the brake fluid, the O-rings that seal the caliper pistons are the most fragile components in the system. After several heat cycles—and believe me, they get hot—they will get brittle. If you ignore the calipers and don't rebuild them regularly, you run the risk of a leaking caliper or having a piston freeze up, which will cause brake drag and poor braking performance. When you flush the fluid in the system, go ahead and rebuild your calipers, too.

LEFT: Every curve in the brake duct hoses reduces the velocity of the cooling air. Keep the hoses as direct as possible from the inlet to the brakes, but also make sure they won't be rubbing the wheels at full lock right or left. More than once, I've seen the wire from a torn duct hose cut down a tire because it was rubbing.

BELOW LEFT When you combine the vibrations that come from racing and high heat, which can cause expansion of the materials involved, it's easy for the bolts connecting the rotor to the hat to work themselves loose. A brake failure can be expensive, disastrous, or both, so make sure to always safety-wire your rotor bolts.

ABOVE: Few racing organizations spend more time testing in a wind tunnel than Nextel Cup teams, but you can take advantage of the tricks that they have learned.

chapter 12

Aerodynamics

If you have followed the Nextel Cup or Busch Series over the last few years, you have probably heard plenty of discussions about aerodynamics. That's because we have just realized in the last decade just how important it is, and there are a lot of people in lower-level racing series who are still catching on. In my experience, if you have a car that's aerodynamically sound, you can get by with the mechanical setup being a little off. But if you have a car that is aero-deficient and you're going up against teams with cars that are sound aerodynamically, you can't overcome it with chassis adjustments.

I know if you are racing a short track program, you are probably thinking: "Wait a minute. Aero may be a big deal to the Cup guys running two-mile tracks, but I run a half mile every Saturday night. Aero doesn't affect me." I know when most of us think about aerodynamics we think about Daytona and Talladega, but trust me, if you are running even close to 100 miles per hour on the race track, there is a lot you can do to make your race car better. My philosophy is if your driver has to get off the throttle anywhere around the racetrack, then you need more downforce. Yes, reducing drag is a good thing, but when it comes to just about every track except Daytona and Talladega, it's always a fight to get as much downforce as you can in the car.

In my years as a crew chief, I've been fortunate to be with some organizations that had access to wind tunnels. When I look back on my career, I believe I have more than 600 hours spent testing in wind tunnels. Of course, that's nothing compared to the aerodynamicists who have thousands of hours of experience in wind-tunnel testing. Fortunately we've learned that there are rules that airflow follows and ways you can take advantage of it. For the most part, the aerodynamic philosophies that we use to

get the most from a race car are pretty consistent. What will work on a Nextel Cup car will work on a Late Model, too. It may not be quite as noticeable on a car with a top on-track speed of 110 miles per hour versus a car that hits 190, but it is still there. So even if you know you will never get anywhere near a wind tunnel, you can still use what we've learned to make your program better.

DRAG VS. DOWNFORCE

The two main aspects that affect us as racers when it comes to aerodynamics are drag and downforce. *Drag* is the resistance that the exterior of the car creates as it moves through the air. In Nextel Cup, the only two racetracks that the driver never lifts off the throttle are Daytona and Talladega, so we've always paid extra attention to reducing drag when preparing cars for those tracks. But for 90 percent of the racetracks that we went to, we mostly paid attention to *downforce*, which is when differences in high- and low-pressure air pockets actually push down on a race car and help it stick to the track. The high-pressure air is created when the air collects, or bunches up, against the top surfaces of the car—especially the nose of the car,

BELOW: In the foreground is the nose for a down-force car. The nose in the background is a Nextel Cup car that is raced at Daytona and Talladega, where downforce is sacrificed in order to reduce drag.

RIGHT: Notice how Dale Jr.'s team keeps the front end taped up to present a nice, clean profile that cuts smoothly through the air. The corners of the nose are also rolled back to give the nose more of a bullet shape.

the windshield, and the rear spoiler. Low-pressure areas are created underneath the car. The differential between the high-and-low pressure areas literally suck the car to the ground.

Drag is drag no matter where it is created on a race car, but the locations where downforce is created are significant. There is front downforce and there is rear downforce, and keeping the two in balance is important. Assuming a car's mechanical traction is balanced, too much front downforce will cause a car to be loose, while too much rear downforce will cause it to push. Downforce adds to the tires' traction limits, so the real-world result of adding downforce is the same as adding mechanical grip.

We've already discussed in detail how you should try to correct a loose or tight condition when it comes to mechanical grip. Remember, it's usually a bad idea to try to fix a loose car by "unhooking" the front end. Reducing the grip on the front of the car may make it feel more balanced, but you are only reducing its overall capability to grip the track. Instead of unhooking the front end on a loose car, you should always try to find a way to make the rear tires grip better. This gives you the double advantage of a balanced race car and increased grip. The same approach applies to aerodynamic downforce. Always try to find ways to add downforce to the end that is losing traction first instead of taking downforce away from the end that is sticking. In other words, don't punish the end of the car that's actually doing what you want it to do.

UNDERSTANDING AIRFLOW

No matter if you are studying air movement through an engine or over a race car, the behavior is the same. In a lot of respects, air is just like water. It likes to follow a curve, and when it flows past a sharp angle it will strip away from whatever surface it is following.

The first thing the air "sees" as the race car rolls through it is the nose. You want to keep the air attached to the car as long as you can, so the more you can do to make your whole car appear like a big radius so that the air will stay attached, the better. The reason is you want to guide the air onto the rear spoiler to give you plenty of rear downforce. What you don't want to do is force the air to attach itself to and detach itself from the race car at several points along the body. Whenever that happens, you are increasing the drag. The goal is to guide the air along the race car and hold on to it until you are done with it. Then when you are done with it—at the rear spoiler—get rid of it cleanly.

BODY LOCATION

A lot of racing divisions, including Nextel Cup and the Busch Series, have locked in the body location relative to the wheels. Still, how the body is mounted on a race car has a lot to do with its aero balance. Even though you may not be able to make big adjustments on body location, you may still have some leeway within the rules. If so, this is definitely an area you want to take advantage of.

Let's start with just a few ground rules about body location. We can move the body way ahead or way back, and what the wind tunnel will tell us is those changes don't really change the drag numbers. The big changes come at what we call the center of pressure. The center of pressure is usually right around the front of the roof. You can move the center of pressure by moving the body forward or backward. For most racers who run short tracks, what I've always preferred to do is move the body as far back as I can. The reason is that moving the rear spoiler back creates leverage because it increases the distance between the spoiler and the rear

BELOW: The nose on this car has been shifted to the driver's right but only slightly, so it can be difficult to see at first glance. Notice how you can see more of the decals on the left fender because it is angled out more than the right fender.

wheels, and that increases rear downforce. There are more ways to increase the front downforce, like adding tape or pulling out the fenders, at the track than there is the rear, so anything you can do to add rear downforce really helps. But moving the body back doesn't just add rear downforce because you are shortening the nose of the car—it also shortens the front fender in front of each wheel. By shortening the fenders, you also increase the angle as those pieces of metal extend out from the side of the bumper to the tire. And increasing the angle of the front fender actually adds front downforce.

BODY LENGTH

You may be able to push things only so far with your rules when it comes to body location. Another idea to consider is to make your body as long as you can. Stretching the body helps give the rear spoiler more leverage, like I just mentioned above, and it also makes the body smoother to the air. A longer decklid gives the air more time to come down from the roof and get hold of that rear spoiler. Again, most rule books have limits on where the body must be placed in relation to the wheels and how long it can be, but there is almost always a range within which you are allowed to fall. When you hang your body, make sure you fall on the long side of these ranges.

GREENHOUSE LOCATION, AND SHIFTING THE NOSE AND DECKLID

One area where you can have a big effect on the car without going crazy with major changes is the greenhouse location. The greenhouse is everything from the bottom of the windows and windshield up. Its size and location relative to the wheel openings and the rest of the car can play a big role in the car's downforce balance. Unfortunately, adjusting the greenhouse isn't easy. To do it means cutting almost the entire body off the race car and starting over, so you want to get it right the first time. A good, sound philosophy is to always center the greenhouse between the wheels. Even if you have pushed the body back two inches, keep the greenhouse centered. That gives you some predictability and your best chances for keeping the downforce balanced.

After you have the greenhouse located, you can shift a few other components to help maximize downforce. The first is the nose of the car. If you can move the nose to the driver's right one or two inches, that will help the front downforce. The main reason for this is it puts more angle into the left front fender. Because of physics, you aren't going to have any problem getting the right front down, but keeping the left front tire down against the track is one of the toughest jobs a crew chief has. Increasing that left front fender angle increases downforce on that corner and helps considerably. Making that left front fender curve outward slightly from front to back will also help you build in additional downforce.

The other thing you can do is shift the decklid to the right. I know we are shifting major body components and moving them to the right side of the car, but in the case of the nose and decklid, it's worth it. The most critical part of the front of the car is the left front fender; the most critical part of the rear is the right rear corner of the spoiler. The greatest problem we have with the spoiler is that the greenhouse shields it from the air as the car moves through it. By shifting the decklid to the right, you are exposing more of the right side of the spoiler to "clean" air, and it can do more work for you. Shifting both the nose and the decklid one inch to the right is a good, safe amount that should work well for every situation. Of course, this guideline applies only if you can do it and stay within your rules.

Beyond just the location of the nose, the shape of the front of the car also plays a tremendous role in creating downforce. It's the most important section of the car in terms of aerodynamics, because it is the first thing the air sees, and thus, it directs where the air goes across the rest of the car. If your rules will allow it, the first thing you want to do is round

the corners and lay the headlight area back. A nice, smooth, bullet-shaped nose is great for creating downforce and reducing drag.

The nose of the car is also the area where I see one of the most common mistakes—right on the valance. The simple rule is no matter what race car you have, make sure that the bottom of the race car, which is that front valance, is the farthest point forward on the nose. In other words, if you ran the car into a brick wall, the very first thing to touch would be the bottom edge of the valance. If the front of the valance is pulled back so that it is behind the bumper, you are creating lift, and that's the last thing you want. The father you can stick out that valance, the more front downforce you create.

BELLY PANS AND VALANCE RETURN FLANGES

The valance return flange is a lot like a belly pan, except that belly pans are illegal in most forms of stock car racing. A valance return flange is a lip that turns back at the valance so that it is parallel to the ground and runs underneath the nose of the car. In the Cup Series, NASCAR says we can run only a 90-degree, one-inch-thick flange underneath the car, but that's better than nothing and actually helps create downforce. The wider you can run it, the better it's going to work for you. Just always make sure the flange runs straight back. If it angles either up or down, it's going to hurt the car. But if it's straight back, it can be a big help.

If by chance your rules don't forbid running a belly pan, then I definitely recommend you try one out. A belly pan is simply a big sheet of aluminum that seals the bottom of the car from the front valance all the way back to the wheels—and farther if you can make it. A belly pan eliminates air from swirling up and around the engine compartment and will really plant the nose of the car. So a belly pan will be especially helpful anywhere you are having trouble getting your car to turn.

If you aren't allowed a belly pan, a good trick is to use your radiator duct as a small belly pan. By flattening out the bottom of the radiator box and getting it just as low as you dare get it, that area can

LEFT: Believe it or not, the shape of the transmission tunnel is important aerodynamically. A nice, smooth transition from the firewall to the transmission tunnel helps direct air in the engine compartment out the back of the car. Making the transmission tunnel as large as possible also helps.

RIGHT: Raising the rear bumper cover helps evacuate the air trapped underneath the car. It is the differential between the high-pressure air above the car and the low-pressure air below the car that creates downforce.

act like a small belly pan. You can't go all the way to the bottom of the valance (or you will tear up the sheet metal and lose your airflow to the radiator), but you can run it a lot lower than the bottom of the grille opening without any problems. Most places don't have any rules about this because, hey, everybody has got to run radiator ductwork to keep the engine from overheating, right?

TAPE IS YOUR FRIEND

When it comes to aerodynamics in racing, I normally tell people that there is no free lunch. That means everything comes with a cost. In terms of aerodynamics, the cost of adding downforce is almost always additional drag. The one exception to that rule is taping up the nose. Normally you tape the nose for qualifying, and it's a good idea because tape on the nose adds downforce and often actually reduces drag. That's because you are sealing the radiator box and brake ducts, which add a lot of

drag to the car's aerodynamic profile.

If you are allowed to make changes to the car between qualifying and the race, take advantage of this and tape up the front of the car as much as you can—as long as the car doesn't overheat within those two qualifying laps. Even if you can't make changes between practice and qualifying, it's still a good idea to have a roll of duct tape handy. If you normally race at one track but go to a different race track that's faster, that extra speed is going to help cool the radiator and brakes. Maybe you can tape up a little more of the front of the car without overheating anything. If it is a cool night, tape over one of the NACA ducts you use to cool your driver. Or you can even install a dummy NACA duct in the bottom front corner of your passenger-side window and tape it up. Anything you can do to block up the windows will help, too. Remember, though, that the window should always be large enough for the driver to get out of with his helmet on. If you make it tough for your driver to get out of the car quickly, you are putting him in danger in an emergency.

SEAL THE COCKPIT

Sealing the cockpit may not be an obvious aerodynamic issue, but it can help your car. The bonus is it's also a safety issue, for reasons I'll explain below. Any way you can, seal up that driver's cockpit. I used to tell my guys: "If I take a water hose and

You Can't Fight the Wind

I remember when it first really dawned on me just how important a good aero program is in racing. I was with Richard Childress Racing when we went to Las Vegas for the first time in 1998. We still had the old Monte Carlo, and Ford had just come out with the new Taurus. Even when we got our first glance at the thing, we knew we were in trouble. It just looked smoother, and you knew it was a better car aerodynamically than what we were racing. It turns out it did have some pretty awesome downforce numbers.

I was at the 3 car with Earnhardt that year, and we finished eighth. We were the only Chevrolet that finished on the lead lap, but we struggled just to do that. In fact, we were the only Chevrolet in the top 16. The thing about it was, throughout that race I was banging my head against a wall trying to figure out how to make Earnhardt faster so he could get up with those boys. But he'd radio me and say, "Larry, I don't know what to tell you to do. The car is driving good, but when they get to me they just turn down underneath me and go on."

That was not springs and shocks and sway bars—that was the power of good aerodynamics. We were just beaten, and there was nothing we could do about it.

stick it in the window, I want that driver's compartment to fill up with water. And I don't want to see water leaking out anywhere."

The reason that became such an issue with me was about 1988 or '89. We built a brand-new Buick Regal when I was with the 26 car and Ricky Rudd. We took the car to Detroit in raw sheet metal. It had the windows and rear spoiler and everything on it, but it was only about 80 percent complete. We just stuck a dummy engine and headers in it just to have something mocked up. We didn't usually do that, but we had just about missed our wind tunnel date because the car wasn't done.

When we put this dummy transmission in it, we didn't have a shift lever on it. Somebody stuck a

shifter boot on the transmission tunnel to fill the hole but didn't fasten it down. So we put the car in the wind tunnel, and I believe it was absolutely the worst car I've ever seen. The car was terrible; it had terrible downforce numbers, and the drag numbers were off the meter. I thought, "How in the world can we build a car this screwed up?"

After about four or five runs, the car wouldn't respond to anything. I think you could have taken that rear spoiler off and it wouldn't have made a difference. Finally, we realized that we just needed to stop and look at this race car a little bit. One of the other guys looked in the car and noticed that the shifter boot was over in the right side against the door. We didn't put much stock in it, but before we

BELOW: The design of the window opening is also important. This is Dave Pletcher's Pro Cup car, but it uses the same philosophies we do in Nextel Cup. Notice the front and top edges are nice and sharp to strip air away from the car so it won't enter the driver's compartment. The B-post, however, is curved because you want it to help pull air out of the cockpit. The bottom edge also has a nice, wide ledge.

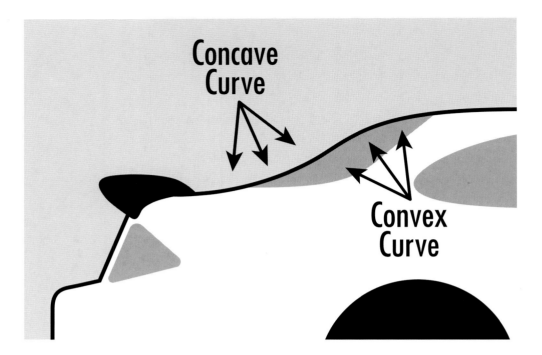

Concave Curve

Convex Curve

started again we actually attached the shifter boot over the transmission tunnel and put tape over the hole that normally would be filled by the shifter.

On the next run, it was like we had a totally different car in the tunnel! The difference sealing that shifter hole made was amazing. So from that day forward, I've been a real stickler about making sure everything is sealed up tight. That includes anything that separates the three compartments in a race car. Don't just stop at the cockpit; make sure the trunk is sealed up well, too. It isn't too hard. A lot of the holes can be sealed with silicone, and the benefit— even if you don't see any aero advantage—is that less fumes are going to get to the driver, and his cockpit is going to stay cooler as well. In the event that a race car catches fire, it almost always starts either in the engine compartment or the trunk, so a well-sealed driver's cockpit also helps protect the driver in case of a fire.

WINDSHIELD ANGLE

If your series uses a full-body template like they do in the Cup Series, there is only so much you can do with the windshield angle. But that doesn't mean you can't take advantage of what they give you. I know a lot of people will try to lay the windshield back to minimize drag, but we have found that it is worth the extra drag to stand the windshield up as much as we can. On a Cup car, the engine is fed air through the cowl opening just in front of the bottom edge of the windshield. By standing the windshield up just a little bit, we can cause a high-pressure area to form above the cowl opening and increase

the amount of air getting to the engine. If you feed air to your engine through the front grille instead of using a cowl, then this won't help you. But if you use a cowl, try standing the windshield up a degree or two, slide your cowl opening as close to the bottom of the windshield as you can get it, and see if that makes a difference in how your engine runs.

The windshield should also not be flat from side to side. Keep it flat in the center, but as you move laterally to the A-posts, the windshield should angle backward at an increasing radius. That helps flow the air around the car. You should also try to make the transition from the windshield to the A-post as smooth as possible. Air doesn't just flow up over the windshield—it gets pushed out to the sides, too—so if you have any ridges where the windshield meets the sheet metal A-post, you are going to create drag. Also, continue the radius you created with the windshield in the angle of the A-post.

REAR WINDOW

The job of the rear window is to direct air onto the spoiler. Remember, to do that you have to use gentle curves. First of all, you want to pull the top of the roof and the back glass out of the way as much as you can to give the air a clear shot at hitting the rear spoiler. You can do this by pulling the back of the roof down as much as your rules will allow. From there, the glass should make almost a saddle shape as it goes from the top to the bottom. There should be a convex curve at the top that transitions into a concave curve at the bottom so that the window pulls air off the roof and directs it down, then catches it and straightens it back out to give it a straight shot at the spoiler. See the illustration for a better explanation of how this works.

WINDOW OPENINGS

First off, make the window opening as small as possible. There are also things you can do to make the window appear smaller to the air. On the bottom, pull that doorsill up to the top of the door so that it is flush. On the top, we always ran the halo bar all the way out to the edge and then filled in the gap between the bar and the roof (see photo on page 104). Just make sure you don't do anything to make the actual opening so small that the driver can't get out with his helmet on. We sat on the pole for the Daytona 500 in 1995 with Dale Jarrett, thanks to aero tricks like this. But in the process, we closed off the window opening so much that Dale had to take off his helmet just to get out of the car. I cringe now when I think about it. Sitting on the pole wasn't worth what could have happened if Dale's car had caught fire.

Believe it or not, a window net helps smooth a car's shape. Keep that net as far to the outside of the window as you can get it and use the thick webbing instead of the little stuff. Finally, keep that window net tight so it's not flapping in the breeze, because that creates turbulence.

You don't want air entering the cockpit from the window opening, so use your rules of airflow to keep it out. You want a sharp edge on the top and bottom

of the window as well as the back side of the A-post. This allows the air to separate from the car at the window openings instead of following the curve into the cockpit. Yes, you want air to get to the driver, but use air ducts for that. It's more efficient.

You also want to use the window opening to pull air out of the cockpit. You can do this by creating a smooth radius at the back of the widow opening (the front of the B-post). If you are allowed to run a side window, and this includes your quarter windows, make sure you make them stiff with a brace behind them so they won't be buffeting in the wind. Just like the windshield, make sure the windows are flush to the sheet metal and present a smooth surface for the air to flow along. (NASCAR rules say that the passenger window must be inset three-

BELOW: This view shows how much the left front fender can be pulled out in relation to the wheel and door panel behind it. It is difficult to get that left front tire to work, so anything you can do to add downforce to that corner helps. Just make sure you don't do too much and get yourself in trouble with the tech inspectors.

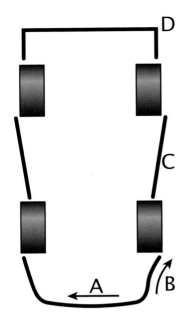

RIGHT: No matter what type of car you race, you can take advantage of a few aero tricks that you can count on helping you. First, sliding the nose of the car slightly to the right (A) creates more area for the left front fender. You can create additional downforce on the left front corner of the car by putting a concave curve into that fender (B). This is helpful because it is always a challenge to get the left front wheel to stick to the track, and additional downforce here helps. You also want to create a wedge shape in the sheet metal from the back of the front wheels to the front of the rear wheels (C). And finally, the transition from the side of the car to the rear bumper cover (D) should be a sharp edge to help the air separate cleanly from the side of the car.

BELOW: This is a Craftsman Truck Series truck built for short track racing. Notice how much room there is between the wheel and the sheet metal. This helps evacuate air from the engine compartment and also protects the tires from getting cut if the fenders get banged in.

quarters of an inch, but you don't want to make it any deeper than you have to.) And finally, under no circumstances do you want the windows to be concave or bow in. Actually, you want the windows to be slightly convex, so that they will be flat if the air pressure pushes them in.

The C-post is the area between the quarter and rear windows that attaches the roof to the back of the car. Its shape is important because you use it to direct air toward the spoiler. From the point that the C-post begins at the back of the rear quarter window until it ends at the side of the rear window, you want it to be a nice, smooth angle. Also, try to angle the C-post so that it makes the back of the greenhouse as narrow as possible. That will allow more air to work its way around the greenhouse in time to make contact with the spoiler.

REAR BUMPER

When it comes to the rear of the car, wider is always better. A wider spoiler is an obvious advantage, but even if your spoiler width is limited, just having a wider decklid will help rear downforce. Moving over to the sides, you've probably noticed how Nextel Cup cars have a sharp corner where the sides of the car transition to the rear bumper cover. That sharp angle helps the air that's traveling down the side of the car to separate from the body at that point instead of pulling around the back of the car and causing drag. Those edges also help create a low-pressure zone, and that differential

between low pressure below and behind the spoiler along with high-pressure air stacked up in front of the spoiler creates downforce. That's also why you want to make the spoiler just as big as the rules allow. If you think you have too much rear spoiler at a track, instead of cutting it down, lay it back a few degrees. That always seems to help more than cutting off some of the spoiler.

When it comes to the bumper cover, I wouldn't run one at all if possible. That's usually not allowed, so pull the bottom of the bumper up just as high as you can. That allows the air that is trapped underneath the car to escape out the back more easily. You want the front valance to be just as low as you can get it to push air up and over the car, then keep the rear bumper high to help get rid of any air that does get under there. I don't know how many times I've seen a car get in a slight wreck and have damage at the rear end. The driver would come in and the crew would cut off the rear bumper cover. Next thing you know, that car is faster than before the accident.

WHEEL OPENINGS

For short track cars, one thing we found to do was always make the wheel openings just as big as we could. Especially on the front of the car, big wheel openings help evacuate air from underneath the hood, which creates front downforce. They help keep the tires cooler, too, and they also limit the chances of a bent fender rubbing on a tire and cutting it down.

The shape of the wheel opening is also important. From the bottom front of the opening all the way around until about 10 o'clock, I want the edge of that metal just as sharp as I can get it. That way the air will separate from the fender and go on around the car. On the back side of the opening, I want a small radius, maybe with the sheet metal bent in a little bit. That's the same concept we are using at the rear of the window opening. The radius will help guide air out of the wheel opening.

If you can get by with it, bending a Gurney lip at the front of the opening will help downforce. A Gurney lip is just rolling the metal out to about a 45-degree angle at the front edge of the wheel opening. You see big Gurney lips on the road-race cars all the time. You don't need anything that big, but just a little bit helps.

DOORS AND BODY SIDES

Shape the sides of the car so that they create a wedge shape, with the car getting slightly wider at the back of the car. Pull the sheet metal in just as far as you can behind the front tires and out as far as you can in front of the rear tires. In between, keep the metal nice and straight. That creates balanced downforce at both the front and rear tires,

and doesn't cost you too much drag. What you definitely do not want is "crowned sides," where the middle of the door bubbles out. Crowned sides create turbulence along the side of the car.

Looking down the car, you also want to keep the sides as flat as possible going down toward the rocker panels. Doors that curve in at the bottom help draw air underneath the car, which is bad. Keep the bottom of the doors out as far as you can get them, and join the rocker panels to that sheet metal at a nice, sharp angle.

When it comes to rocker skirts, we've found that they only really help on the right side. As you go through a turn, the car is in yaw, or sideways, in relation to the air. A rocker skirt on the right keeps air from sneaking underneath the car along the side, while the absence of a rocker skirt on the left side allows air to escape from underneath the car more easily. You still want to run nice, wide rocker panels on both sides of the car, but run a rocker skirt only on the right side.

BELOW: Even if you are racing a series that requires prefab bodies, you can still mix and match pieces that give you the greatest aerodynamic advantage. This Late Model stock uses a rear bumper cover with nice sharp edges on the side to keep air from collecting behind the car.

ABOVE: Transmissions built for racing allow multiple ratio choices for each gear. This way, you can get the perfect splits—especially from third to fourth—to get back up to speed quickly on restarts.

chapter 13

Gears and Gear Selection

Crew chiefs rightfully spend most of their time concentrating on their race car's handling, but don't forget that there is a lot to be gained—and lost—in the transmission and rear end. You may have the hottest engine on the track, but if you aren't transmitting the engine's power to the rear wheels efficiently, it can be just like you are down on power.

Gears are also critical because your selection of ratios can be the difference between a car that can pass the competition anywhere on the track and one that can't seem to get out of its own way. A car has to be geared correctly in the transmission so that it can get up to speed quickly without bogging down. If you have been around racing any amount of time, you've probably come across somebody who wasn't too fast around the track but always seemed to have your number on the restarts. That's probably because his transmission ratios were just about perfect for that track. The gear ratio you choose for the rear end is also vital because it determines if your engine is able to run at its peak power-making rpm range. Too little rpm, and the engine bogs and won't accelerate; too much, and it's wheezing for air all the way around the track—or worse, it's breaking parts.

TRANSMISSION OPTIONS

The laws of physics say that turning sets of gears requires power, so some horsepower losses in your drivetrain are unavoidable. However, there are things you can do to minimize the losses.

Your first concern with your transmission is gear choices. Actually, what's important is the size of the gaps between the gears, or the *splits*. The secret is to keep the splits as close as possible. In other words, every time your driver shifts gears, you want the rpm change to be as little as possible. If the split is too great, it will cause the engine to drop too much rpm, and it will lug and not be able to accelerate the car. So keep the splits as close as possible so the engine stays in the desired rpm range and keeps plenty of torque at the rear wheels. The simplest way to test your splits is just to practice a few restarts in a test session. Notice if there is a shift that makes the engine drop more rpms than the rest. Maybe it is first to second or third to fourth. If it makes the engine bog down, try tightening up the ratio split between those two gears.

Of course, if you are running only 35- or 50-lap features, it is easy to think that worrying about your gear splits is a waste of time. The races aren't long enough to require pit stops, so why bother, right? Don't forget about restarts after a caution, which can be a huge opportunity to pass two or more cars if you play your cards right. It can be awfully hard to pass on short tracks, and if your driver can out accelerate the guy in front to the first turn on a restart, then that's one less guy he will have to pass later on.

LUBRICANTS AND GEAR COOLING

When it comes to gears, the enemy is heat. Friction produces heat, and heat leads to durability issues.

BELOW: Passing on short tracks is all about acceleration on the exit of the corner. No matter how strong your engine is, you have to have the correct gearing to take advantage of it.

Heat also hurts power because it reduces the oil's ability to lubricate the gears. Modern synthetic oils are much better at withstanding high temperatures than mineral oils, but they do still have their heat limits. A second advantage to synthetics is they

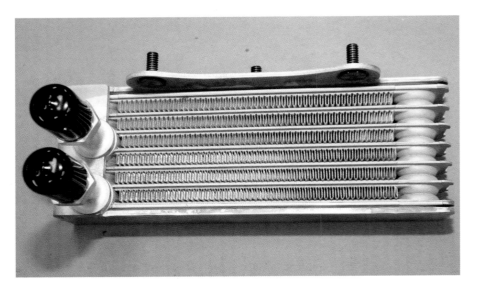

ABOVE: Oil coolers for the rear end or transmission are simply small radiators built to handle thicker fluids like oils instead of water. In order to be effective, they must be mounted in a location with plenty of airflow.

work better at lower temperatures. When using a mineral-based oil, you know it is going to be too thick and cost you horsepower until it warms up. You don't have that concern with a synthetic oil, which can be a big advantage for qualifying when your car isn't up to operating temps.

Besides running quality gears in good-quality oil, the fluid level also plays a role in controlling temperatures. Just like in the engine—where, if the crankshaft is splashing in the oil, it's creating heat and sucking up power—too much fluid in either the transmission or the rear end isn't a good thing. So the lower you can run the lubricant level without starving the gears for oil, the better—that's less heat and less friction. And you don't need to assume that the location of the fill hole is also the ideal fluid height. For years we simply filled the transmission with gear oil until it began running out the fill hole and then capped it. But later we found out that the fill hole on the transmissions we were running was located in a random spot. The manufacturer had

picked a nice flat spot on the housing to drill a hole. We were burning up transmissions because we were running way too much gear oil.

Of course, there's also a fine line between too little and too much. You might think, "If too much will burn up a set of gears, then I'll just drop the level in my transmission and rear end way down." But if you starve the gears of oil, it will do the same thing—only quicker. If you aren't running some type of oil cooler, then you probably aren't running a pump and, depending on the gear, are splashing in the oil to provide lubrication. That means there is a certain level you cannot go under or else you won't get that splash lubrication.

If you are running a cooler, you can get by with lower levels in either the transmission or rear end because you can use the pump to direct oil onto the gears. Gear oil is pulled out of the transmission or rear end at the lowest point in the case and is generally returned through a line that connects to the top of the housing. Make sure that return line directs the lubricant onto the gear and not the side of the case. This way, you can lower the fluid level to the point that the gears aren't splashing in oil that's pooled in the bottom of the case. You can keep plenty of volume in the system because you still have lubricant flowing through the pump, the assorted lines, and the cooler.

There was a misconception for many years that synthetic lubricants didn't make good gear oils. I think that used to be true, but it isn't any more. Today, you can be comfortable qualifying and racing on good synthetic gear oil. Just make sure it is engineered for racing.

GEAR CHOICES

There are no easy guidelines to determine what gear you should be running at every racetrack. You have to match your gear to a lot of conditions: the size of the track, your engine's capabilities, traction, etc. Ideally, you want to use the gear that keeps the engine in the sweet spot of its rpm range. Your engine builder can tell you what that is. Also, you have to determine the best location on the track for passing and gear the car so that it is strongest there.

Normally, at short tracks you beat people from the center of the corner off. Martinsville is a good example of that. It may look like drivers are passing getting into the corner, but the pass actually started at the exit of the previous turn. The driver was able to take the position away from the car in front of him and take the preferred line into the entrance of the next turn.

Part of that passing ability is due to the chassis; if your car turns well and the driver has confidence that the tires are going to hook up when he puts his foot in the throttle, you are going to be fast and should be able to beat people off the corner. If you have the chassis so that the car is driving and turning well, you want to gear the rear end so that the car will lunge up off the corner. If you are having trouble with the setup and the driver is spinning the tires every time he gets into the throttle, then you will have to put a higher gear into it (a lower numerical gear) to take away some of the torque at the rear wheels. That will help reduce wheel spin, but it comes at the expense of acceleration off of the corner.

So at short tracks, you want to optimize performance as the car accelerates out of the turn. At bigger tracks, it's different. Passing is more

ABOVE: An external, belt-driven rear-end pump is simple and dependable. It doesn't require much horsepower to run because the pressure requirements are very low.

Gear Changes Can Affect Handling

This may sound odd at first, but remember that when making gear changes at the last minute, you may also be affecting the car's handling characteristics. It's obvious at a short track where going too low with the gear can cause wheel spin, but I remember always having to be careful at bigger tracks like Michigan, too, where a high gear is always pretty good, but if you went too high it could cause problems for the driver. When he put his foot in it, if the rpms were too low, the engine would bog down. Not only will that hurt acceleration, but it can also make the car push on the exit of the corner. That's why I always recommend getting in at least one quick run with your final gear choice before practice ends. That way, you know if your gear change affected anything in a way you weren't expecting.

ABOVE: Electric oil
pumps are available, but
they still aren't as popular as mechanical pumps.
The biggest advantage
these offer is that they
can be mounted remotely
and don't rob power
unless you have to switch
to a stronger alternator.

OPPOSITE: Whether
you build your own rear
ends or have someone
else do it, make sure to
have the ring and pinion
mesh checked all the way
around.

common down the straights, so you want to gear
the car so it isn't nosing over halfway down the
straightaway. Acceleration out of the turns isn't as
big a deal at bigger tracks because you aren't braking as much before turn entry and the rpms don't
fall as low in the corners.

As a general rule, you want to race with a slightly
lower gear than you qualify with. During qualifying you are on fresher tires, the track normally
isn't oiled up, and there's no traffic to deal with.
Everything is optimized. In a race the pace slows
down, which drops the rpm levels. That means you
will need a lower gear to get the rpms back in the
ideal range. A lower gear also helps if you are trying to maneuver in traffic. Of course, a lot of racing
series won't allow gear changes between qualifying
and the race—NASCAR even limits gear choices in
the Nextel Cup Series now—but this is also a good
thing to keep in mind if you spend your entire practice time trying to pick up speed in qualifying trim.
You may have to give up a little bit in order to be
competitive once the race starts.

REAR-END COOLERS
Unless you are doing a lot of shifting, it is unlikely
you need a transmission cooler. But if you are running races of any length, you will need to run a
rear-end cooler. Keeping the rear-end lubricant cool
isn't just important for the gears—it's also needed to

keep locker springs from breaking.

To run your oil through a cooler (a small, specially
made radiator specifically for thicker fluids), you
obviously have to pump it. I'm a big believer in the
pump driven off the input shaft on the rear end.
You can either run a belt off the shaft to an external
pump or use an internal pump that connects right
to the end of the pinion shaft and drives that way.
(It works a lot like the way the oil-pump driveshaft
fits into the end of the distributor shaft.) Either way,
everything is right there together, so when you need
to change a gear, you just pull everything off.

If you are running a belt-driven oil pump, it's
always a good idea to fabricate some type of shield
to keep a ball of rubber or anything else from flying
up and knocking that belt off the pulley. It doesn't
have to be anything that weighs a lot; it can even
be a piece of screen. Whatever it is, you just need
something to protect that belt.

Some people still like to run the electric pumps
because they can be mounted remotely and don't
rob any horsepower from the driveshaft. Of course,
you have to figure that if the electric pump is pulling
amps, requiring you to switch to an alternator that
produces more power, that's going to cost you more
horsepower, too. Electric pumps are also cheaper, but
it has always been my belief that they can be more
prone to failure. The single-stage mechanical pump
is just a simpler piece. It's a lot like an external oil

pump on your engine, so it's almost bulletproof.

No matter what type of pump you are running, you want to make sure you are pulling the oil from the lowest part of the case. A cheap insurance policy is to run the oil through a small inline filter before it gets to the pump. Then run it through the pump and push it to the cooler. You want to push the oil through the cooler rather than suck it because that reduces the possibility of getting air in the lines. After the oil goes through the cooler, pump it back into the housing from the top so that it can run down onto the ring gear.

MAINTENANCE

If you are racing Nextel Cup, then you have a guy tearing down your gears and transmissions after

LEFT: An internal oil pump is the most expensive option, but it is also the simplest and best protected. It is driven by a shaft that plugs right into the end of the pinion shaft.

OPPOSITE: If you have wrecked the car bad enough that you suspect the engine has moved, don't forget to check the transmission tail housing as well as the input and output shafts for damage.

every race and rebuilding them to make sure you won't have a problem. But that kind of expenditure isn't possible in most other series. If you are a budget-conscious racer competing in shorter events, say, 20 times a year, then you don't require the same program. Just like motor oils, however, gear oils tend to break down over time with use. I would recommend simply changing the gear oil in the transmission every four or five races and changing the lube in the rear end after every second race. Remember, you won't cause any problems changing your lubricants too often, but you can mess things up by waiting too long. That also gives you an opportunity to pull off the covers and check your gears for excessive wear or damage. Look for pits or spiderweb cracks.

If you are running a nine-inch rear, take the gear out and look at the pattern on the ring gear where the pinion is hitting. You want to make sure it isn't hitting too deep or too shallow, and you want to make sure it is hitting plenty of each tooth on the ring gear. Also make sure to look at the whole gear and not just one section, or you won't get the whole story. Spin the gear and make sure that it isn't too tight.

While you are at it, keep a close watch on your axles. Look at the splines on the axles, especially on the ends at the drive plate. Sometimes all it takes to twist the splines is to spin the wheels on a restart or on pit road; then your axles are weakened, and Murphy's Law says they are going to break at the worst possible time. Keep your axles lubricated with a good high-temp grease.

Finally, check your old lubricant for clues to what's going on inside both your transmission and rear end. Burnt gear oil has a distinct smell, and once you smell it the first time, you will never forget it. If the oil smells burnt, you know you are overheating your gears. Also, get a little of the lubricant on your fingers and feel it. If it feels gritty, then you probably have metal shavings off the gears in there, which is a definite sign you have a problem. When you are putting everything back together, make sure to take a good look at all your gaskets if you are going to reuse them. If it starts leaking at the track,

it's going to cause you a lot of grief. A lubricant leak is likely to cause your car to smoke, and your driver will probably be seeing the black flag soon after that.

WRECK CHECK

Anytime you take a hard lick on the nose and it looks like the motor may have moved, you want to make sure to have your transmission checked out to see if the input shaft is bent. If the car hit hard enough that there is no more room between the transmission and the driveshaft yoke—in other words, the driveshaft has no play in it—then you may need to look at the tail housing. The output shaft or the seals may have been damaged.

SHIFTER MAINTENANCE

One of the biggest failures you see, especially with short track cars in which the transmission hasn't been taken out in a long time, is a shifter failure. That's because the shifter is all about grease and lubrication. When you run short tracks week in and

week out, you get a lot of dirt and grit blowing up underneath the car, and the next thing you know your shifter is bound up. So what I recommend, and we used to do this every race morning, is to take some cleaner and shoot it up in that shifter to clean out all the dirt and grit. Then use white lithium grease and lubricate the shifter really well. Spray graphite also works well, you just don't want to use an oil or grease that's going to be a magnet for grit.

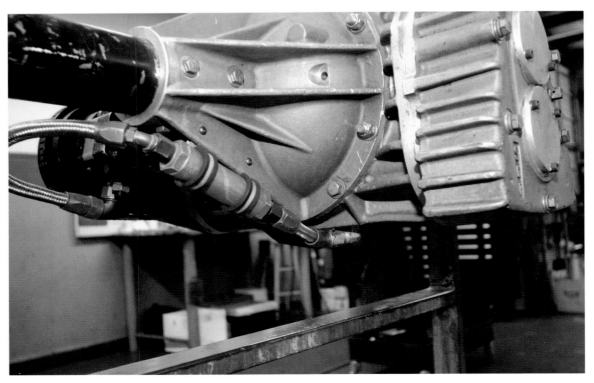

LEFT: **LEFT:** A good way to reduce friction and improve the lifespan of your gears is to have them polished. This removes imperfections and makes the surface of the teeth smoother.

Educated Guesses for Gearing at New Tracks

NASCAR held an exhibition race at a racetrack in Motegi, Japan, in 1998. No one had been over there to test, and there were no plans for anyone from the Nextel Cup Series to test that track before we went there to race. The problem was we had to pack our race cars, along with all the extra parts we would need, into containers and ship them two months before the race. Obviously, we couldn't haul every rear gear we owned over there, so we really had our work cut out for us to figure out what we needed to race a track we had never seen before.

Not too many race teams travel regularly to Japan, but this is a problem most of us have when going to a new track. If you hope to be competitive, you have to be willing to do a little homework.

Even though nobody had raced stock cars at Motegi, I knew the Champ cars in CART had already been over there. I was friends with Rick Rinaman, who at the time was Little Al Unser's crew chief, because we had done some promotional posters together for Snap-On. So I called Rick and asked about what gears they ran.

I know that comparing Cup cars to Champ cars is a lot like comparing apples to green beans, but there are ways to work around that. I asked Rick what racetrack he had been to in the States that compared to Motegi. He said there was no doubt it was most like Homestead (this was before Homestead had been reconfigured). We hadn't raced at Homestead yet, but we had tested there. Even though I didn't care a bit what ratio the Champ cars raced at Homestead, I knew what gear worked best for our cars there. That gave me a good idea what would work for us at Motegi. Thankfully, that phone call paid off, because Mike Skinner got the win there.

ABOVE: The first item of business when testing is finding a level area where you can work. This is especially important if you are trying to scale a car.

Testing

Nextel Cup racing teams all approach racing a little differently. Different crew chiefs may have completely different ideas on how certain things should be done. But if there is one thing that is common to the most successful teams, it's that they all believe a good testing program is critical to winning.

Testing, however, is a pretty broad term. We can be talking about renting a track for a day and spending it testing different shock packages or about the one hour of track time you may get at your local facility before qualifying. Either way, making the most of your time during a test session is critical. After all, if you aren't learning anything during a test, you aren't doing anything more than burning laps and wasting money.

PREPARATION

Just like a race, a proper test requires plenty of preparation back at the shop. You want to have your car completely ready so that when you get to the facility you can spend the most time possible with the car on the track. Prepare your car just as you would for a race. That's important for two reasons: First; a fully prepped car minimizes time spent wrenching in the pits, and second; for the test to be valid, you have to mimic conditions that you can predict will affect you during the race—this especially includes your race car.

Of course, the whole point of testing is to make changes to the car to see what works best for you and your driver. Making changes to the chassis is expected, but what you don't want to do is start making changes without a plan. As the crew chief, it is your responsibility to provide your team with the game plan every time it is at the track.

The setup you choose to put under the car for your first laps on the track depends on the scenario.

If you are testing at a track you have experience with, you can go ahead and start with the setup that has worked best for you in the past. This will give you a baseline from which you can judge your progress for the rest of the day. If you are testing a track you have never been to before, there is going to be more guesswork involved. Hopefully, you can contact someone who can give you a good idea of what the track is like and maybe even suggest a setup. If not, start with something basic that your driver is familiar with. Even if he isn't used to the track, he should be able to know how the car is going to behave.

Once you have done that, you can go ahead and start planning your test from there. There are different types of tests, and what you want to do next depends a lot on what you are trying to achieve. One common situation is trying to get a feel for how a certain setup will affect the race car. For example, you may be testing a new family of shocks, and you want to know how they are going to react with your preferred spring packages. In this situation, you aren't really concerned with dialing in the perfect setup for that particular track; you are more interested in gathering information that will help you

BELOW: Whether you have rented the track for a day or are just on the track for an hour's practice before qualifying starts, starting with a good plan is a must if you hope to make the most of your testing opportunities.

make good decisions at every track you go to. This is sometimes referred to as an "ABC" test because you are testing package A, then switching to B and then C, one right after another, to get a feel for how they compare. You are doing all the test runs in a batch as quickly as you can because you want to eliminate as many variables as possible (air temperature, track temperature, humidity, etc.). In this case, you can basically plan out every step of the test.

The second type of test is when you are trying to perfect your setup for that particular track. These tests are tougher because you cannot plan out everything specifically. In these situations, I always wanted to have some type of "what if" plan. What if the car is pushing? What if it is loose? Normally, I would spend at least a couple of hours coming up with my "what if" list. (You will see an example of this on page 174.) You may not have much spare time to sit down and come up with a list like this, and I didn't either. A lot of times I would make up my game plan in the car on the way to and from the race shop. You can do the same thing on your way to work. Of course, I definitely don't recommend you try to write your list and drive a car at the same time. The solution I found was to keep a microcassette recorder in the car all the time. That tape recorder can be a great tool, because that time you have alone in the car is perfect for thinking problems through, and the recorder will help you

remember what you came up with.

Even though I normally came up with a pretty extensive "what if" list with likely fixes for every potential handling problem I could imagine for that track, I never felt the need to stick with that plan no matter what. There is no way to predict everything perfectly, and once you get to the track, you are better able to observe what handling problems your driver is experiencing. Still, having a plan of some sort ready when you arrive at the track can save you a great deal of time and frustration.

TESTING ROUTINE

No matter what you are testing, there are some things you and your crew can do to work as efficiently as possible and avoid mistakes. By the nature of testing, you are going to be making a lot of changes to the car. Time spent working on the car doesn't teach you anything; it's laps on the track that are valuable, so you want to minimize time in the pits.

First, from your plan you should already have an idea what shock and spring packages you want to try. Set them all up at the shop beforehand, including scaling out the car. Count up the rounds on the jack bolts and write down that information for every package. Now when someone installs that shock and spring package, he can just count the rounds and know everything is right.

Of course, during the course of the test you may also want to make changes you hadn't anticipated and need to recheck frame heights. It's also a good idea to check frame heights as a backup to make sure you aren't getting off track. An easy way to do that is to put a piece of tape on all four fenders and, while you are at the shop on level ground, mark a line on the tape at a consistent height for all four corners. Find the most level spot you can at the track and use that for your pit. Measure those four marks again and log the heights. They may change because the ground isn't perfectly flat, but you know the car is set up correctly. Now every time you make a change, you can easily refer back to those marks above each of the four fenders to determine if the frame height has moved.

Whether you are simulating long green-flag runs or just a couple laps to simulate qualifying, some things your crew should check every time the car comes in are the air pressures, the air-pressure buildup in all four tires (the air pressure when the car left the pit versus the pressure when it came back), and shock travel. You have to be careful on the shock travel because, whether it's a zip tie or a rubber grommet, one bad bump on the racetrack can fool you. Shock travel may be minimal except when your driver hit that hole that moved the travel indicator four inches, so don't forget that the travel indicator is just for max travel. Still, travel indicators are good to see if your chassis change has affected shock travel.

TIRE TEMPS VS. WEAR

Just like the shock travel indicator, reading your tire temps as the car comes off the track can give you lots of good information, but it can also mislead you. Generally, the hotter a tire is, the more it is working. You want to try to balance the tire temps all the way around the car so that all four wheels are sharing the load. But reading temps can be tricky. First, you have to get the temps off the tires as soon as the car gets to the pit, but even that may not be good enough. If the driver takes a slow lap around the track before coming down pit road, that can throw you off. Or if he hit pit road too fast and slid the rear end, the rear tires may be too hot.

#_____ — Engine_____ Laps

Day_____   <CAR>   _____Miles

DATE	EVENT	CHASSIS #	LAP DIST.	TEMP
TRACK	DRIVER	ENGINE #	TOTAL MILES	WEATHER

RS
___

LS

AIR PRESSURE
(GOODYEAR)

I -   I -
O -   O -
I -   I -
O -   O -

<REC>
_ _ _ _ _ _ _
"TIRES"

| FRONT   " SWAY BAR |
| GEAR   : |
| REAR SPOILER   ° |
| SHOP WEDGE |
| TOE-OUT |
| L   R |

CAM
CAS

SPRINGS

SHOCKS

FRAME

MISC.

PANARD BAR
L   R

LAP	TIME	CHANGES	COMMENTS
1			
2			
3			
4			
5			
6			
7			
8			
9			
10			
11			
12			
13			
14			
15			
16			
17			
18			
19			
20			
21			
22			
23			
24			
25			
26			
27			
28			
29			
30			
31			
32			
33			
34			

ABOVE: During a test, try to collect every piece of information you think might be helpful later on. Recording brake temps is relatively easy with an infrared temp gun.

going to reflect what the car is really going to do in qualifying.

As a rule, I always wanted to keep five fans going in my work area: one on the driver and four blowing on the tires. If you are going to accurately simulate qualifying laps, you want your tires to be the same temperature every time the car leaves the pits.

Although reading tire temperatures isn't always reliable, I do believe that the tires are capable of giving you lots of valuable information about how the car is working. The way to understand what they are telling you is by reading the tire wear. Cup tires have a row of five holes across the width of the tire. By monitoring the depth of these holes, we can determine how much of the rubber is worn off of the tire and in which area.

The first thing to do is to get a wear check on the holes when the tire is brand-new. You might think that the tread-depth holes on a new tire would be consistent, but they aren't—and we are reading down to $1/32$ inch, so precision is vital. So while the tire is still new, mark and number your sets, record the depth of the holes, and keep that information handy.

Once you've run a good number of laps on a set of tires and taken them off, you can recheck the tread-depth holes. For the sake of our example, let's say you've run 50 laps, and you pull the tires and do a wear check. The main thing you are looking for is if the car is balanced. If it is, the holes will have consistent wear patterns on each side. You can compare the wear patterns against your database. Wear doesn't change, so you don't have to check the tires right away, and it doesn't matter how the driver came off the track.

Look at the right front versus the right rear. If the right front is wearing more, then the car is pushing; if the right rear is wearing more, the car is loose. Then look across the front tires, which will tell you if your camber setting is off. Tread depth is measured in increments of $1/32$ inch. In a perfect world, I always like to see the right front wear one-half to three-quarters of $1/32$ inch more on the inside than the outside due to negative camber.

Still, you always have to be aware of the temperature of your tires and what they are doing to the car's handling characteristics. Not paying attention to that can make a crew chief throw down his stopwatch in frustration. After qualifying, they will say, "Dad gum, we were four-tenths [of a second] faster in practice!" But what they don't consider is that the fast lap in practice came on the fourth lap on a run. During qualifying they may have gotten only two laps on the track, and you don't get the time to get the same amount of heat in the tires. The other thing is teams will make a three-lap qualifying run, come in to make a wedge adjustment, and go right back out. They didn't allow enough time for the tires to cool back down, so the time with warm tires isn't

On the left front, I like to see it wearing just a little more—maybe a half of $^1/_{32}$ to $^1/_{32}$ inch—on the outside versus the inside because you run positive camber there.

Wear can also give you some insight into your tire pressures. If you are wearing more in the center of the tread than the outside edges, that's an indication you may have too much air pressure. The opposite tells you that there is probably too little.

CLOCKING SEGMENTS

A stopwatch can be a crew chief's best friend; after all, it is the best scientific tool available to tell you if the changes have made the car faster or not. But if you are only clocking lap times, you aren't evaluating all the information available. Robert Yates taught me years ago how to clock segments on a racetrack, and I think it is one of the most valuable pieces of information I know.

When you clock segments, you are essentially breaking down the racetrack into smaller sections and timing the car through those sections. This way, you can determine on which areas of the track your driver is strongest and on which areas he and the car need help.

You have to be careful when clocking segments and not try to do too much. I've seen people at a short track trying to clock turns one and two, the backstretch, turns three and four, and the front stretch. That's four segments per lap, and I don't

know anybody who can get all that right consistently. Instead, get two stopwatches and pick two areas of the track to clock. Remember, we aren't measuring seconds; we're measuring tenths and sometimes half-tenths of a second.

What I try to do is focus on one end of the track. Pick good, distinct points and hit the watch when your car crosses those points. It can be lettering on the wall, a telephone pole, or even a tree in the distance. It can be anything, as long as it is distinct and isn't going to move.

Once I have my points, I'll start clocking my driver to get a feel for how he's doing. If he is complaining that he's loose in the turns, this allows me to clock just the turn and see if the changes being made are improving his times. An experienced driver can normally tell you if a car is faster, but sometimes he can confuse a comfortable car with speed, and you need the corner times to know for sure.

Once I have a good feel for where we're at, I'll start clocking the competition and give my guys feedback on the best cars out there. That's our mark so we know what we are up against. Then I'll break it down even further. Instead of clocking from the entrance of

LEFT: When making chassis changes throughout the day, it can get easy to lose track of some of your critical measurements. One easy way to keep track of frame heights is with a piece of tape marked at a specific height. When the car is on level ground, a quick check with a carpenter's square will tell you exactly where you are.

Reading "Hand" Language

If you pay attention as a crew chief, your driver can tell you a lot about the car even if he isn't a good communicator. I worked with Joe Ruttman in '86, and he was terrible about telling me what the car was doing. The way he looked at it was he was the driver, and whatever you gave him, he would drive. That's good, but it doesn't help you much when you are trying to give him the best car possible.

When we went places to test, I'd make Joe put on a pair of white gloves so I could see his hands. Your driver might not be able to tell you much, but his hands aren't going to lie. If he has both hands on the steering wheel and they are turned so far you can hardly see them above the door, then you know the car is pushing or not turning well. Likewise, if you see his hands turning the wheel back to the right, you know the driver has a loose car and is trying to keep it from spinning out. If the car is driving well, the driver's hands should make nice, smooth motions on the wheel and be consistent from lap to lap. If his hands are sawing back and forth, then he's fighting the car. Any time a driver and the car are fighting each other, you can count on both of 'em being slow.

turn one all the way through the exit of turn two, I'll clock just the entrance and just the exit.

If a faster car is beating you on the exit of the turn, it's normally a sign that the other driver is able to get on the gas sooner and stay in it. If it's the entrance, normally the driver is staying in the throttle a little longer than your guy because his car is turning well or simply isn't as edgy on turn entrance as your car. This information just helps you and your driver identify your strong and weak points.

Unless I'm at a really big track, I rarely worry about clocking the straights. On short tracks, it's the turns that are important. If you do clock the straightaways and you are getting beat, there is only a slim chance—and I do mean slim—that you are actually getting beat on straightaway speed. I'm not saying that people won't be down on power or you will never miss the mark with the gearing, but more often than not, the problem is that your driver isn't carrying enough speed out of the turn.

Pocono is a perfect example of this. I don't know how many times I've clocked the front stretch there, turned to my motor man, and said, "Look, they are beating us by four-tenths down the straightaway."

But then I'll go and clock turn three and find out the same guy is beating us by three-tenths there. That means he's getting into the throttle sooner and carrying that extra speed all the way down the straightaway. If we can get our car to turn better, then the driver can carry more speed through the turn, and we can improve our front stretch times, too.

So unless it's a big, big racetrack, don't get caught up in straightaways. Again, you beat people at short tracks through the corners. If you can get the car to handle, you will be amazed at how well it looks going down the straights because the driver can get into the throttle sooner.

OBSERVATIONAL TOOLS

When your car is on the track, there is a lot you can learn just by observing it. Use your ears to tell you when the driver is getting off the throttle and when he's picking it back up. Use your eyes to tell you what the suspension is doing.

Of course, a lot is going on out there, so it can be difficult to tell anything at all unless you know what you are looking for. One of the big challenges anywhere you race is keeping that left front wheel

BELOW: Watch the gap between the tire and the fender to tell you what your car is doing through the turns. If you can see that left front open up significantly, you know the car is experiencing a lot of body roll. If the left rear closes up on turn exit, the rear end is squatting under throttle to give the rear tires plenty of bite.

down. If that wheel is down on the track, then you know it is working pretty well. Watch the wheel opening above the tire. You know what kind of gap there is when the car is sitting still, so use that as a frame of reference. If the gap really opens up as the car rolls through the turn, it is either rolling over on the right side or rolling back on the right rear. That big gap tells you the left front wheel probably isn't getting much work done.

Also watch the left rear wheel opening and relate what you see with what you hear. When your driver gets into the throttle on turn exit, does the rear end really squat down? That means the rear tire is getting a good bite into the racetrack.

DON'T FORGET TO CHANGE YOUR TIRES

If your car is just pushing and pushing when you are practicing, and all of a sudden you start making drastic changes and nothing happens, there is a good chance that through those runs when you were pushing so badly, you used up that right front tire. Chances are, no matter what you do, you aren't going to get that push out. Your only option is to put on a new set of tires or at least new right sides. Sometimes you have to bite the bullet and put on a new set of tires in order to realistically evaluate what a chassis change is doing.

The same deal holds if you have gone out for four or five runs and been loose the whole time. If you have just been sideways loose, there's a chance

you've burnt the right rear off of it. Any time your car has been really loose or tight and you don't get it taken care of in four or five runs, those tires might be shot. If you don't change them, you can actually overcorrect the car and not know it until you put on a fresh set of tires and start the race. Then you are in a world of hurt.

DIALING IN THE TAPE

You want to be able to tape up the front of the car as much as you can. As I mentioned in chapter 12, tape on the front end of the car adds front downforce and reduces drag, so you want as much as you can get without overheating the engine.

The problem is that the correct amount of tape may change from one weekend to the next, depending on the weather. So every time you finish a run, before your driver leaves the track, make sure he checks the water and oil-temp gauges and gives you that information. Add or remove tape until you get your temps at the levels your engine builder recommends.

RECORD KEEPING

There is just no substitute for good note taking—whether it is at the shop or at the track. But that's especially true at the racetrack. There is no right or wrong way to keep notes, just as long as you do it.

The method I recommend is to document your beginning setup, as described in chapter 10. Other information to record is time of day, track temperature, air temperature, and any other variable you think might affect performance. Keep up with every lap, even if it's just going out and warming up, because if it is a long race you will need to calculate your fuel mileage. You also need to document all your laps, because motor guys and gear guys need to know how many laps are on their equipment.

Document every lap time. When each run is over, document the driver's comments, the air pressures, air-pressure buildup, shock travels, and tire temperatures. Maybe even make some notes to yourself on segment times and any other observations you have made.

LEFT: Measuring tread wear is one of my favorite ways to find out how the car is doing on the track. Before you can do that, however, you have to scrape away all the rubber that a hot tire will pick up as it rolls back to the pits.

Don't Fight Things You Can't Control

As a crew chief, it's easy to get caught up in excuses like, "Our motor isn't running right." Another popular one is, "Our driver isn't into it today." There were times I firmly believed that was happening when we were at the track. But the driver is who he is, and the motor is what it is, and there is nothing you can do at the track to change those things. Work to get your package the best you can and don't worry about the rest. Always assume—and there's a word I try to avoid—that your driver is going to give you the best he can. You've got to give him all *you* can, and that means not only a car that drives well but also good information.

I think that when you get caught up in the things you can't control at the racetrack, that's when you get into trouble. Don't ever forget that you are in charge of the handling package, and as far as you are concerned that's the most important thing. At the end of the day when somebody wins, especially at a short track, they aren't going to talk about how good their motor ran—they're going to talk about how well their car handled.

Not worrying about the things you cannot control doesn't end at the driver and the motor. I don't care how good you are—you can't control the weather, rule changes, other cars, flat tires, and things like that. The list goes on and on. Focus on the things you can control and don't let anything else distract you.

Going into the next run, write down any chassis adjustments you made. Document every change and how much you changed it, not just the big stuff. When you put fuel into it, make sure you write down how much fuel it held. Keep up with all the hard laps on the tires. All that information is going to be valuable to you. When you make a change later and the effect isn't exactly what you expected, you can look at your notes and see what other variable was involved that caused the difference.

COMMUNICATING WITH THE CREW

It doesn't matter if your crew is three guys or 13 guys; everybody needs to be wearing their radios. Radios simply speed up everything in a number of ways. First, as the driver is coming off the track, you and he can be communicating about what the car is doing and what you want to do next. When you decide, you tell your crew what you want over the radio, and everybody knows at the same time. If a guy is in the back of the hauler working on shocks, he knows, too, and you don't have to wait until he comes out to tell him. People think you wear radios only during the race, but the crew needs to wear radios all the time, even in the garage. If other race cars are running around you, it's easier to talk to a guy on the other side of the car over the radio than trying to yell at him.

As a crew chief, my spot during a test session or practice was on top of the hauler. When my driver was on the track, I was observing the car. I'd talk to him and the crew over the radio, and they would make the changes. While they were doing that, I'd use the time to clock the competitors. Then we'd run and I'd return my focus to our car.

Additionally, whether it's a race or practice, I always tell my guys to put notebooks in their pockets. Then, if someone wants to tell me something, he should write me a note. I may not have time to have a conversation right then, but if you give me a note, I will have a look at it as soon as I can. Plus, that way I won't forget. It doesn't have to be a letter, just enough to get the thought across.

Whether you are testing or practicing before a race, you can't always push your crew without giving them a break—lunch, a five-minute break while you talk things over with your driver, whatever. But one thing I've always preached to my guys is never quit looking at your race car. If it is sitting on the jack stands and we don't practice for two hours, get a creeper, roll underneath it, and just look around. You might see something leaking or a crack in something. You don't always have to be working on your race car, but never quit thinking about and looking at it. You might just find something that could cause you trouble when the car is on the track.

COMMUNICATING WITH YOUR DRIVER

Any time you are dealing with your driver, you aren't just his lead mechanic. You've also got to be his coach as well as a poor man's psychologist. This is just as true for testing as it is for the race. If you are testing a new track for the first time, remember that you have to get your driver acclimated to the track just as much as you have to learn the best ways to set up the car for it.

If you are at a track for the first time, it might not be a bad idea to bring a driver who has experience at that track to help you set up the car. Or if you are in a practice session before the race, maybe you know an experienced driver who would be willing to come over and drive the car for a few laps. That

might not be likely, but if you can do it, it'll help you get the car at least close to where it needs to be so your driver can concentrate on learning the line and finding his braking points. Also, if this is your driver's first time at a facility, don't send him out in the car right away. Take him up to the top of your hauler and, together, both of you watch how other drivers drive the track. You can learn a lot by watching other people's lines, which may be hard to discover from the driver's seat.

When you are testing for qualifying, the only thing that matters is the stopwatch. You aren't as concerned with how comfortable the car feels because your driver has to stand it only for a lap or two. Speed—as long as he can keep it off the walls—is the only thing you care about. But when you start practicing for the race, you have to be as concerned

with how the car feels to your driver as you are with the stopwatch. Yes, you still have to keep an eye on the stopwatch because a driver can be fooled into liking a car that's so comfortable it's slow. But you have to make sure both the car and the driver are as fast on lap 50 as they are on lap 10. It's the guy who's the fastest for the longest who will win most of the races, and that's what you are trying to do. I'm rarely ever concerned about the guy who sets the fast time during practice, because if he can hold that speed only for the first 10 laps, then it isn't going to do him any good.

When a driver has made his final practice run before a race, I want to debrief him right then. The first things I'm going to ask him don't have anything to do with how the race car is handling: "Are you comfortable? Is your seat OK? Are your mirrors

ABOVE: Don't assume that radios are to be used only during a race. They can significantly improve communication even in the garage.

BELOW: Consistency is the key when trying different setup packages. Varying tire temperatures can mask the true result of any chassis changes you make. To reduce this as much as possible, it's a good idea to keep fans on your tires whenever your car is in the pit.

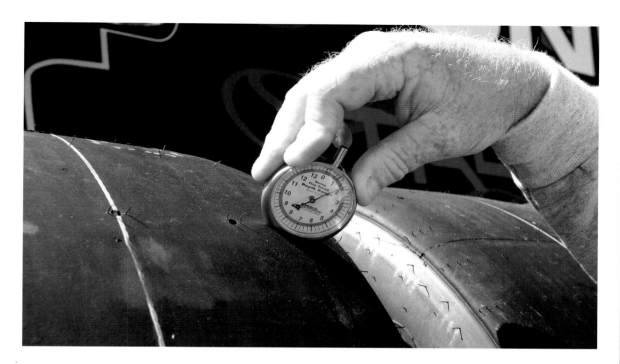

LEFT: Most race tires have a row of tread-wear holes across the width of the tire. Checking wear is simple with a depth gauge.

OK? Do you feel any heat coming from anywhere? Do you have enough air blowing in on you?" It's the things he might not think about because he might not get long stretches in the car during practice. But at lap 50 or 100, he's on the radio saying, "Man, my butt is burning up. I meant to tell you that after practice, but I forgot."

There's plenty you can do about a problem like that after practice, but during the race your driver is up the creek. He needs to concentrate on his driving, but now his backside is burning and that's taking his concentration away from racing. I have found you have to get information like that from the driver while it is still fresh on his mind. Once you feel you have sufficiently done that, then you can move on to how the race car is handling.

Another trick I used as a crew chief was drawing the track and breaking it down into sections. Don't just ask your driver how it went and let him lead the conversation. Break the track down into segments and make the driver explain exactly how the car handled in each section all the way around the track. You have to pick his brain. He collects so much information from the driver's seat that a lot of times he's going to remember only the last thing that happened. I don't know how many times that has happened—and I'm talking about with all my drivers: Dale, Mike, Davey, you name them. I'd ask a driver about a specific segment, and he'd say, "I'm glad you mentioned that because the thing is getting a little loose under braking." That would be the first I'd heard about that all weekend long. So you can't

interrogate or debrief your driver too much.

At the end of the day, you have to please two things: your driver and the stopwatch. The driver wants a car that handles well and doesn't beat him up so he will be able to drive his best. And the stopwatch...well, you know what the stopwatch wants. Normally, if you can please them both, you are going to have a pretty good car. Sometimes you can please the driver, and the stopwatch won't show too well. That's when you've got to sit your driver down and tell him, "I know you are saying the car is good, but our times are just off. You may need to get over wanting the car to feel a certain way so we can do some things to make it faster."

Then you may have the times on the stopwatch looking pretty, but the driver isn't happy. That's probably the worse situation of the two, because if the driver isn't comfortable with what the car is doing, then one of two things are likely to happen: Either he's not going to race hard, or he's going to wreck trying. I don't have to tell you that neither of those options is good for winning races.

I don't care where you are testing or what your intentions were for the test. At the end of the day, your job as the crew chief is to provide your driver with a car that is both fast and raceable. By "raceable" I mean that the car is comfortable and predictable, and it gives the driver confidence that he can race with anybody. Sometimes that's a pretty hard combination to achieve, but if you can give that to your driver at the end of the test, you can consider your day a success.

ABOVE: Taping up the grille opening and brake ducts improves the car's aerodynamic profile. It's one of the few times you can increase the car's downforce and decrease drag. Just be careful, because adding tape to the nose increases front downforce and can make the car loose if you aren't prepared for it.

Qualifying

These days, a good qualifying program is more important than ever because, no matter what series you are racing, it can be very difficult to pass on the track. It only makes sense that when you want to be the first to cross the finish line, starting at the front gives you an advantage. At most tracks racing on Saturday nights, you don't have the luxury of 500 miles to try to work your way to the front. You may have only 35 or 50 laps of racing, and if you start in the back, your chances at winning might be shot before you even start. Plus, you never want to run in the middle or the back of a big pack of cars if you can help it. When you are in that position, the chances of you getting swept up into a wreck somebody else caused is raised by a factor of 10. When you are up front, there aren't as many people in your way, you don't have to work your car as hard trying to get around people, you can set the pace, and you can keep your radiator and front end in good, clean air.

When I was a Nextel Cup crew chief, we had a lot more options when it came to optimizing a car for one or two qualifying laps. That changed for 2005; the series now impounds the cars at most of the events between qualifying and the race. That means you essentially have to qualify the car in race trim since you cannot change anything before the race starts except a few minor things like tape and maybe wedge. I applaud the move because I think it is a good way to save teams some money. This is also in line with what a lot of lower-level racing series have been doing for years. But even if there are limits to what you can do to your race car between qualifying and the race, there are strategies you can employ to help maximize your speed for a single lap and get a top qualifying position.

PRIORITIES

Let's start with the situation that the sanctioning body says no work can be done on the car between qualifying and the start of the race. They may allow you to pull some tape off the grille or adjust the air pressure in the tires, but that's it.

Even in this situation, you still have some decisions to make. Do you sacrifice a little drivability to get the fastest car possible? That may hurt your chances of being able to race in a pack of cars, but it will help your qualifying effort. Or do you prepare your car thinking solely about what your driver will want from the car during the race? Obviously, if you have a backup—like provisional points—this is definitely the way you want to go. But if you are new to a series or don't otherwise qualify for a provisional, you know you are going to have to make the field on speed. Even if you have the best-prepared car for the race, if you can't qualify, it doesn't do you

any good. You have to lean toward preparing a car that you know will qualify well and hope for the best once the race starts.

In a scenario where you have only one practice for qualifying and the race, I encourage you to work smart. The most effective way that saves you the most steps is to begin the practice session working on your race setup and then switch in the second half of the session to qualifying. That way, once practice is over you should just about be dialed in for your qualifying lap. If you finish practice in race mode, you have to switch to qualifying setup and then back to race setup once qualifying is over. Even if all you can do is change the tape, air pressure, and wedge, that's still extra work you have to do.

BUILD YOUR DATABASE

I've talked a lot about record keeping already, but it keeps coming up in just about every chapter because it is so important. When you are qualifying, there is absolutely no room for error. There isn't another lap to make up lost time if the driver overshoots a corner. So you have to do everything in your power to make sure your driver can nail that one perfect lap. You can't have any surprises at the last minute to throw you off.

The way to make sure you are prepared for everything is to build your database for the track and the driver. If you are racing at the same track week after week, you have a good opportunity to learn its tendencies. For example, you practice in the middle of

the afternoon, and the track temperature is normally 120 degrees. Qualifying starts at 6:30 p.m. when the sun is setting, so from experience you can predict how much the track typically cools off. If the car always tightens up, you can be prepared for that.

You can also build your database on your driver. If he's like most drivers, he's putting everything he's got into that lap because it really counts for something. So he's getting out of the throttle later on turn entry and getting back into it sooner on turn exit. He might not even be aware he's doing it. I've had drivers say they were driving the lap just like they did in practice for qualifying but always complaining that the car was loose. That's because they were over-driving it. But if you see this week after week, a light should go off in your head. Even if your driver isn't aware he's overdriving, you can take steps to tighten up the car in the final practice. Now he might com-

plain about the car being tight in practice, but you know what's going to be best for him because he's going to be on the throttle sooner when he qualifies.

TAPE

Tape is one of the most useful tools at your disposal when it comes to qualifying. It's also unique because, as we discussed in chapter 12 on aerodynamics, it adds downforce without adding drag. More downforce and less drag mean better speeds on both the turns and the straights. If you are allowed to remove it after your qualifying run, taping up the nose of your car can definitely help your times. Because you have to run only one or two laps, you don't need all the airflow to your engine and brakes like you do under racing conditions, so you can afford to tape up the radiator grille and brake ducts. This even includes the NACA ducts in the side windows. Generally, the more tape you can run, the better off you are.

Obviously, cutting the airflow that's going to the radiator is going to heat up the water more quickly. It's only a matter of time before the engine overheats. So it is very important that you start your run with a cool engine. Most race teams don't have the luxury of a cooling station to flush the engine with cold water, but there are other things you can do. If practice runs right up against qualifying, don't run your car up until the last minute. Give it time to cool off. Also, raise the hood and use fans to blow air on the outside of the engine. If you keep the hood down, there is no flow of air through the engine compartment and that trapped air just serves as an insulator. If nothing else, a fan keeps that air moving and helps cool the engine. Finally, don't crank the engine before you have to. Push the car out to the starting line. If the water temp is already at 240 degrees Farenheit and you go out there with the nose taped up, you can count on that car beginning to overheat before you even finish your warm-up lap.

Remember that adding tape to the nose will increase front downforce. It really pins the front of the car to the track, which can make it loose. If you have been practicing all day and the car has been

LEFT: If you are racing radial tires, bringing up the air pressure by as much as 10 or 12 pounds will help the tires heat up more quickly for your qualifying lap.

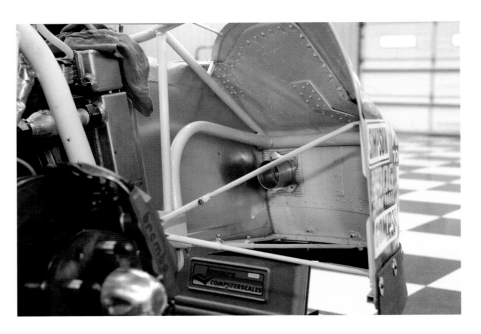

ABOVE: If you are allowed to do it, pulling in your fenders is a good way to bring the car's downforce back into balance after the nose has been taped up. It also reduces drag. Few series allow you to run adjustable fender braces like these, but even if you can't, braces aren't difficult to remove and replace.

to the engine through the cowl opening, but many cars racing on Saturday night depend on some air getting through the grille (and maybe even past the radiator) to feed the engine. Keep an eye on your stopwatch. If you see your car slow down once the grille is fully taped, you might be starving your engine for air and need to leave a hole to allow some airflow.

FENDER WIDTH

As the front end gains downforce, you can make spring changes (if allowed) or a wedge adjustment to compensate for it. You normally don't want to adjust the air pressure in the tires because that's a tool we can use for another purpose. If you aren't prohibited from doing it by the rules, adjusting the fenders is even better. Normally, you want the front fenders—especially the left front—pulled out as far as you can get them to add front downforce and help the car turn. But pulling in the front fenders can help return the car's balance and reduces drag at the same time if adding tape to the front of the car has upset the car's downforce balance.

When I was at Richard Childress Racing, we documented every car we had in the wind tunnel. That included downforce added by taping up the nose. For example, let's say car number 2 had 20 square inches of grille opening and the fenders were 75 inches wide. Before we ever raced that car, we knew from wind-tunnel testing that if we taped the grille solid, to return the downforce balance the front fenders needed to be pulled in to 70 inches. Now, unless you are a Nextel Cup team, you probably don't have the resources to do that. But you can do the same thing with a little time spent testing. Just be aware that if you are able to adjust the front fenders, you can use that to your advantage.

UP THE TEMPS

Other than engine coolant, everything in a race car wants to be warm: engine oil, gear lube, brake pads, bearing grease, tires, you name it. The warmer you can have those things, within reason of course, the more free-flowing they will be, which will free

on the loose side, when you tape the nose it's going to get even worse. Because of that, you don't want to put all the tape on at one time. If you do that on your last practice run, you stand a chance that the car is going to be way too loose and spook the driver. It has been true with almost every driver I've ever worked with: Whatever the car feels like on the last lap is what he remembers. The last impression is the lasting impression. No driver wants to loop a car during qualifying and not get the chance to race, so if the car is too loose on the last practice lap, he will get gun-shy and run his qualifying lap too conservatively.

To avoid this problem, add tape to the front end a strip or two at a time instead of just taping the grille solid all at once. It's what we called "sneaking up on the tape." That way we could track how the car was handling and adjust as it gained front downforce.

Finally, don't assume that just because you saw Dale Earnhardt Jr. qualify with his front end taped up solid, the same thing will work for you. If your car is aerodynamically sound, there is no reason tape shouldn't help it cut through the air better. But you can also be starving your engine of air, which can slow you down. Nextel Cup cars feed all the air

up horsepower. All those things will make you run faster. That's why Nextel Cup teams use heaters whenever possible.

Another trick is to make a run at the end of practice to keep all the fluids warm. You can also jack up the rear end of the car, crank the engine, and allow it to run with the transmission in gear. That will warm up everything except the front wheel bearings and the tires. That works for teams in the Nextel Cup Series because they have a cold-water cooling system to cool the engine down before qualifying. Most teams don't have that piece of equipment, nor are they allowed to have a bunch of heating elements in the car. But what you can do is use blankets to insulate the oil tank if you are using a dry-sump system. Keeping the oil warm is better than nothing, and if you think you can get by with it, you can try a heater pad on the transmission and rear end.

AIR PRESSURE

Adjusting the air pressure in your tires is more of a tool if you are racing radials than if you use bias-ply tires. Changing air pressure doesn't really affect stagger on radial tires, so you can pump up the pressure and not throw off the car's handling.

At most short tracks, even with Cup cars the issue is getting the thing to hook up on cold tires. Upping the air pressure will get heat into the tires faster. Increasing the gas pressure on the shocks will do the same thing, but you normally cannot change shocks between practice and qualifying. You normally can, however, adjust the air pressure in the tires.

It's not unusual to see guys go up as much as 10 or 12 pounds of tire pressure, especially on the right side. The key seems to be getting the car to turn during qualifying. The more you can open up that air-pressure split between the left and right sides, the better that car will turn.

If you are racing bias-ply tires—and I know a lot of short track series still do—then all that goes out the window. There is nothing wrong with bias-ply racing tires—some of the best Nextel Cup races ever were back when we were racing the bias-plys—you just have to be aware that they react differently than belted radials. Instead of using air pressure to control the tire's spring rate, you use it to control stagger.

Because a bias-ply doesn't have the steel bands in it, it is a lot more flexible. You can add stagger to the tire, which is the measurement of the circumference. In oval track racing, you want the right-side

ABOVE: The lubricants in your race car are designed to work most efficiently at operating temperatures, so cold oils in your car only cause excess drag. If you can use them, powered heating elements in your oil tank, transmission, and rear end can make a real difference in your qualifying times.

RIGHT: If you can't use heating elements, a common trick is to put the rear end of the car on jack stands, crank the engine, put it in gear, and let it run a while. This will at least heat the transmission fluid, rear-end lube, and the grease in the rear bearings. Be careful, however, not to heat up the engine coolant too much before heading out to the line.

tires to have more stagger, or be bigger around, than the left-side tires. That helps the car turn. The perfect illustration for this is to place a Styrofoam cup on its side and roll it. It is always going to roll in a circle with the smaller end of the cup on the inside.

Back when we raced bias-ply tires in Nextel Cup, our stagger was usually somewhere between 1 and 1¼ inches. That number can vary greatly depending on the type of tire and car you are racing. What is consistent, however, is how you can use stagger to tune a car. Changing the stagger split (the difference between the left and right sides) on the rear tires affects how the car turns under acceleration. This

makes it a good tuning tool to affect how the car handles from the center of the turn through the exit. If the car is loose on the exit of the corner, you can either add pressure to the left rear or let air out of the right rear, and that will tighten up the car.

Front stagger works the opposite way. The more front stagger you add, the less the car will want to turn. Front stagger also affects the car more from the entrance of the turn through the center. This makes it easy to know where you want to make stagger adjustments—the front or the back tires—based on where in the turn you want to change how the car handles.

THE "THROWAWAY" LAP

There are other things you can do when getting heat into your tires is a problem. A lot of times at the short tracks, you are given two laps for qualifying with the best lap counting as your time. When this is the case, instead of teams making two attempts at a fast lap, many teams treat the first lap as a throwaway lap. In other words, the driver will use the first lap to get the tires warmed up so that they will stick on the second lap when he goes for a fast time.

When you are doing a throwaway lap, you cannot simply go out there and bomb the lap. If your guy overdrives the corner working too hard to get heat into the tires, he can overwork the right front. If that happens, the car is going to push even worse on the second lap. On the other hand, if the driver allows the car to get wicked loose, he's going to overwork the right rear and it's going to be loose the next time around. So that's something your driver has to work on. If he's going to make a throwaway lap, he can't afford to mess up that second lap. And when it's very cold, it's even more of an issue.

HEAT THE BRAKES

As a rule, brake pads don't grip well when they are cold. It doesn't take much to get them to heat up and into the zone where they work best, but if your driver goes full throttle into the first turn with dead-cold brake pads, he is not going to get the response he expects, and it's going to throw off his lap. The easy solution to this is to have your driver lightly drag the brake just for a second when he is going down the backstretch on his warm-up lap. This accomplishes two things: It gets the brakes up to operating temperatures, and the radiant heat from the brakes also helps heat up the tires.

The only concern with this, especially if you are in a Late Model–type car that doesn't have a lot of power, is you have to make sure you are up to speed when you take the green flag to begin your timed lap. You don't want to do anything that will keep you from being at maximum speed coming off turn four as you approach the green flag.

When a driver does have a bad qualifying lap,

quite often the problem isn't anything he did on that lap—it was his approach that hurt him. Remember, it doesn't matter how much time it takes to run the warm-up lap, so instruct your driver to roll out of the throttle a little early as he goes into turn three, set up well for the exit, and get back on the throttle as quickly as possible getting out of turn four. Carrying a lot of speed out of that fourth turn can make a world of difference when it comes to your timed lap because you gain so much front stretch speed.

DEALING WITH THE DRIVER

We've saved the most important task for last. Like I mentioned in chapter 14, as a crew chief, you must sometimes get into the psychology of the driver. That doesn't mean you have to trick him into running a fast lap, but you do have to understand him enough to make him comfortable running the best lap he can.

Earlier in this chapter, I said that a driver's last impression is his lasting impression. I think that's true with even the very best drivers out there. Even with Dale Earnhardt, what he felt in his last practice before qualifying is what he anticipated on that qualifying lap. That's why we always set up the car to be able to make a really fast qualifying run at the end of practice.

I'll give you an example at the extreme end of the spectrum. At Darlington, if you are all taped up with new tires, you can run a lap in the 29-second bracket. But on a race run at Darlington, that rough asphalt will eat into the tires and make them start giving up after just a few laps. So 20 or 25 laps into a run, you might struggle to run 31 flat or 31.50. You can't ask a driver who finished practice with a 30-lap run to go out and qualify at 29 flat when the last lap he ran before that was 31.50. When that qualifying lap comes, if he's any kind of a competitor, he's going to try to run that lap as hard as he can, but if he doesn't have a good mental reference to work from, he's not going to have all the tools he needs to do it. So consider making one last short run in qualifying trim at the end of practice. You may even want to consider bolting on a new set of tires.

ABOVE: Rules make it hard to have a definite speed advantage over the rest of the field. Often, it's good race strategy and preparation that allow you to separate your car from the rest of the field.

chapter 16

Race Strategies

We have now reached the fun chapter in the book. You have already put in the late nights at the shop, you have tested, and you have sweated the details. Now it's time to go and race. Might as well make the most of it, right?

RACE PLANNING

You have to start planning your race strategy well before the green flag falls. And your plan has to be a little more involved than, "We're going to go as fast as we can." You don't know what's going to happen when all those cars get on the track together, but you do know how many laps that race is going to be, and you can plan around that.

First off, if the race is short, you simply cannot afford to start in the back of the field. The first step in your race strategy has to be to do everything you can to get a good qualifying time. We talked about how to do this in chapter 15. Sometimes, especially if you aren't allowed to make significant changes between qualifying and the race, you may need to sacrifice the perfect race setup in order to get your car to make a really fast lap.

In longer races, you will have the opportunity to work your way to the front if you have a bad lap in qualifying. Long races also mean pit stops for fuel and fresh tires. In a competitive race, the 14 to 20 seconds you spend in your pit are an eternity. Even if you make only one pit stop during a race, that stop may be the key to getting a win.

Because it takes so much time to get down pit road, make your pit stop, get off pit road, and get back up to speed, the one thing you definitely don't want to do is make any more stops than you have to. If you eliminate a pit stop under caution, that's positions you gain without having to pass a car on the track. If you eliminate a pit stop under green

and everyone else has to make a green-flag pit stop, that's even better because you are essentially putting a lap on the field.

The way to do that is to plan your pit stops. Of course, you cannot plan when cautions are going to come out, but if you know how long you can go between pits, you can take advantage of whatever comes your way. I always tried to plan my races backwards. If the race was 300 laps and I knew I could run 75 laps on fuel, then I knew if I pitted on lap 225, I could go the rest of the way. If I pitted on lap 150, I knew I could go the rest of the way on one more stop. Just work your way from the checkered flag all the way back to the green flag.

With this strategy, you are essentially racing the track. Guys started doing this at the road courses. Paul Andrews did it first with Geoffrey Bodine in 1996 at Watkins Glen. Paul broke that 90-lap race into three segments and had Geoffrey pit on laps 30 and 60; whether it was a green flag or yellow didn't matter. He just went out there and raced the track and didn't care about the competitors. At the end of the race, Bodine was first and everybody else was saying, "Where did he come from?"

BELOW: If something happens and repairs have to be made to your car during a race, your first priority no matter what is the safety of your crew. You can't possibly have a plan for every damage scenario, so use your radios to communicate as you work on the fly.

I've seen the same strategy work on the oval tracks, especially where it is hard to pass. Teams in the truck series know they can get around 55 laps at Lowe's Motor Speedway between pit stops. When they hit that 55-to-go mark, smart teams hit pit road on the very next caution. Then, as other teams have to pit, they slowly work their way to the front because no matter what, they can stay out the rest of the race.

Keep in mind that this strategy really works only at tracks that aren't too hard on tires. When we went to Darlington and Rockingham, pit strategy was easy. Those tracks eat up tires so badly that every time the caution flag flies, the best idea is always to come in and get four fresh tires. If you are in this situation and limited with how many tires you can use, you probably will be better off to try to hang around the lead lap as long as you can and hold a fresh set of tires in reserve for the late laps. That way, you can make a charge for the lead at the finish.

CALCULATING FUEL MILEAGE

Knowing how long you can go between pit stops means you have to know how long you can go on a tank of gas. Calculating your fuel mileage isn't as difficult as most people think, but it does require

constant attention. That's why so many crew chiefs assign a person on the crew, normally the gas man, the job of keeping up with it. Still, when the car runs out of gas on the track, you are the one who gets blamed, so you have to always be thinking about fuel mileage, too.

You can't begin calculating your fuel mileage during the race; you have to start in practice. You can get a good idea of how long you can go from previous races, but every change you make to the car—not to mention the weather conditions—can affect fuel mileage. So that's not always dependable information. During practice, fill the fuel cell and make a long run. At the end of the run, have your gas man use a full fuel can and refill the fuel cell. By refilling the fuel can afterward, you can find out how much fuel you put into the car, which is the same amount of fuel you burned during that run. Divide the laps run into the gallons of fuel consumed to get the gallons of fuel burned per lap, which will normally be a figure in tenths of a gallon. For example, let's say you ran 100 laps and burned 20 gallons of fuel. Twenty divided by 100 gives you 0.2 gallons per lap.

At first it may seem to be easier to figure the number of laps you can get per gallon, but knowing how much fuel you burn per lap is what you really need. That way, if you have run 35 laps, you just multiply your figure by 35 to find out how much fuel you have consumed.

Miles per gallon (mpg) is also easy to calculate. Multiply the number of laps run by the size of the tank (in gallons). Take that figure and divide it by the gallons of fuel burned, and the result is your miles per gallon. Knowing your miles per gallon isn't really that helpful, but once you have that information, you can easily calculate how many laps you can run on a tank of fuel. Simply multiply the mpg by the capacity of the fuel cell (in gallons). Divide that figure by the size of the track (in miles), and you have the number of laps you can run on a full tank of fuel.

Those figures, however, are only for laps run under green-flag conditions. Caution laps still need to be factored into your mileage calculations, but

BELOW: Even under the best of conditions, a pit stop is organized chaos. Make sure beforehand that every member of the crew knows exactly what his job is.

LEFT: Giving your driver lap times when he's racing door-to-door with another car is a waste of airwaves. All that matters now is that he clears the other car quickly and cleanly.

not nearly at the same rate as a lap at race speed. In the Nextel Cup Series, it takes four caution laps on a half-mile track to equal one green-flag lap. On midsize tracks like Richmond or Rockingham, we normally figured three caution laps burned the same amount of fuel as one race lap. And on anything bigger than a mile, caution laps are figured at a two-to-one ratio.

Finally, you cannot assume that all fuel cells—or cars, for that matter—are built the same. Sometimes we'd come across a fuel cell that actually held more than 22 gallons from the factory, and we treated that cell like it was gold. The fill tubes and fuel lines in cars can also be run differently, which means that the capacity of the lines will vary from car to car. The only way to know how many gallons of fuel a car holds—and that includes everything from the fill line to the fuel cell to the fuel lines that feed the carburetor—is to fill it up and see. During a test session, drain the cell to within a half gallon of empty. Go out and run the car until the driver sees the fuel pressure drop, and then have him shut off the car immediately. (You don't want the engine to shut off from lack of fuel because that can cause a lean condition and burn pistons.) Now, in the pits, fill the car and see exactly how many gallons of fuel it will hold.

Of course, even with all that information, calculating fuel consumption is still not a perfect science. Nobody in stock car racing pays more attention to fuel mileage than the Nextel Cup teams, and you can still see somebody running out of fuel at the end of a race. Again, that's because so many things affect how quickly a race car burns fuel. If a car is pushing, it's going to use more fuel. That's because the front wheels are sliding, which binds up the car

and increases its rolling resistance. You also have to watch your lap times. Let's say you are at a racetrack where your driver has been averaging 22 seconds a lap. You make a pit stop to add fuel, change the tires, and make a chassis adjustment, and now he's running 21.50 laps. Now that car is burning more fuel per lap. The driver has cut his lap times because you made the car turn better. Turning better isn't going to use more fuel, but now your driver is able to get into the gas sooner, which makes the car use more fuel. Of course, you are happy to burn a little more fuel if it means faster lap times; it's just something you have to be aware of.

Generally, a car that is handling poorly will consume more fuel as well. This time it's not because the driver is in the throttle more; it's because he's having to get in and out of the throttle a lot to keep the car under control. Every time you mash that gas pedal, the boosters in the carburetor squirt extra fuel in there, which uses a lot more fuel than a steady pedal. There is no way to take all of this into account on every lap—even if you could, you would drive yourself crazy. But what you can do is continually update your mileage estimates. Check your total fuel consumption after every pit stop and recalculate your gallons-per-lap figure. You just keep adding information to your database so you can more accurately predict how far you can go when you get to the final laps.

If you think you have a handle on calculating fuel consumption and are attempting to play the fuel mileage game in a race, make sure you communicate that with your driver. I see this mistake being made all the time, even in the Nextel Cup Series. If you are trying to stretch fuel to turn a 95-lap run

BELOW: A car that's loose, like the 0 here, or otherwise handling poorly will use extra fuel because the driver must constantly work the throttle to keep it under control. Every time he does this, the fuel squirters dump extra race fuel into the carburetor's venturis.

into 100 laps, don't tell your driver on lap 90 that he needs to start conserving fuel. The way a driver saves fuel is to get out of the throttle a little earlier and get back into it a little more slowly coming out of the turns, but he can do only so much before he's coasting around the track. The earlier you get him involved, the better.

CONSERVING THE CAR

In the Nextel Cup Series, we think of tires as resources that are consumed just like fuel. We use 'em up and put on new ones at the next pit stop. But there are a lot of races out there that are just too short to make pit stops a good idea. Racers

have to make their tires last the entire race. In that situation, you have to consider those four tires just as much a part of the car as the engine.

Now you have to adopt a strategy like we were racing 25 and 30 years ago in the Nextel Cup Series. You had to be careful not to race too hard early and use up your car. David Pearson was so great back then because he would save his car by running just fast enough to stay on the lead lap. Then, in the final laps, he would make a dash to the front and outrun everybody because he hadn't used up his car or tires.

I don't care how good your driver is, nobody is going to stop a 100-lap race after the first 20 laps

Strategy Games

When you have the fastest car on the track, race strategy gets a lot simpler. But if your car isn't the fastest, you sometimes have to pull a rabbit out of your hat if you hope to win. One of those times I can remember trying to steal a victory on strategy came in 1998 at Watkins Glen.

Mike Skinner, whom I was working with at the time, has never been what you would call a renowned road racer. When we went to a road course, we felt that if the stars lined up just right and nobody made a mistake, we might be able to come home with a top-15 finish. As long as the car came home straight and we finished somewhere inside the top 15, that was a good day.

At Watkins Glen in '98, that's just about exactly where we were running, somewhere between 12th and 15th all day. At the time, we could run about 33 laps on a tank of fuel, if memory serves me correctly. Well, a caution came out with 38 or 39 laps to go. The obvious choice was to stay out on the track and wait to make a pit because, let's face it, five laps around that 2.5-mile track is an extra 12.5 miles. That's a long way. If you figure you are getting 4.5 miles to the gallon, that still leaves you almost three gallons of fuel short. So you can imagine everyone's surprise on the crew when I told Mike to come on in. One of my guys looked at me like I had two heads, but I just said, "Work with me on this one.'"

If we followed conventional wisdom, we'd just be following the pack, and the way we were running that day, the best we were going to be able to do was somewhere between 12th and 15th. But a road course is a pretty good place if you are trying to save fuel. There are plenty of turns for the driver to roll through, and you can also shift into higher gears sooner to save fuel. So we decided to take our chances knowing everyone was going to have to pit in the next five to 10 laps regardless of whether there was another caution.

Still, when Mike came down pit road by himself, that was an awful lonely feeling. Before he even left the pit box, I was on him to start conserving fuel. If he didn't work for mileage, there was no chance we could go the rest of the way on one tank of fuel. Once the race went back to green, I reminded Mike on every lap to watch the throttle. Then, the rest of the field started pitting under green, and the next thing we knew we not only had the lead, but we had about 20 seconds on the second-place car.

The problem was Jeff Gordon and Mark Martin had plenty of fuel and fresh tires, and were coming fast. We couldn't match their pace or we would run out of fuel. I kept calculating how many laps we had to go and how fast we had to run to keep them from eating into our margin before the finish. Mike had to stay within about two seconds of the lap times they were running or they were going to blow us off the track. I thought we were going to run out anyhow, but it was worth the risk.

They ended up catching us with three laps to go, and we finished third. But the gamble paid off because we would never have finished third if we had just followed the crowd and not broken off and done our own thing. The sad thing is I stayed on Mike so hard about saving fuel that we had almost two gallons left in the fuel cell at the finish. It was enough that I could have allowed Mike to run a half second a lap faster and maybe he would have won the race. We ran so far that we caught NASCAR's eye. After the race they tore us to pieces trying to see if we cheated. They pulled our fuel cell, pulled our fuel lines, and then even drilled holes into panels. Still, it was a good day because there was no way we would have finished third without trying a strategy that no one else dared to.

and declare you the winner. If you use up or overheat your tires early, they aren't going to come back no matter how much you lay off of them. So keep on your driver to use his head early on. Stay out of trouble and keep the leader in sight, but don't use up what you've got until it's time to get down to the real racing.

If there is a drawback to this strategy when racing on short tracks, it is that you don't have to be far off the pace to get lapped. If you are starting at the back of the field, by the time you take the green flag, the leader is already halfway down the backstretch. Now you don't have any choice but to push it just as hard as you can to keep from going a lap down. If, however, you qualify well and start near the front, you can take things a lot easier on your car. Cautions in short track races are common, so you can just about count on a caution every so often to help you catch back up with the leaders. That's

just another reason why qualifying is so important. It may not pay money to sit on the pole, but it sure helps you to be in a position to claim the money at the end of the night.

COMMUNICATING WITH YOUR DRIVER

Once the race has started, it's important to give your driver the information he needs, but the biggest part of your job is to be a cheerleader. There might be some exceptions, but most drivers want to feel that their crew chief and spotter are running the race with him. Some may want to hear a near-constant chatter over the radio and others, like Dale Earnhardt, didn't want a lot of talking. But every driver I've worked with needed to feel that I was involved in what was going on. That means you are ready with lap times when he asks, and you know whether that car he is about to pass is for position or if it's a lapped car.

OPPOSITE: In stock car racing, calculating fuel consumption is a difficult game, but it's one that must be played well if you are going to limit your car's trips to pit road.

Communicating with the radio is a useful way to give your driver good information, but be careful not to overwhelm him. Consider lap times, for example. As a crew chief you always want to track lap times to see how the car is doing, the pace your driver is setting relative to the leader, and things like that. But if your driver is in traffic or racing for position, you are wasting airwaves trying to give him lap times. He's racing that car in front or beside him, and that's all that matters. Maybe you can offer some words of encouragement or maybe an observation that the other guy is sliding up half a lane in turn three, but otherwise leave him alone so he can concentrate. If the driver has half a straight on the field or is otherwise by himself out there, he needs to know his lap times. That enables him to start moving around and see if maybe another line is working a little better. What you don't want to do, though, is starting giving your driver segment times. I think that is just too much information to process during a race.

UNDERSTANDING THE SPOTTER'S ROLE

If you are sitting on the pit box, your view is probably obstructed for most of the track. That's why the spotter's role is so important. During a race, the spotter is normally talking to the driver as much or more than the crew chief.

Make sure you place your spotter at the top of the stands or someplace where he has an unobstructed view of the entire track. At the very least, make sure he has a good view of the backstretch, which you normally can't see from the pit box.

As the crew chief, your attention has to be split between your driver and your crew. There were times when I had to have a conversation with my tire guy or my car chief about something during the race. You don't want your driver to have to listen to a bunch of chatter over the radio that doesn't involve him, so, depending on who the driver was, I'd either radio over and let the driver and spotter know they were on their own for a bit, or I'd just leave them to it. We'd usually use two channels. Everybody was on one channel, but if I wanted

to talk to someone without the driver hearing, I'd motion for that person, or persons, to switch channels. That way we weren't talking over the spotter.

The worst thing you can do as a crew chief is talk over the spotter. I know that happened to the 31 car once in the Nextel Cup Series. The crew chief was talking, and the spotter was letting the driver know another car was coming up inside. The driver didn't hear him and turned right into that car. When you are racing, and especially at a short track, the spotter has the priority when it comes to radio time. It's his job to make sure the driver is aware of any hazards on the track and what other cars are doing.

That doesn't mean the driver and crew chief cannot talk; you just need to be smart when you talk, and don't talk to him for two solid laps. You also want to make sure you don't distract your driver. Some drivers will tell you it doesn't matter, but I have always tried not to chatter at a driver in the turns or when he's racing hard with another car. Think about it; he's in there trying to focus on hitting his mark, using a little brake at just the right moment and feathering the throttle, and you come in out of the blue talking about what a good lap that was. It has to be distracting. So even if the driver says he doesn't care, I always try to talk to him only on the straights. Then he can answer me whenever he feels like it. I think that's also a good idea for the spotter to follow. Sometimes the spotter has to give information when a car is under the driver's corner in a turn, but otherwise, try to limit the chatter to the straights.

Besides lap times and whether he's clear of the car he's trying to pass, one piece of information a driver always likes to know is how he's doing compared to the leader. If he's stuck in traffic and can't see the leader, just give him a reference to let him know where the leader his. You don't need to give him times; just say, "Leader at the line now." He knows where the start/finish line is, and if he's entering the third turn, then he knows how far ahead the leader is.

One of the things you may not think about is that the advancements we've been making in driver

ABOVE: In situations like this where your driver is battling door-to-door with other drivers, the spotter has to remember to keep his eyes on the entire track and not just the action around his driver. If there is trouble ahead, the spotter has to be able to give his driver as much advance notice as possible.

safety have actually made the spotter's role even more important. Putting a driver in a cocoon may help protect him better, but it also eats away at his peripheral vision. Your spotter has to be aware of this and help out. As the race gets going, a lot of cars normally fall off the pace. A car on fresh tires is going to be a lot faster than a car on old tires. You've got to make sure the driver is on top of his game, or he can run over somebody in a hurry. This just means that the spotter has to be aware of everything on the track, not just wrecks or the cars right around your car. If there is a car out there puttering around on six cylinders, give your driver half a lap of warning because the speed difference can be substantial. Don't always assume your driver can see everything that's going on out there.

KNOWING YOUR DRIVER

In the heat of competition, you cannot expect your driver to be as analytical as a computer. It is your job to hear what he's telling you, match that with the information you are gathering on your own, and make a good decision about what the car does or does not need.

Mike Skinner is one of the most competitive people I've ever had the pleasure of working with. But his personality was always to overstate what the car was doing. One a scale of one to 10, if the car was loose on a scale of two or three, he'd make it sound like eight or nine. As a crew chief, you want to give your driver whatever he needs, so my first reaction was to say, "My gosh, we've really got to make some changes to get this car where Mike can drive it." Of course, after we made major adjustments to the car—which was maybe a little loose before—it would be so tight it wouldn't turn in a 40-acre field.

Ernie Irvan was on the other end of the spectrum. If Ernie ever came over the radio and told you the car was a "little bit loose," you knew you'd better get to work on the next pit stop—if Ernie said it was loose, you were going to be looking at the right-side door numbers when he came around the next turn.

Part of the trick is getting to know your driver's personality, but you also have to be able to use your own eyes. If the driver is complaining the car is loose, but you look at your stopwatch and realize you are only half a tenth of the pace the leader is setting, well, maybe you tell him to just hang on a bit. The car isn't bad off as it is, and if you spend 20 seconds in the pits while everybody else is out on the track, you are really going to put your driver behind the eight ball. I've always tried to get my driver to describe what the car is doing on a scale of one to 10. Everyone's definition of a "four loose" or a "six tight" may be different, but once you learn your driver's scale, you at least have a better idea of how severe the situation is.

COMMUNICATING WITH YOUR CREW

A mistake during a pit stop can absolutely kill your track position. And the biggest cause for mistakes during a pit stop is poor communication. I don't know how many times, even in Nextel Cup, I've heard about a crew that was supposed to put wedge in and actually took wedge out. Then that wastes another stop, because you've got to come around and pit again just to fix that mistake. That kind of stuff happens more often than you would think, because there is just so much going on in the pits.

That's why I definitely recommend, as I mentioned in chapter 14, that everyone in the pits who has a responsibility on the car wears a radio. If you are trying to scream to your crew or depend on one person to go around and talk to everyone individually, you are inviting mistakes. That's why, even when everyone was wearing radios, I would double-check and make everyone on my crew confirm that they knew exactly

what they needed to do. People may have thought I didn't trust them enough, but it was just because we couldn't afford a mistake due to poor communication.

REPAIRING WRECKS

It is easy to think you have to have a plan for every situation when it comes to wreck repair in the pits. But after all, if you have to repair crash damage during a race, you are probably out of the running anyway. If you try to plan for every situation, you usually wind up with a book full of notes, a crew that's overloaded with information, and nobody who is exactly sure what to do in any situation.

By the end of my career as a crew chief, I had settled on assigning general duties to the crew for these situations. First and foremost is safety. If the rear end was jacked up, I made sure somebody was responsible for getting jack stands under the car. After that, I simply tried to match people with the responsibilities that were already closest to their jobs. Tire guys were responsible for pulling out busted fenders. If there was an engine problem and the hood had to be raised, the engine tuner was responsible for making sure the hood pins were back in the car before it left the pits. You get the idea.

Really, the best plan when it comes to wreck repair is to depend on your radios and communicate. You can't really know what needs to be done until you get a look at the car. It's the guy who has his head underneath the rear bumper of the car after it has been rear-ended that can tell you what needs to be done. Everybody can hear what he has to say, then they can all hear you say what you want done and can all get to work.

What I do have to stress is that one of the most dangerous times at a racetrack is when a crew is working on their car in the pits. They are out of their usual routine and they are rushing—both are leading reasons for mistakes. Above all, make sure that your crew members are looking out for each other in this situation. There are always jack stands under the car, and the car doesn't leave the pits until everyone on the crew is accounted for. That way, at least a bad night won't turn into a disastrous one.

ABOVE: Wheel bearings aren't something that absolutely must be replaced after every race, but you at least have to check them to make sure they still spin freely.

chapter 17

Weekly Maintenance

When it comes to Nextel Cup and the racing held on Saturday nights at tracks across the country, there really isn't that much difference mechanically between the cars: tube frames, V8 engines, solid rear axles, and double A-arm front suspensions. If you have worked on a Late Model, you have a good idea of everything that's going on in a Nextel Cup car. The biggest difference is the stakes that are involved. Millions of dollars are on the line every time a team travels to a Nextel Cup race. Those millions aren't just prize money; they also come from sponsors, souvenir sales, and everything else that hinges on a team's success. Because of all the high stakes and the pressure that exists, a part failure that creates a DNF can be quite devastating. It still happens occasionally, but the extent to which a Nextel Cup team rebuilds a car between races is something that most teams simply cannot afford.

Even if you are racing at the Busch and Truck levels, a realistic approach has to be taken to weekly maintenance. You are still going to have to check high-wear parts every week, but replacing those parts with new ones between every race isn't mandatory. The best weekly maintenance program for your operation is going to be dictated by the division you are running, the length of the races, the number of people working on your car, and the money you have available to spend. It's a hard truth that you can only do so much, but by being smart and prioritizing your needs, you can do a lot with a little.

TEARDOWN

For most Busch, Cup, and Truck teams, the actual process of what happens to a race car after a race is basically the same. Normally, the car will be brought in and thoroughly washed. Any wreck damage is removed or cut away so the car will be safe to work

on. Then the vehicle gets all of its suspension and steering components stripped, including the rear end. Painted parts are sandblasted down to the bare metal because sometimes it can be hard to tell if a crack is in the metal or just the paint. Powder-coated parts aren't stripped, but they are checked. Many of the components are also magnafluxed. Next, all the wheel bearings are serviced and repacked with grease. Normally, we replace all the ball joints. Tie rod ends are usually replaced after every two races. That also depends on where we've run. Some tracks, such as, Dover, Bristol, and Darlington, work the car so hard in the corners and give the cars such a beating that we will replace the tie rod ends automatically rather than take a chance. But even if we are running a part like a tie rod end for two or more races, we'd still magnaflux it.

If you are racing a Late Model, you probably don't have the resources to do this every week. What I've just described requires a lot of manpower and money. If you are running 30- to 50-lap features once or even twice a week, this is obviously more than you need. If you are racing at this level, you should consider completely servicing the car after

BELOW: Even if your car doesn't suffer any obvious damage at the track, you should still make a complete and thorough inspection back at the shop. You have to keep an eye on normal wear and tear so you can fix small problems before they become big ones.

eight or 10 feature events. If you are doing a lot of practicing and testing with the same car, you should try to do it once a month. When you do, try to at least pull and repack all the wheel bearings, physically check the ball joints and tie rod ends, look for cracks in all the steering and suspension components, and generally go over everything with a fine-tooth comb. You don't necessarily have to pull every component off the car, but if there is anything you can't properly inspect while it is installed, go ahead and pull it. Checking the ball joints, tie rod ends, and the steering box is important because if you have any slop in the steering system, it's going to be hard for the driver to get a good feel for what's happening on the track. Worn steering components will give the car a lazy or unpredictable feel to the

driver, so they may need to be replaced even if they aren't showing signs of failure.

Even though you hand-check all the components in your steering system, it can sometimes be difficult to tell exactly how much they have worn. Checking your bump steer is a good way to tell if you're getting slop in your steering system. I always check bump steer twice. If you do it twice back-to-back and get different results, that's a sign you might have too much slop in your system. Something is moving around in the steering system that isn't designed to. A thousandth or two isn't too bad, but if you are getting different numbers that are greater than ten thousandths or more, then it bears more investigation.

Keep in mind that if you don't have a magnaflux machine in your shop, you should be able to

find either a race shop or a machine shop that will do this check for you. Even when I ran a little Late Model operation in Alabama many years ago, I would pull some of the suspension components after eight or 10 races and take them to a local machine shop. It's definitely worth the effort to find someone, because magnafluxing parts is one of the best ways there is to catch minor problems before they become major ones.

BRAKES AND WHEELS

You may not want to replace or repack the wheel bearings every week, but it's a good idea to pull the hubcaps off the wheels and take a look at the wheel bearings after every race. If the grease is discolored or smells funny, it is probably burned from excess heat. That could mean a mechanical problem or that your brakes were simply pretty hot during the last race. Either way, you need to repack the bearings with fresh grease and check to make sure you don't have a mechanical problem.

For Late Model guys, problems from brake heat often occur at the end of the season when they start running the longer big-money features. Up until then, they've been running 50-lap features and never had a bearing problem. Then they run a 150-lap feature and don't think to check the bearings. During that long race, the brake heat really has an opportunity to cook the bearing grease.

While you are checking the bearing grease, you should also check the bearings themselves for wear. After you have washed off all the old grease, the bearing should spin freely in your hand and not be discolored from excess heat. Another check for bearing wear is to bolt the wheel back on the hub, grab the top and bottom of the tire, and give it a good shake. There should be a little bit of play, but not much at all. If you can shake the wheel back and forth, that's a sign your bearings are worn and allowing too much slop.

Also, it is interesting that the wheel bearing that gets the most abuse is the outside bearing on the

LEFT: Checking bump steer is a good way to see if you are getting any wear-induced slop in the steering system. If you bump one wheel twice and get two different figures that are more than 0.010 inch off, you may have a problem.

Check, Check, and Triple Check

As crew chief, a lot of your job is coordinating your crew at the shop and the track to make sure everyone is working together. But I've always felt I needed to spend plenty of time with the car myself. I mentioned in chapter 14 that you should encourage your crew to never stop looking at the race car, and I think the crew chief should do the same.

When I was working as a crew chief in the Nextel Cup Series, I always tried to find time to go through the race car myself. Sometimes it was in the evening when everyone else was gone. Sometimes I just moved the car to the back corner of the shop where I could be out of everyone's way. With the car on jack stands, I would get a creeper and go over every part of that car. I didn't take things apart, but I did visually inspect it all.

By spending an hour or more just looking over your race car, you can accomplish a lot of things. First, I sometimes noticed things that had been missed but needed to be taken care of—everything from loose fittings to leaks to cracks in the frame—before the car went to the track. Second, spending time alone with nothing on your mind except the race car gives you a good opportunity to think through solutions for handling problems or ideas for improving your car. Give it a try sometime—you might be surprised at the things you come across.

RIGHT: You can make a quick bearing check with the wheel still on the car. Just grab the wheel at the top and bottom, and give it a good shake. Some movement is OK, but too much play tells you that you have a bearing going bad.

OPPOSITE: OK, this is a worst-case scenario, but even with the nose of the car in place, a radiator can get pretty clogged up with rubber, oil dry, and other debris off the track. Cleaning the radiator regularly will help your cooling system work efficiently.

left front wheel. When the car loads in the turns, it's always trying to pull the left front wheel off the spindle, and that really stresses the bearing.

RADIATOR

Over the course of a race, a lot of junk collects between the fins of your radiator, even if you have a screen in front of it. It's a big mix of tire rubber, oil dry, pebbles, dirt, and who knows what else. If you don't regularly clean your radiator, the cooling system will become less and less efficient. As we talked about in chapters 12 and 15, which covered aerodynamics and qualifying, it is important to keep as much tape on the nose of the car as possible because it helps both downforce and drag. If the radiator isn't cleaned, over time you will find yourself pulling tape off the front of the car or even opening the grille to larger dimensions and wondering why your car isn't cooling like it used to.

The first thing to do is blow or hose out as much of the junk as you can. Make sure you do it from the back of the radiator and blow everything out the front. If you blow on the front of the radiator,

you will just wedge most of that stuff in farther. Periodically pull the radiator from the car and do a more thorough cleaning. If you can, buy or build a vat that is large enough to submerge the entire radiator. Fill the vat with lacquer thinner or Varsol, plug the openings, and just allow the radiator to soak. That will help loosen up the rubber that gets wedged between the radiator fins. At some shops, we even ran a hose on the bottom of the vat and pressurized it so that air bubbles were always stirring up the solvent, which helped even more. Just remember that the stuff we normally use is flammable, so keep the vat outside the shop and keep a lid on it.

FUEL

A lot of things at the racetrack are out of your control, and one of those things is the fuel you are getting. You have no idea how long that fuel has been in the holding tanks or if it's of good quality. Check your fuel filter weekly to see if there is any water in your fuel. If there is, drain your fuel cell and flush the lines.

Also, if the car is going to be sitting for more than a week or you plan to do any welding work, I encourage you to go ahead and drain the fuel cell. From a safety standpoint, it's a lot better to work on a car that isn't loaded with a flammable liquid like race fuel.

SETUP CHECK

Even if you had a good night and didn't hit a thing, I don't recommend you leave your car sitting on the trailer until you head for the track the next week.

First of all, there is no way you can truly know that nothing is broken or leaking until you can crawl around and under the car to at least visually inspect all the major components. And before you can do that, the car has to be unloaded from the trailer and cleaned. Even if you are just going to run your car through the quarter car wash, keeping a clean race car is a good habit to get into. Besides making it a lot easier to spot leaks, a clean car is a lot easier to work on, and it also helps a team feel more professional. After all, it's hard to demand that everyone on your team be meticulous about their work when you are giving them a dirty race car to work with.

When you are washing your car, be careful to keep water out of the places it can damage. Put a plastic bag or some other protection over the air cleaner and brake fluid reservoirs. It is also a good idea to mount your ignition box, or boxes, onto a removable panel. That way you can pull most of the electrical system right out of the car before you start hosing things down. Also, try to keep from soaking the seat belts. It doesn't do the strength of those belts any good if they are allowed to get wet and then dry out over and over again.

Once the car is clean and back in your shop, go ahead a do a few of the more important setup checks. Check your toe, caster, camber, bump, ride heights, and wedge. If you are racing the same track again the next week, you don't have to go through everything, but those few checks will tell you if anything has changed. You don't have to be in a wreck to knock your setup off. It can happen by bumping another car or just plain old wear and tear. Jack bolts also turn with all the vibrations and bumps a race car is subjected to, and that can change the wedge.

After finishing your setup checks, put the car up on a set of jack stands. I know it is tempting to leave it sitting on the ground or even roll it up on the trailer and have it ready to go, but with the soft front-spring setups that are common these days, the weight of the car will effect those springs over time. Keep the weight off them as much as you can, and they will serve you better.

The Weekly List

Every team's weekly maintenance list will be different based on their needs and resources, but here is a short list of tasks that you should at least consider doing after every race.

- Wash car.
- Check for cracks in frame, driveline, and suspension.
- Charge battery.
- Check fluids and lubricants.
- Check valve lash.
- Clean radiator.
- Check wheel bearings.
- Check filters.
- Measure critical suspension points (caster, camber, wedge, toe, etc.).
- Check brake rotors.
- Check valve spring tension.
- Grease all fittings.
- Check that crush panels still seal properly.

BRAKES

Look at your brake rotors when you pull off the wheels. Short track racing is hard on brakes, and the heat cycles week after week can cause cracks to form in the rotors. Look for cracks, especially where the hat joins the rotor. Small spiderweb cracks are OK, but longer cracks can be a sign that the rotors are about to fail.

Every couple of weeks, pull the calipers even if the pads are still good. Check the pads for glazing and inspect the caliper pistons. If the seals are torn or the pistons look badly scratched or otherwise damaged, you need to take a closer look and have them rebuilt.

LUBRICANTS AND FILTERS

You don't necessarily have to change every lubricant in the race car weekly. Engine and transmission lubricants can probably make it a couple of races as long as you aren't running extremely long features. The same thing goes with filters. You would be surprised how long an air filter will last if you keep an eye on it and blow the dust and dirt out of it after every race.

Still, you need to keep an eye on your lubricants and filters. Check all your fluid levels after every race, and give them the smell test while you are at it. Lubricants, just like bearing grease, have a distinct smell after they have been exposed to excessive heat. Even if you have never smelled burned lubricant before, you will notice because it doesn't smell nearly the same as when you put the stuff in there. Some lubricants, however, should probably be changed regularly. Changing the gear oil in the rear end after every race is a good idea, especially if you are not running a rear-end cooler. If you even suspect you have boiled the brake fluid in the last event, go ahead and change it. Never take chances with brake fluid, because once it is broken down it will never work right again. Also, go over the car and grease every fitting every week. A joint will never go bad because it has been overgreased. Of course, don't grease it until you see the grease coming out and then give it two more pumps. That just makes a car tough to work on.

THE ENGINE

This is a book about race car handling and working with the chassis, so we haven't talked much about engines. Still, engine builders aren't in the habit of making weekly trips to race shops unless they are getting plenty of money, so it's a good idea to have a maintenance program for your engine, too.

Fluids, filters, and belts are definitely the first thing when it comes to keeping an engine healthy. I've said that it isn't necessary to change the oil every week, but for specifics I would recommend speaking with your engine builder. He can give you guidelines on everything required to keep it healthy and winning races for you. You should especially talk to him about setting up a program to monitor your valve springs.

Valve springs are easily the most stressed part of any race engine because the

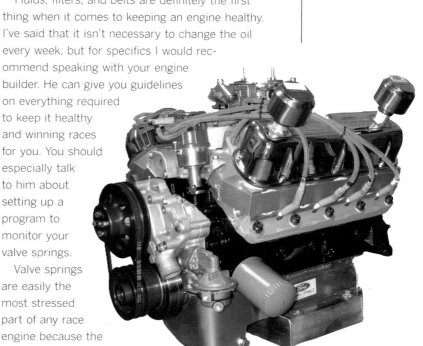

BELOW: Even if you run a wet-sump oil system and use a canister-type oil filter, you can still inspect the elements for signs of engine damage. Several companies sell special tools that will cut off the casing and expose the filter element for your inspection.

rpm levels are now so high. The bad news is that when one fails, it often has catastrophic results. Bent valves, chewed-up pistons, and broken cylinder heads are just a starting point. Fortunately, the good news is they usually give you a warning before they fail—if you know what to look for. When new, springs will normally lose a bit of pressure during the break-in period and then settle out. Before failing, they will start losing pressure again. Most manufacturers recommend you perform a random spring check after every race or test session. Log your findings. When a spring begins losing pressure that second time, it should be replaced. If more than two start losing pressure around the same time, replace the whole set.

Engine filters are also critical. Filters not only keep contaminants from harming your engine, but they can also tell you a lot about an engine's health. Check fuel, air, and oil filters regularly. If you have a dry-sump oiling system, then you probably have an Oberg filter, which is easy to remove and check. If you run a wet-sump system, you are likely stuck with a standard canister-style filter. These are not as easy to monitor, but they do make tools that allow you to cut the filter apart and check the element. When inspecting your filter element, look for metal shavings. If they are aluminum (if you cannot tell by sight, use a magnet—aluminum isn't attracted to magnets, while steel is), they are most likely off the bearings. As long as you don't have an excessive amount of shavings, you are probably OK. If the shavings are steel, contact your engine builder. Steel shavings in the oil filter element mean something inside the engine is chewing itself up.

After you have done all that, you should perform a lash check at least after every couple of races. If you are running solid lifters, the valve lash needs to be checked regularly because it will change. Checking lash is simple, and your engine builder can show you how to do it in a few minutes. He's also the best person to tell you what lash figures you should be checking for.

While we are on the subject of engines, don't forget to keep an eye on your headers and tailpipes.

It is especially easy for the tailpipes to get knocked around or dented during a race. If they develop a leak, it can harm your performance as well as allow carbon monoxide into the driver's compartment. If the tailpipes are hard to remove or install, that's a sign something has gotten knocked around and the bolt holes are no longer matching up well. The same thing goes with header pipes. The pipes are tuned to make the exhaust ports scavenge properly, and any leaks can have a significant impact on power. Leaks at the header gasket are common and commonly overlooked. Occasionally, when you first crank your engine and before it gets too hot, run your hand around the exhaust side of the cylinder heads and see if you can feel any leaks. If you can, chances are you've blown a header gasket.

BEFORE YOU LEAVE THE SHOP

The most important part of a good weekly maintenance program is that you get it all done before the last minute. I think Murphy's Law applies particularly to racers. Whatever can go wrong will at the worst possible moment. Whenever you are completely prepared, fewer problems catch you by surprise. If you leave any type of maintenance for the racetrack, there is no telling what you will discover when you finally get around to it.

That's why I think it is better to spend a late night at the shop the evening before the race than it is to get a good night's sleep and leave work for later. A well-prepared team is a team that has thought of every possibility it can and expects to win no matter what. There is simply too much to be done at the racetrack to try to do anything that should have already been done back in the shop. If you don't believe it, keep an eye on the teams that regularly win at the racetrack and see how they do things week to week. Besides, being prepared just makes a day at the racetrack a lot more fun, and you just can't beat that.

OPPOSITE: Ball joints are a high-wear item because of all the abuse they take. They don't necessarily have to be replaced every week, but do make sure to check often to make sure they aren't bent or binding up. Also, coating the threads with anti-seize will make your life a lot easier the next time you tear down the suspension.

ABOVE: Pressure changes work a lot like the springs. If you are trying to correct a problem on turn entry through the middle, make a pressure change to your front tires on the next pit stop. For problems from the middle of the turn through the exit, make a pressure change on the rear tires. For problems turning, increase the split by increasing the right-side pressures versus the left.

chapter 18

Adjusting on the Fly

In my years as a crew chief, I think one of the most rewarding aspects of my job was making the correct decisions that made the race car better and helped my drivers get to victory lane. Yes, it is nice when you unload with the fastest car because that means you might not have to work as hard. But to me, few things feel better than taking a car that was no better than 10th place when the race started and making it a winner by the time the checkered flag fell.

One of the places where a crew chief really earns his pay is at the racetrack, where he's got to make those race-time decisions on how to improve the car. I've always liked that there are several ways to attack any handling problem a race car may have. But there are so many tuning options on a race car that it can get confusing as to which change will be best. The stakes are high—often a single wrong decision will doom your chances for a win. This chapter contains all the tricks I've learned over the years for tuning a car at the track. Some of it I may have already mentioned in earlier chapters, but you can consider this chapter one big cheat sheet for handling fixes.

Often, a crew chief will struggle because every time he thinks he's fixed something, the car starts having trouble somewhere else on the track. That's because everything on a race car affects something else. Maybe that softer spring on the right front helps the car turn in better, but now your driver is complaining that it makes the car want to turn too much when he's on the gas coming out of the turn. Was that the right change? What is your next move to correct the problem caused by the first change?

When I was working as a crew chief, I kept a list handy of every change that was available to me. I often had the list taped to the back of my clipboard and would use it during practice to remind me of all my options. Some changes you could make during a pit stop, and some you couldn't. Later in this chapter, we will quickly go over each tuning option.

DETERMINING PROBLEMS AND PRIORITIZING

On an oval-shaped track, begin by breaking down the turns at each end into three sections: entrance, middle, and exit. When you are talking with your driver, make sure he is specific about exactly where in the turn he is having a problem. If it is a problem all the way through the turn, that's fine—just make sure you know where it is affecting the driver, because that plays a role in determining your solution. Also, as I discussed in chapter 16, make sure your driver describes how bad the problem is. I recommend using a scale of one to 10. If we are talking about a loose condition on a scale from one to 10, one is just slightly loose and 10 is fighting to keep from spinning out at the start/finish line. So if a driver tells me his car is loose and it's about a two, then that gives me an idea what I need to do to correct it. For a two, I know I can probably fix it by adding a piece of spring rubber instead of making a complete spring change.

Green-Flag Fixes

There is a lot of information presented in this chapter. Unfortunately, much of it is no good if you are trying to fix a handling problem during a race. During competition, you are limited to changes that you can do quickly so you won't put your driver a lap down.

The best option is to make an air-pressure change. That can be done before the stop to the tires about to be mounted on the car while the driver is on the track so it doesn't increase time spent in the pits. Track bar and wedge adjustments are also common, but they do increase time in the pits. In general, wedge adjustments are used to correct problems that affect the car from the center off. Track bar changes are normally used for problems that show up on entrance and exit. Tire pressure changes affect a car all the way through a turn.

Begin by walking your driver through the corner. Let's just say the car is loose getting into the corner. There are several things you can do to fix that, but remember, everything you change affects something else. So "loose in" may not be the whole story. The car might also be tight off, and you need to know that before you begin, because your correction for loose in might just make the tight off problem even worse. So even if the driver tells you the car is loose getting in, always follow up by asking him how it was the rest of the way through the corner.

Next, take it another step further. If the car is loose getting into turn one, ask if it is also loose getting into turn three. Even though many racetracks look like both sets of turns are identical, few actually are. That plays a role in finding the best setup, because rarely are you able to perfect the car at both ends. If the problem shows up at both ends of the track, find out if one end is worse than the other.

Finally, find out whether the driver's use of either the brakes or throttle is part of the problem. Brakes can play a role in upsetting the car, and often all that is required is an adjustment to the bias. Especially at tight-radius, slow-corner tracks like Martinsville and road courses, brakes can cause a car to be loose getting in. All that is required is moving the bias a little to the front.

Once you have all the information you feel you need, it's time to plan your attack. My theory has always been to fix first what your driver feels first. If you are OK getting in the corner but push through

the middle and then get loose off, fix the push first before you move on to fixing the loose situation. This is because fixing the first problem often actually helps the second.

Let's keep going with our example. If the car is tight in the middle, then the driver is probably continuing to turn the wheel and slow down because the car keeps going straight. When the front wheels finally do catch, they are steered way too far to the left, and whoops! Now the car is loose. The loose condition on turn exit can be attributed partly to the driver overcorrecting on the push. So fixing that push means the driver won't be turning the wheel so hard, and the car will be smoother all the way through the turn.

FIXING PROBLEMS VS. BAND-AIDS

A Band-Aid is a solution that doesn't exactly fix the handling problem—it just covers up the symp-

RIGHT: Flatter tracks put more side-loading on the tires. For that reason, you need more negative camber, or negative camber gain, on the right front on flat tracks and less on tracks with greater banking.

toms. We've discussed this before, but I believe strongly that you should always work on the end of the car that is giving you trouble. A loose car means the rear wheels are giving up grip before the front wheels; a tight car is just the opposite. If you increase the spring rate on the front wheels, you can make a loose car tighten up, but you aren't fixing the problem. That just makes the front wheels give up sooner so the car feels more balanced. Still, your driver now has to deal with having less overall grip.

That's why I believe you should always try to add traction to the end of the car that is struggling. If the car is loose, concentrate your efforts on increasing grip at the rear wheels so that they better match the grip at the front of the car. When you succeed at that, you've not only balanced the race car, but you've also given it more grip overall.

Sometimes, of course, time just doesn't allow for that option. If you have been fighting a tight car all day and there are only 10 minutes left in practice, then OK, go ahead and do something to unhook the rear end. We all live in the real world, and sometimes you have to do what you have to do to get the car balanced. That's OK—just keep that for a last resort.

ACKERMAN

Don't even bother playing with ackerman settings unless you have a day to test, because it is so difficult to predict how an ackerman change will affect the car. Plus, there are a lot of other adjustments that are far more effective. Positive ackerman turns the inside wheel more than the outside to reduce tire scrub and improve driver feel. Normally, most of my short track cars were set at half a degree of positive ackerman when the wheels were turned 15 degrees. Race cars usually respond well to more positive ackerman at short, tight tracks and less at bigger tracks.

AIR PRESSURE

Air pressure in the tires works a lot like spring tension. Less air generally increases grip, while more reduces it. There are limitations that you have to live with. If you run your air pressure too low, the tire will roll right off the rim in the first turn before it gets a chance to heat up. If you run it too high, the pressure will be too great when the tire heats up. In a radial tire, a small change in air pressure makes a big difference in how the car handles. I've seen a one-pound change in air pressure make the car react like a 15-pound spring change.

If you are loose, you can put a little more air in the right front or take some out of the left front. Normally, the two front tires are more sensitive to air-pressure changes from the entrance of the turn into the center. That's when the driver is on the brakes and the weight of the car is concentrated on the front wheels. Adjusting the rear tires has greater effect from the center off. So if you are loose to the center, you are probably better off to make a pressure change to the front wheels.

Although air pressure doesn't affect stagger

when you are racing radial tires, air-pressure splits between the left- and right-side tires do help the car turn better. This is especially helpful in the middle of the turn. If the driver says the car is OK getting in and coming off but skates a little through the middle, I'd recommend dropping the left-side pressure a little.

BUMP STEER

Zero bump steer is your goal, but that's often just not possible. Always make sure bump steer increases toe out as the suspension travels and never creates a toe in condition. If you are careful, bump steer can be a good way to add toe out just in the turns where it can be helpful, while minimizing it down the straights where it contributes to tire scrub.

Remember, increasing the toe out on the right front will help correct a car that's loose on turn entry.

CAMBER

You can't typically adjust rear camber at the race-track because it requires changing the entire rear end, so we're just talking about camber in the front tires. Before I make any camber change, I want to see the tire wear. Reading tire temps can fool you, but nothing will mask tire wear.

Camber is normally a good adjustment when you are having trouble getting the car to handle on the entrance down to the middle of the corner. If your driver complains that the car is tight in the middle of the corner, and when you check your tire wear you see that you are wearing the outside of the right

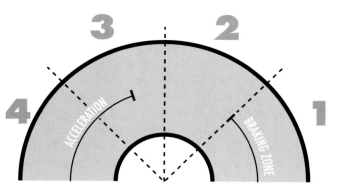

front a little more than the rest of the tire or even wearing evenly across the tread, then you definitely can dial in some more negative camber. If you are maximizing your tire patch in the turns and making the entire width of the tire work, then you can't help but ride the inside of the right front tire on the straights. Wear is always measured in 1/32 inch increments, and we're comparing the wear on one portion of the tire to another portion of that same tire. On the front, I like to see between 1/64 to 1/32 inch more wear on the inside of the right front than the outside, and the same amount of additional wear on the outside of the left front tire versus the inside. If the car is loose, I want the opposite.

CAMBER GAIN

Camber gain is controlled by the upper A-arm length. A shorter arm increases the negative camber gain rate, while a longer arm slows it down. You don't want positive camber gain. Part of the soft spring/big sway bar package is using longer upper A-arms to slow down camber gain. This is important because the soft springs allow so much wheel travel. Adjusting camber gain is especially helpful at bigger tracks with longer straights where you don't want a lot of static camber. You don't want the tires rolling on the edges a lot at big tracks, but that's less of a concern at smaller tracks where the car spends most of its time turning.

Tune your static camber so that the car turns well getting into the corner. By the middle of the corner, the car has traveled the suspension enough that camber gain really comes into play. Once you have the static camber so that the car feels good from turn entry to the middle, use camber gain to tune the middle of the turn.

CASTER

Caster is something you can never change during a race, but it is an important tuning tool at the track. It is mostly used to make the driver feel comfortable in the car. Still, I would rarely change the caster in the right front wheel; that corner of the car is just too important. If my driver tells me the car feels pretty good through the center and getting off the corner but a bit loose getting in, that's a sign that a caster change may help. You can put a little more right front spring in it, but that probably will cause the car to be too tight through the middle and on turn exit. So closing up the caster split by adding some positive caster to the left front can help tighten up the car on turn entry without affecting it the rest of the way through. If the car is tight, increasing the split by adding negative caster can make the car easier to turn. That's a trick we always had to do to get the cars to turn on the entrance of the corner at places like Rockingham and Darlington. Just be aware that significant caster changes will also affect wheelbase and bump steer.

FENDER WIDTH

In Nextel Cup, we normally adjusted fender width to compensate for the increased downforce when we taped the nose of the car for qualifying. Simply put, widening the fenders increases front downforce and drag, while narrowing the fenders does the opposite. If you are allowed to adjust your fender width, this can be a good way to balance the front and rear downforce.

GEAR SELECTION

Rarely in a race will you run as fast as you qualified. Prepare for that by running a slightly lower gear than you might pick for an empty track. This will also give your driver more acceleration out of the turns for passing.

Gear selection can also affect how a car drives. Because a lower gear provides more torque at the rear wheels, it can make a car easier to turn from the middle of the corner out. If you go too low, however, it can also make a car loose if it creates wheel spin.

FRONT PERCENTAGE

Front percentage is the percentage of the car's total weight that is over the front wheels. More front percentage tightens the car up; increasing the rear

LEFT: When trying to determine what adjustments need to be made to the car, make sure you understand exactly what is going on. Begin by walking the driver all the way through the corner. Break down the corner into distinct sections, and also make sure you ask your driver if the problem is a product of braking or acceleration. All of this information can influence exactly how you want to attack a problem.

percentage will help the car be freer on turn entry. Remember that the front percentage increases over the course of long green-flag runs because the fuel level drops in the fuel cell. So dialing in the front weight percentage during test runs with the fuel cell continually being topped off is not a good idea. The car will likely be too tight for the majority of the race.

LOWERING BLOCKS

Lowering blocks perform the same function as raising or lowering the trailing arm mounts. Adding lowering blocks between the top of the trailing arms and the bottom of the rear end increases the angle between the center of the wheels and the front of the trailing arm mounts, and increases bite. Lowering blocks were also useful at tracks like Daytona and Talladega when we ran very soft springs. The blocks were useful because they created space between the upper and lower shock-mounting points, which gave the shocks more travel room and kept them from bottoming out.

Whenever you add lowering blocks, you have to be careful to crank down on the rear jack bolts to return the car back to legal ride height. As a rule, I don't recommend running lowering blocks if you can help it, because they are really nothing more than spacers and can add slop between the rear end and the trailing arms no matter how tightly you crank down on the U-bolts that secure the rear end.

REAR-END STEER

Use this only as a last resort. Whenever you go to a

new track, I recommend you always leave the shop with the rear end square to the chassis. But if you just can't seem to get the car to turn from the center off, try using the eccentric on the right trailing arm mount to push that right rear tire back 1/32 inch. That will steer the rear end of the car to the outside of the track and help the car get through the turn. Pulling the right rear tire forward has the opposite effect and can help a car feel more stable on turn entry.

REAR SPOILER

Besides the way the body of your race car is built, one of the most important things you can do to make your rear spoiler effective is keep enough spring in the back of the car to hold it up in the air. Yes, soft springs may help the rear tires grip, but if they cause the decklid to settle so that the spoiler doesn't see as much air, you can actually make the car looser.

Always make your rear spoiler as large as you are allowed. If you feel it is creating too much drag or unbalancing the car with too much rear downforce, reduce the angle instead of cutting it down. I believe a spoiler actually helps downforce at the front and rear because air stacks up all the way to the front of the car.

FRONT SHOCKS

A modern racing shock absorber provides almost endless tuning options, and everything changes depending on the rest of the package. The following are a few guidelines, but I highly recommend thoroughly testing any shock packages you plan to work with.

Compression works a lot like springs. Increasing compression in either the right front or both front wheels will tighten up a car; decreasing compression will increase grip and free up a car. Rebound is more difficult to predict. Increasing rebound is hard on the tires but can increase front grip because it pins the nose of the car to the ground and increases the aerodynamic downforce.

REAR SHOCKS

The left rear shock is one of the trickiest parts of

a race car. Although you can predict what certain changes will do most of the time, it never works all of the time. Testing any changes made to the rear shock/spring combination is a must.

Normally, reducing rebound in the left rear shock will help a loose car. If the car is loose from the center through the turn exit, reducing compression in either the right rear or both rear shocks helps. If, however, it gets loose just as the driver gets into the throttle in the center of the turn, try adding some compression to the left rear. If the driver is having trouble accelerating or getting the rear tires to hook up, try adding rebound to both rear shocks. That will hold the rear end down and help the tires really grab the track. Increasing the stagger in the rebound (more in the left rear than the right rear) is also a good way to help a car turn from the center off.

SPRINGS

Although I said that air pressure works a lot like springs, there are some differences. For example, if the car is loose getting in, you can increase the pressure in the front tires. But increasing the spring rate in the left front doesn't do the same thing. On the left front, to correct for a loose-in condition, you want to soften the spring, which keeps the car from rolling over on its right front wheel so much.

Springs can be used to help a tight or loose condition, but they can also be used to help keep a car from rolling over. Excessive roll does two things you don't want: One, it reduces the downforce on the left-side tires, which reduces grip. And two, it puts too much strain on the right-side tires, which can make them give up too soon.

The formula for rear springs is fairly simple. Spring split in the rear is pretty common, with the left-side springs significantly softer than the right side. That helps a car turn from the center off. If the car is loose while accelerating, that's because the car is driving too hard off the right rear tire and overpowering it. Stiffening the left rear spring will help that. A good thing about increasing the left rear spring rate is it doesn't do anything to take the spoiler out of the air, which is critical for rear down-

force. If you are struggling to get the rear tires to bite under acceleration, which is common at short tracks, you may even try softening both rear springs

Normally, stiffening the right rear spring will help a car from the center of the turn through the exit. However, when using soft-spring packages, upping the spring rate on the right rear at high-speed tracks can actually tighten up a car. That's because the stiffer spring holds the right rear corner up in the air, and that corner of the spoiler stays exposed. This is usually a consideration only at faster race-tracks, but as teams are going with softer and softer front springs, it is becoming more common to see this happen.

ABOVE: The rear track bar is a valuable tool for correcting problems at the rear of the car. During the race, the only change commonly made is the right-side height where the track bar mounts to the frame. Raising it makes the car looser, while lowering it will tighten a car up.

ABOVE: When making rear spring changes, always remember that part of the right rear spring's job is to hold the right side of the rear spoiler up in the air. If you make the right rear spring too soft in an effort to get that tire to stick, you can actually make things worse. A right rear spring that is too soft allows that corner of the car to droop, and that corner of the spoiler essentially "hides" behind the roof where the air cannot get to it.

SPRING RUBBERS

Spring rubbers not only help you make minor spring-rate changes, they also introduce a progressive quality to your springs. At first a spring doesn't notice the rubber, but as it continues to compress, that rubber causes the rate to spike.

This is useful if you are fine on turn entry but struggle in the middle of the turn when the springs are compressed the most. Of course, this works only one way. You can only make a rubber increase the spring rate as the suspension compresses. If you need to make smaller changes, then use partial rubbers instead of a full loop. Spring rubbers are also made of materials of different hardness levels, and that can provide you with the ability to make finer adjustments.

STEERING RATIO

A fast ratio, like 12:1, makes a car respond quickly to a driver's inputs on the steering wheel. It can, however, make a car feel like the steering is too quick on the big tracks. Twelve-to-one ratios may be fine on the tight tracks, but for bigger tracks where the driv-er needs to be really smooth on the wheel, consider slowing the ratio down to the 14:1 or 16:1 range.

If you are racing a rack-and-pinion steering system, this isn't as easy. A solution I have found with my son Brandon's Bandolero is to change the size of the steering wheel. When he first started racing he moved the steering wheel a lot, and any time you turn the wheels on a low-horsepower car, it scrubs off speed. Switching to a steering wheel with a larger diameter gave the steering a slower feel to him and helped him drive the car more smoothly.

FRONT SWAY BAR

The front sway bar stabilizes the car by tying the motion of the front wheels together. In traditional big-spring setups, a bigger bar tightens up the car, while a smaller bar does the opposite. That's not always as predictable with soft-spring setups. A bigger sway bar can actually stick the front end because it keeps the left front corner of the car pulled down in the turns. That makes the car more aerodynamically sound and increases the downforce on the left front corner. Unless you have experience with specific sway bar changes on a particular track, I do not recommend making sway bar changes without the opportunity to test the results.

REAR SWAY BAR

Rear sway bars seem to have fallen out of favor with the popularity of soft front-spring packages, but they can sometimes be useful to help loosen up a car in the middle and on the exit of the turn. A driver doesn't like to feel a rear sway bar on turn entry, which is what happens if the bar is mounted solidly to the rear suspension with heim joints. Another option is to use a length of chain on one end that's long enough so that the sway bar isn't always under tension. If the sway bar is mounted underneath the rear axle, the chain should be on the left side. If it's above the rear-end housing, move the chain to the right. The idea is that the suspension doesn't pull all the slack out of the chain on the sway bar until the car reaches the center of the corner and the right rear suspension is fully traveled. When the chain kicks in, it frees up the car and helps it turn from the center off. You won't run a rear bar anywhere near the size of the front bar, because you want its effect to be much less dramatic than at the front.

TAPE

Taping over the grille opening and brake-duct openings at the front of the car has the dual advantage of increasing downforce and making the car cut more efficiently through the air. Because qualifying is only a lap or two, you can usually afford to tape the nose solid. This isn't possible during races because it will cause the car to overheat. Still, during practice it is always a good idea to find out how much tape you can run in racing trim and still keep the engine within its proper working range. Also, if you can tape only a portion of the grille opening, keeping the tape on the left side of the opening will help the downforce on the left front wheel.

TOE OUT

This may sound odd, but toe out has always worked well for me on anything that I've raced on asphalt. When you set your toe out, put it all on the right front tire and keep the left front pointed straight ahead. This helps the car feel more stable on turn entry. At the racetrack, leave that left front alone and make all of your toe adjustments on the right front.

Toe out affects a car most on turn entry, but it also contributes to tire scrub. If you can do it and keep the driver comfortable with the car, reduce the toe out all the way down to $\frac{1}{16}$ or $\frac{1}{32}$ inch to reduce tire scrub as much as possible. You don't want to run zero toe, because if the bump steer causes the

Davey and the Slanted Dash

Low-snout cars with a low front roll center caught on in the early '90s. Low-snout cars have a lot of advantages, but some drivers didn't like them because they always gave the sensation of being loose getting into the corner, even if they weren't, because they allowed more body roll.

Davey Allison loved the feel of a low-snout car, but that body roll in the corner gave him trouble. He had this pet peeve that he never wanted to feel that the dashboard in the car was leaning down from left to right. That gave him the feeling that the car was loose. It didn't matter if the car was really loose or not; it was just a sensation that he didn't like. And because of the extra body roll that was a characteristic of the low-snout design, he always seemed to notice that the dash wasn't level. Davey knew that the car wasn't really loose, but he couldn't get over that feeling. No matter what we did, he always kept coming back to the dash.

Finally, Gary Beveridge, one of our fabricators and a pretty sharp individual, came to me with an idea. He simply said, "Why don't we build a little angle in the dash?" So we tried it, and amazingly enough, it worked. We didn't try to trick Davey with it or anything, but the dash was level when he went through the turns, so it was OK.

The "What If" List

During the chaos of a race, sometimes it can be easy to forget some of the adjustment options that are available to you. So at the racetrack, I always kept this "what if" list handy to remind me of all the options I had available to adjust the car throughout the race. If the driver said the car was feeling "a little loose on entry," I could quickly scan my list for what I thought the best fix might be.

IF LOOSE	IF PUSHY
Wedge in.	Wedge out.
Track bar down (RS).	Track bar up (RS).
Close up LS to RS air pressures.	Open up LS to RS air pressures.
Air in RF.	Air out of RF.
Air in LR.	Air out of LR.
Air out of LF.	Air in LF.
Air out of RR.	Air in RR.
Air in front tires.	Air out of front tires.
Air out of rear tires.	Air in rear tires.
Pull tape off front-end openings.	Check temps. If OK, add tape to front-end openings.
More rear spoiler.	Less rear spoiler.
Push in RF fender.	Pull out LF fender.
Unhook rear sway bar.	Hook up rear sway bar.

LS—left side, RS—right side, LF—left front (normally refers to tire), RF—right front (normally refers to tire), LR—left rear (normally refers to tire), RR—right rear (normally refers to tire)

wheels to toe in, that will cause the car to unpredictably feel very loose to the driver. Short tracks usually like more toe out. At places like Martinsville, teams run as much as one-quarter inch of toe out in the right front.

TRACK BAR

The track bar, or panhard bar, is one of the most useful tools available when it comes to controlling the rear end of the race car. On most cars, the track bar is connected on the left side to the back of the left trailing arm and moves with the rear end. On the right side, it is connected to the chassis at a point that is normally higher than the left side. In a race, only the right side is adjusted.

There are three adjustments available with the track bar: moving just the right side, moving just the left side, and moving the entire bar up or down equally. Moving the mounting points on either side changes the angle of the bar, while moving the entire bar changes just the height, not the angle. Dropping the right side, dropping the entire bar, and raising the left side all tighten up the car. Raising the right side, raising the entire bar, and lowering the left side are all options to make a car looser. As I mentioned, during a race the only options available to you are raising and lowering the right-side mounting point. During practice, however, all three options are at your disposal. In my experience, changing the bar's overall height has more effect on a race car in

the middle of the turn and coming off. Changing the angle of the bar helps some on turn entrance and a lot on turn exit.

Remember that how much and at what location on the racetrack a track bar has an effect is influenced by the rest of your setup package. These guidelines worked for me, but spring split and wedge (cross weight) can have a big influence on how it works for you.

TRAILING ARM LOCATION

This is specifically for the truck arm cars, but parts may also be applied to three-link cars. The general rule of thumb is the lower the front of the trailing arms are mounted to the chassis, the more forward bite it will give the car under acceleration. Too much forward bite, however, will give the car a push. The trick is to find that balanced point where the car drives forward hard without killing the steering.

One way to fight the push created by too much forward bite is to mount the front of the left trailing arm slightly lower than the right. That will loosen up a car under acceleration. Staggering the arms also seems to give the driver a little more secure feel from the car as it gets into the corner.

VALANCE RETURN FLANGE

In chapter 12, I discussed the downforce advantage a short 90-degree valance return flange can provide. Remember, the valance return flange must extend back from the bottom of the valance and must always be parallel to the ground. If it points toward the ground, it is going to cause lift instead of downforce. Most sanctioning bodies regulate how long the lip can be, and normally you want to take that to the limit, but you can also use it as a tuning tool. If you are having trouble keeping the left front wheel planted, running a larger flange on the left side of the valance than the right can help. It's great if you can do this by increasing the size of the flange on the left side, but if you have to do it by reducing the size of the flange on the right, that's OK, too.

WEDGE

Wedge, or cross weight, affects a car all the way through the turn. In the ideal situation, you want to set up your car so that the wedge increases as the driver turns the wheel to the left. That way, wedge goes up on turn entry and comes back off on turn exit. That can be done to a degree by using different kingpin angles in the right and left spindles.

Generally, more wedge tightens up a car, while less wedge does the opposite. A good rule of thumb is to use wedge only for minor adjustments. If you make extreme wedge changes, you can create a three-legged car, or a race car in which most of the car's weight is on two wheels and that teeters from side to side on the other two.

WHEELBASE

Because you want the rear end straight and different caster in the front wheels, the wheelbase is rarely even. Still, you can use it to influence handling. Keeping the wheelbase on the left side of the car just a few fractions of an inch longer than the right will help a car turn through the middle of the corner. The difference should be only one-eighth to one-quarter inch. The downside is that at high-speed tracks that differential can make the car feel a little loose getting into the corner. In that case, you may want to slug the front A-arms to even it back out. Some chassis use eccentrics on the lower A-arm mounting point to do the same thing.

BELOW: The best gear ratio for qualifying is rarely the best choice for the race. During a race, especially on a short track, traffic stacks up, and the driver will depend more on acceleration to pass rather than flat-out speed. This normally means a rear gear that's one or two notches lower.

Afterword

This book has been the most fun that I think I've ever had on any project. I want to thank David Bull, my publisher, for encouraging me to attempt a second book. This time around the purpose has not been to talk about my life or career (which I did in *Larry McReynolds: The Big Picture*) but to share some of the philosophies that have helped me become a successful NASCAR crew chief. I know how much I could have used something like this when I was starting out in racing working on Late Models in Birmingham, Alabama in the late '70s. There was nothing out there at the time, and I know I would have valued any information that could have helped me rather than having to learn so much by trial and error. Today, there are books out there that try to tell you how to set up a race car and things like that, but I don't think there is anything like this that tries to help with every aspect of a crew chief's job, from setting up the crew to race-day strategies. If you have found just one thing in this book you can use to make your race team better, then I have met my goal. If you have gotten more than one thing from it then that's a bonus to me.

As I mentioned in the beginning of this book, I hope you don't think that I am telling you my way of doing things is the only way. Sometimes there are several different ways to do the same thing when it comes to setting up a race car, and they may all work equally well. I'm sharing what I've found has worked best for me. Please take this information, combine it with your own experience as a racer, and find what works best for you. Maybe by mixing and matching what you know with what I've told you, you will discover something that nobody else has ever thought of before. If you are brand-new to racing and you're using this book as an introduction, then I encourage you to use this information as a foundation and continually build on it. The information in this book is a good place to get started, but don't fool yourself into believing it is everything you will ever need to know.

Racing is constantly evolving. In the year that Jeff Huneycutt and I worked on this book, we had to make several changes just to keep up with what was happening. That's one of the great things about motorsports—it's always evolving. The basics will always stay pretty much the same, but somebody is always adding a new twist or making an improvement somewhere to racing technology. I hope some of that will come from you.

I have presented a lot of information in the book, and I would like to emphasize a few of the most important philosophies that I hope you will always keep in mind.

First, never assume anything. Assuming anything is a shortcut and one of the quickest ways I know of to get yourself into trouble. Test your ideas and any changes you want to make, and don't be afraid to admit when your ideas are wrong or need more work. It's better to find that out in a testing situation than during a race.

Second, I've tried to stress ways to work smarter, not necessarily harder. Yes, if you are going to lead a race team you had better be willing to work hard, but there are plenty of people out there who do that every day. The way to set yourself apart from the pack is to work as intelligently and as efficiently as possible. We all are given only twenty-four hours in a day; the crew chief who makes the most use of his (and his team's) time in the shop and at the track will have the most success.

Finally, I want to leave you with the most important thing I have to say: Please don't ever allow the safety of your driver to take a back-seat to anything else. There are always going to be more opportunities to make your car a little bit better, but you never get a second chance if you make sacrifices with the safety systems that protect your driver and something goes wrong. You are always going to have a chance to race and compete tomorrow as long as everyone you are responsible for comes home safely today. I hope the skills, techniques, and philosophies I've presented in this book will help you develop your own successful racing program and become the winning crew chief we all work so hard to be.